Youth Tourism to Israel

TOURISM AND CULTURAL CHANGE
Series Editors: Professor Mike Robinson, Centre for Tourism and Cultural Change, Leeds Metropolitan University Leeds, UK and Dr Alison Phipps, University of Glasgow, Scotland, UK

Understanding tourism's relationships with culture(s) and vice versa, is of ever-increasing significance in a globalising world. This series will critically examine the dynamic inter-relationships between tourism and culture(s). Theoretical explorations, research-informed analyses, and detailed historical reviews from a variety of disciplinary perspectives are invited to consider such relationships.

Other Books in the Series
Irish Tourism: Image, Culture and Identity
 Michael Cronin and Barbara O'Connor (eds)
Tourism, Globalization and Cultural Change: An Island Community Perspective
 Donald V.L. Macleod
The Global Nomad: Backpacker Travel in Theory and Practice
 Greg Richards and Julie Wilson (eds)
Tourism and Intercultural Exchange: Why Tourism Matters
 Gavin Jack and Alison Phipps
Discourse, Communication and Tourism
 Adam Jaworski and Annette Pritchard (eds)
Histories of Tourism: Representation, Identity and Conflict
 John K. Walton (ed.)
Cultural Tourism in a Changing World: Politics, Participation and (Re)presentation
 Melanie K. Smith and Mike Robinson (eds)
Festivals, Tourism and Social Change: Remaking Worlds
 David Picard and Mike Robinson (eds)
Tourism in the Middle East: Continuity, Change and Transformation
 Rami Farouk Daher (ed.)
Learning the Arts of Linguistic Survival: Languaging, Tourism, Life
 Alison Phipps
Tea and Tourism: Tourists, Traditions and Transformations
 Lee Jolliffe (ed.)
Tourism, Culture and Development in East Indonesia: Hopes, Dreams and Realities
 Stroma Cole
Backpacker Tourism: Concepts and Profiles
 Kevin Hannam and Irena Ateljevic (eds)
Royal Tourism: Excursions around Monarchy
 Philip Long and Nicola J. Palmer (eds)

For more details of these or any other of our publications, please contact:
Channel View Publications, Frankfurt Lodge, Clevedon Hall,
Victoria Road, Clevedon, BS21 7HH, England
http://www.channelviewpublications.com

TOURISM AND CULTURAL CHANGE 15
Series Editors: Mike Robinson and Alison Phipps

Youth Tourism to Israel
Educational Experiences of the Diaspora

Erik H. Cohen

in collaboration with
Einat Bar-On Cohen and Allison Ofanansky

CHANNEL VIEW PUBLICATIONS
Clevedon • Buffalo • Toronto

Library of Congress Cataloging in Publication Data
Cohen, Erik.
Youth Tourism to Israel: Educational Experiences of the Diaspora / Erik H. Cohen.
Tourism and Cultural Change: 15
Includes bibliographical references.
1. Heritage tourism–Israel. 2. Jewish youth–Travel–Israel. 3. Jews–Identity. 4. Israel and the diaspora. I. Title. II. Series.
G156.5.H47C65 2008
338.4'7915694–dc22   2008005746

British Library Cataloguing in Publication Data
A catalogue entry for this book is available from the British Library.

ISBN-13: 978-1-84541-085-8 (hbk)
ISBN-13: 978-1-84541-084-1 (pbk)

Channel View Publications
An imprint of Multilingual Matters Ltd

UK: Frankfurt Lodge, Clevedon Hall, Victoria Road, Clevedon BS21 7HH.
USA: 2250 Military Road, Tonawanda, NY 14150, USA.
Canada: 5201 Dufferin Street, North York, Ontario, Canada M3H 5T8.

Copyright © 2008 Erik H. Cohen.

All rights reserved. No part of this work may be reproduced in any form or by any means without permission in writing from the publisher.

The policy of Multilingual Matters/Channel View Publications is to use papers that are natural, renewable and recyclable products, made from wood grown in sustainable forests. In the manufacturing process of our books, and to further support our policy, preference is given to printers that have FSC and PEFC Chain of Custody certification. The FSC and/or PEFC logos will appear on those books where full certification has been granted to the printer concerned.

Typeset by Wordworks Ltd.

To the memory of

Shlomo (Shlomik) Gravetz *(Israel, 1946–2006), former head of the Youth and Hechalutz Department. He had the vision and the policy courage to launch a long-term research on the Israel Experience programmes without which this book simply could not be possible. To work with him was a genuine and rewarding experience.*

and

Edgard (Lynclair) Guedj *(Morocco and France, 1922–2007), creator of the DEJJ, one of the most important visionary innovators in modern informal Jewish education I had the privilege to learn from directly.*

Contents

Acknowledgements xi

Preface xv

1 Introduction. Jewish Educational Youth Travel to Israel:
   A Special Case of Diaspora Tourism 1
   Data Analysis Methods Used in this Book 3

2 What is the 'Israel Experience'? 7
   Character of the Tours. 9
   Objectives of the Israel Experience 14
      General objectives. 15
      Objectives of the organizers 18
      Goals of the participants 21
      The parents' expectations 23

3 Participation in the Israel Experience 27
   Rate of Participation 27
   Character of the Population 29
      Country of origin 29
      Age. 30
      Gender. 31
      Participants' background in Jewish education and community
      involvement. 31

4 The Historical and Sociological Background of Jewish Youth
   Tourism to Israel 35
   Changes Occurring in the Relations between Israel and the
   Jewish Diaspora. 35
      Stage 1: Establishment of relations 36
      Stage 2: Pride in Israel and Jewish identity: 38
      Stage 3: Reciprocal relationship between Israel and the Diaspora 39
      Stage 4: After the intifada 40
      A typology of Israel–Diaspora relations 41

The State of Jewish Education from 1945 to the Present 43
  General background 43
  Changes in Jewish education 46
  Towards the future of Jewish education in the Diaspora 56
The Sociology of Contemporary Tourism 57
The Nature of Contemporary Jewish Identity 60
  Aspects of Jewish identity 63
  The Israel Experience and Jewish identity 64
  A typology of Jewish identity 65
  Symbols of Jewish identity 68
Adolescence as a Formative Period in Shaping Personal Identity . 73
  Role models 74
  The group 74
  Values 75
  Dating patterns and attitudes towards religious exogamy 76

5 **Survey of Research on the Israel Experience** 80
  Early Studies 80
  The Taglit-birthright Israel Survey 83
  The Ongoing Survey of the Israel Experience Programme 85

6 **Perceptions of Israel** 89
  Pilgrimage, Shelter, Immigration and *Aliya* 92

7 **Satisfaction with the Tour, and Elements of a Successful Visit** . . 97
  Satisfaction with the Tour and Previous Educational Background 105
  First Visit Compared with Repeat Visits 106
  Influence of Programme Duration 107
  Influence of the Size of the Group 109
  Logistics 110
  Preparation and Follow-up 112

8 **Impact of the Israel Experience** 115
  Impact on Jewish Identity 116
  Impact on Attitudes towards Israel 119
  Impact on Personal Identity 121
  Long-term Influence 122

9 **Content of the Programme** 126
  The Modules 126
  Subject-Based Programmes and Specific Content Areas 131

The Holocaust	131
The Exodus programme	136
The kibbutz visit	139
Memorial sites	141
Mifgashim (encounters with Israeli youth)	144
Volunteering	149
Bar/Bat Mitzvah programme	150
Visiting students	151
Class visits	155

10 Informal Education and the Israel Experience ... 157
Balance between Cognitive and Emotional Dimension ... 157
Importance of the Group ... 159
Kahane's Elements of Informality ... 159

11 Staff of the Israel Experience ... 165
Importance of the Counsellors ... 165
Attitudes and Worldview of the Counsellors ... 170
Qualities of an Excellent Counsellor ... 173

12 Marketing ... 176
Expansion Plans ... 176
Obstacles to Participation ... 177
    Cost ... 177
    Security, safety and other parental concerns ... 178
    Alternative summer plans and conflicting obligations ... 179
    Initiative and awareness ... 179
Sources of Information about the Programme ... 180
Reaching Unaffiliated Jewish Youth ... 182

13 Conclusions and Reflections ... 187
The Role of Youth Tours to Israel in Contemporary Jewish Identity 187
Diaspora Tourism to Israel: A Search for an Authentic and
Holistic Jewish Experience ... 189
The Limitations of a Successful Programme ... 190
Rite/Right/Write of Passage ... 194
    Rite of passage ... 194
    Right of passage ... 195
    Write of passage ... 196
Towards a Model of Heritage Tourism and Directions for Future
Research in the Field ... 198

Glossary of Hebrew Terms 200

Appendix: Examples of Itineraries 202
    Sample programme, Summer 2007 202
    Itinerary for a Youth and Hechalutz Department Group,
    Summer 1997. 206
    Sample Daily Programmes 207

References 210

Index 224

Acknowledgements

Writing acknowledgements for a book such as this is difficult, as so very many people contributed. I sincerely hope that I do not forget anyone who contributed to this project. I extend my heartfelt thanks to all those kind colleagues, friends and experts who dedicated their time and attention.

First of all, I would like to express special thanks to the thousands and thousands of Israel Experience participants who gave of their time in Israel to answer our many questions. They are the anonymous contributors to this book. May they see here a sincere gift to them. The various staff members of the Israel Experience programmes, especially the *madrichim* (counsellors), have been our active partners in the complex task of distributing the questionnaires. Their support and patience have been critical in the success of the scientific enterprise.

This project would have been impossible without the exceptional initiative taken by the late Shlomo Gravetz Head of Youth and Hechalutz (Pioneer) Department of the World Zionist Organization (WZO), and by his General Director, Itshak Mopsik, for what became a decade-long research and evaluation of the various programmes bringing Jewish youth to Israel.

I would like to extend our thanks for the help we received from many individuals and institutions while conducting the original research and in writing a preliminary analysis of the data published in Hebrew in 2000, specifically: The Jerusalem Institute for Israel Studies, especially to its President Professor Abraham (Rami) Friedman and its General Director Ora Achimeir; the steering committee for the Hebrew edition, Dr Menachem Ravivi, Shlomi Gravetz and Dr Mordechai Bar-On; and The Department of Education of the Jewish Agency for Israel, and especially General Director Alan Hoffman, General Deputy Director Hasya Israeli, and Aharon Eldad for their initiative, efforts and their support.

For information on the Taglit-birthright israel programme, we would like to thank Dr Shimshon Shoshani, Professor Barry Chazan, Mr Gidi Mark, Professor Len Saxe, Professor Charles Kadushin and Assistant Professor Shaul Kelner.

Thanks to the members of the research team: Maithé Simon, Jeff Boussidan, Almog Sharav, Hagit Oron, Rivka Isaacs, Reuven Amar, Dalia Yisraeli and Naomi Bloom, who laboured to collect, edit and prepare the data for press, and to the staff of the Department of Education at the Jewish Agency and its institutional predecessor the Youth and Hechalutz Department – directors, coordinators and counsellors who helped the research team at all stages of collecting the data.

Thanks to Dr Elan Ezrahi and Dr Susan Elster for data on the MASA programme.

Special thanks to Maurice Ifergan (policy consultant and data analysis), Reuven Amar (mathematics and computer expert) and Marc Selzniov (data organization) for their invaluable contribution.

Members of the Scientific Committee for the Evaluation Studies

I had the honour and privilege to be accompanied by a group of international experts.

Each member of this group contributed to this research according to his or her own style and specific area of expertise. It is a special and enriching experience to receive advice and assistance from such respected and distinguished colleagues when launching a pioneer project. Their presence and their challenging questions were indeed positive contributions to this research:

Professor Ackerman, Walter * – Ben Gurion University,
Professor Adler, Haim – Hebrew University of Jerusalem,
Professor Davidson, Arieh – JTS, New York,
Professor DellaPergola, Sergio – Hebrew University of Jerusalem,
Professor Greilsammer, Ilan – Bar Ilan University, Ramat Gan,
Dr Eisemberg, Rose – Universidade Hebraica, Mexico City,
Professor Kahane, Reuven * – Hebrew University of Jerusalem,
Professor Kriegel, Annie * – Université de Nanterre,
Dr Levy, Shlomit – Guttman Institute, Jerusalem,
Dr Levin, Helena – Universita de Rio de Janeiro,
Professor Lifschitz, Gabriel * – Bar Ilan University, Ramat Gan,
Professor Moscovici, Serge – EHESS, Paris,
Professor Ritterband, Paul – CUNY, New York,
Professor Saxe, Leonard – CUNY, New York,
Professor Tapia, Claude – University of Tours, France,
Mrs Schmool, Marlena – Board of Deputies of British Jewry.

(* *deceased*)

Support team

Naomi Bloom – English editing,
Jeff Boussidan – research in the Zionist Archives,

Acknowledgements

Rivka Isaacs – bibliographical research and programming,
Hagit Oron – editorial assistance,
Almog Sharav – editorial assistance,
Alexander Shekhtman – formatting reference list,
Johanna Yaffe – English editing,
Dalia Yisraeli – bibliography and production assistance,
Data Malal (Jerusalem) – ensured the data processing.

Preface

In 2000, The Jerusalem Institute for Israel Studies published a book in Hebrew written by myself and Einat Cohen entitled *The Israel Experience: An Educational and Policy Analysis* (Cohen & Cohen, 2000). The book was the cumulative result of over a decade of research on the subject conducted by my research team, together with work of my colleagues in the fields of Jewish education and identity. Shortly thereafter, we began working on what we envisioned would be a translation of that book into English. What has resulted, seven years later, is not a translation of the first effort, but rather an entirely new book. Major upheavals in Israel, the Jewish world and the Israel Experience programme itself necessitated not only updating the data, but also a new analysis of the situation at large. The years between the publication of the Hebrew edition and the publication of this English edition were among the most difficult in the more-than-50-year history of the Israel Experience programme, and have witnessed some of the greatest changes in the programme. Owing to the escalating violence and danger of terrorism during the second *intifada*, participation in Israel Experience programmes, like tourism to Israel in general, dropped dramatically. Many programmes were cancelled altogether. Only in recent years has participation begun to recover, partially thanks to a reduction in the number of attacks on Israeli civilians, and partially as a result of the establishment of the free-of-cost Taglit-birthright israel programme. Despite the ideological, logistical and economic difficulties for those directly involved in organizing the programme, in terms of socio-historical research, this situation represents a valuable opportunity. Researchers as well as organizers of the Israel Experience programme are being forced to re-think and re-examine the facts, the assumptions and the meanings attributed to this tremendous and unique phenomenon in the world of heritage and Diaspora tourism.

The concept of Diaspora tourism, exotic only a few years ago, has become widely accepted and the subject has been addressed at major tourism conferences, in books and in journals (see, for example, Coles & Timothy, 2004). The Israel Experience, a well-documented and well-researched example of consciously-designed Diaspora tourism, has been in existence for over half a century. Continued research and documentation of the programme, during difficult years as well as during smoother times, is critical. Specifically by evaluating difficult times, we can gain valuable insights into the most basic foundations of Diaspora tourism in general and the Israel Experience in particular.

It is hoped that this book will be of use and interest to those directly involved with the Israel Experience programme as well as to students and researchers in the fields of tourism, ethnic identity, education, adolescent studies and Jewish studies, at the junction of which we find the phenomenon of educational tours to Israel for Jewish youth.

Chapter 1
Introduction. Jewish Educational Youth Travel to Israel: A Special Case of Diaspora Tourism

This book is the cumulative analysis of a decades-long empirical study of an educational and heritage tour programme that brings Jewish youth from around the world to Israel: the 'Israel Experience', as it has come to be known. The Israel Experience is looked at from many angles, both as a specific case study and as an indicator of broader issues and trends. It is analysed as an educational tool, as an example of youth leisure culture, as a key aspect of Jewish identity formation and as a case study in the growing field of heritage tourism.

Issues central to Jewish studies are explored in depth, for example Israel–Diaspora relations, Jewish identity in various diaspora countries, and the role of the Israel visit in Jewish education. For those involved with Jewish studies as researchers, educators or community leaders, this book offers the most comprehensive data and data analysis available on the widely-recognized subject of Jewish youth tours to Israel. Some pertinent factors, such as the history of the Jewish Diaspora and the role played by the modern State of Israel, are distinctive to Jewish studies and are not precisely paralleled in other examples of heritage tourism. The political, sociological, religious and psychological importance of the relationship of Diaspora Jews to Israel, and thus of the tour to Israel, looms large in the Jewish world, and raises numerous issues and questions close to the core of collective Jewish identity. At the same time, the longitudinal, cross-cultural survey of the Israel Experience provides valuable insights into the relationship of non-Jewish migrant and other diaspora populations to their countries of origin, and the role of heritage tourism in the development of ethnic identity, particularly among other diaspora and migrant youth populations.

The book presents the historical and sociological background to the programme, and a cross-cultural analysis of the impact and meaning of the programme in Jewish Diaspora communities around the world. It develops several typologies concerning various issues touched on by the phenomenon of educational heritage tourism for adolescents. The dilemmas and paradoxes facing organizers and policy makers are explored, along with the significance of various alternatives on the future of the programme and the Jewish public. Thus, the Israel Experience is at the junction of many fields of study: education, tourism, adolescence and ethnicity. The findings of the empirical study are discussed in the context of some of the important concepts and theories from these fields, which are provided not as an exhaustive review but as necessary background to position this case study within the relevant fields.

The field of tourism studies is rapidly growing and changing. Heritage tourism, educational tourism, youth travel and religious tourism are all gaining importance and recognition. This book presents a case study of the longest-running and most thoroughly documented, intentionally organized heritage tour programme in existence. As such, it touches on issues central to contemporary tourism studies, for example: the identity of the visitor vis-à-vis the host in heritage tourism, youth travel to a politically volatile region, travel to a 'homeland', modern-day pilgrimage, education in tourism and more.

One of the primary goals of the youth tours to Israel is to impact the personal, ethnic and religious identity of the participants. Both implicitly and explicitly, in ways that are planned and in ways that are unintended, the educational visit to Israel is a powerful experience. The trip to Israel has come to occupy a key role in Jewish education throughout the Diaspora. The impact on participants and, by extension, on their home communities, is significant, even remarkable, though limited by circumstances. A pivotal experience, it is still only one of the many influences on the identity of the participants. Additionally, only a minority of Jewish Diaspora youth joins the tours. Thus, this study touches on some of the core issues related to identity in the post-modern era, such as the role of youth travel in identity development, the religious and ethnic identity of minorities, particularly during adolescence, concepts of Diaspora and the search for roots.

Since the era of the 'grand tour', travel has been lauded as a valuable part of a well-rounded education (Brodsky-Porges, 1981). Myriad study-abroad and educational travel programmes exist, and have been credited with increasing cross-cultural understanding, broadening the perspectives of the participants, acquiring skill in foreign languages and more (Carlson & Widaman, 1988; Davis, 1996; Kauffmann et al., 1992; Laubscher, 1994). Today's Jewish educators are wrestling with the problem of how to make the religious and cultural tradition understandable and meaningful to young Diaspora Jews who live in highly secularized societies (Rosenak, 1987), or in religious non-Jewish societies (Cohen, E.H. & Bar-Shalom, 2006). The trip to Israel has been cited as an integral part of this goal.

Introduction

The study also explores issues related to informal education in general. As noted by Kahane (1997), informal education plays an increasingly important role in the rapidly-changing societies and career worlds into which today's youth must integrate. My studies of the tour programme as a whole, and of the individual educational units that make up the tour itinerary, touch on educational issues. Some of these issues are theoretical and pedagogical, including the representation of historical events in various contexts, the transmission of religious values in an educational programme, and the interplay between expectation and outcome. Others are practical, such as the impact of tour length and group size, the recruiting and training of personnel, and the preparation and follow-up for participants.

Additionally, as the participants and counsellors in the tours are teenagers and young adults, the findings of this study contribute to the wider field of adolescent psychology and sociology. In particular, we look at group dynamics, the participant–counsellor relationship, differences between groups comprised primarily of younger and older participants, and identity formation at this critical time of social development.

Targeted studies of the tour programme addressed questions such as 'what is the Jewish identity of the participants?' and 'what are the components of a good programme?' This cumulative analysis allows us to frame the questions differently. What does the Israel Experience tour programme tell us about Jewish identity? About heritage tourism? About informal education? Subsequent chapters will explore and elaborate upon each of these questions.

In the half century during which the Israel Experience programme has been in operation, the Jewish people have passed through some of the most dynamic, catastrophic and radical changes in their history. At the same time, global culture is in a state of rapid flux, affecting education, personal and social identity, travel and leisure patterns, and more. The visit to Israel is one of the settings in which young Jewish people may express, experiment, learn about and transform their personal and social identities. As such, it provides a window into how changes in Jewish identity are being addressed and processed within Jewish society worldwide. It also provides a baseline for looking at similarities and differences between this and other examples of educational heritage tourism at the turn of the millennium.

Data Analysis Methods Used in this Book

This book presents and analyses data from questionnaires completed by more than 65,000 participants in Israel Experience programmes. Each questionnaire contained hundreds of items related to the demographics, attitudes, beliefs and behaviours of the participants, and their evaluation of the program. The data may be compared along a number of variables, including nationality, gender and year of participation. In dealing with such large amounts of data and multiple variables, I have found techniques based on the Facet Theory school of thought, developed by the late Louis Guttman, to be invaluable. The intention here is not to champion one technique over another, but rather to familiarize the reader with the techniques used in the analysis of the data from the ongoing survey of the Israel Experience program (for a comprehensive bibliography of Facet Theory publications, see Cohen, E.H., 2005a).

The technique I most commonly use in analysis of the data presented here is known as *Smallest Space Analysis* (SSA). The first step in conducting an SSA is the construction of a table of correlations between the chosen variables. Linear or non-linear correlations may be used. In general, I prefer to use the Monotonicity Coefficient (MONCO) procedure, a regression-free coefficient of correlation (Guttman, 1986: 80–87). Correlations range from –100 to +100. The correlation between two items indicates the extent to which respondents who give a certain answer to one item are likely to give the same answer to the second item. The non-linear MONCO correlations are always greater than linear correlations because MONCO measures whether or not two items increase or decrease in the same direction. It is more sensitive (though less useful as a predictor), and recognizes a wider variety of correlations as 'perfect'. Zero indicates that there is no correlation between the responses to two given items.

The Hebrew University Data Analysis Package (HUDAP) (Amar & Toledano, 2002; Borg, 1981; Canter, 1985; Guttman, 1968, 1982; Levy, 1994) is then used to perform the SSA. The SSA is used to graphically plot the information from the table of correlations on a cognitive map. The SSA represents each item as a point in a Euclidean space called the 'smallest space'. The points are plotted according to the principle that, the greater the correlation between two items, the closer they are on the map; conversely, the lower the correlation, the further apart they are (Guttman, 1968; Levy, 1985, 1994). The map helps in perceiving the various relationships among the items by revealing distinct regions of correlated data (Canter, 1985; Guttman, 1968, 1982; Levy, 1994; Shye, 1978). By definition, a structure can be found for any data in $n-1$ dimensions, where n equals the number of items in the table of correlations. Hence, the smaller the number of dimensions necessary to discern a structure, the stronger the significance and reliability of the findings. The SSA map is interpreted on the basis of content. The plotting of the points is objective, but the division of the map into regions is subjective, guided by the theoretical basis of the study.

Various structures may be found: a sequence of horizontal, vertical or diagonal regions (i.e. from 'least' to 'most'), a series of concentric circles (i.e. from central to peripheral) and a set of wedge-shaped regions emanating from a common centre. This last structure, known as a polar structure, indicates that the content regions have equal status (that is, neither weak vs. strong, nor central vs. peripheral). They may be arranged in sets of opposing pairs. In this case, items with weak or negative correlations are pushed to opposite sides of the map. An item equally correlated to all other items would be placed towards the centre of the map.

After the basic map is generated and fixed, it is possible to introduce and integrate other variables (such as sub-populations) as 'external variables'. This feature distinguishes SSA from other, similar, multi-dimensional data analysis techniques. First, the correlation is calculated between each external variable (for example, female participants) and the set of selected primary variables that were used to generate the SSA map. The correlations between the external variables themselves are not considered. The external variables are plotted, one by one, in such a way that the structure of the map is not affected, in correspondence to their correlation with the primary variables, which are fixed. In this way we see the relationship of each of the sub-groups to the primary variables, but not their relationship to one another. The external variables tool permits comparison of many different sub-populations within the context of the primary structure (Cohen, E.H. & Amar, 1993, 1999, 2002).

Another data analysis technique used is the Multi-dimensional Partial Order Scalogram Analysis (M-POSAC). This tool also graphically displays the structure of the data but, while the SSA portrays the data according to content variables, the M-POSAC portrays the data according to profiles of the respondents surveyed. It shows the various patterns of responses, and thus enables the researcher to develop a typology of response styles.

To give a simple example of a series of five yes/no questions, respondents answering affirmatively to all five questions (yes, yes, yes, yes, yes) could be given the profile 2-2-2-2-2; those answering in the negative to only the first question (no, yes, yes, yes, yes) could be given the profile 1-2-2-2-2 and those answering negative to only the last question (yes, yes, yes, yes, no) could be given the profile 2-2-2-2-1.

However, there is an inherent difficulty in comparing this set of profiles. A 'perfect' order or scale may be found only if every pair of profiles within the sample is comparable, that is if they vary in only one direction (elements of one profile are the same or higher but none are lower than the elements of another profile). Perfect orders are rare. In most cases, profiles vary in both directions.

In the example given above, the first profile may be compared with the second or third because the data vary in only one direction; that is, all of the responses in the first are equal to or higher than the responses in the other profiles. These may be arranged in what is called a 'perfect order'. The second and third profiles are 'non-comparable'. It is not possible to say one profile is higher or lower than the other because in the second profile the first digit is lower than in the third profile, while in the third profile the final digit is lower.

The M-POSAC is designed to deal with such situations by creating a partial order, which could be called the 'best fit' among the set of non-comparable profiles. The profiles are plotted along two axes, each axis representing one of the variables that the computer programme determines are the most relevant in discriminating between the profiles.

These data analysis techniques have consistently proved valuable in dealing with large survey populations and many variables.

Chapter 2
What is the 'Israel Experience'?

Jewish society in the Diaspora is facing an existential issue: the question of continuity. Many Jews are gradually assimilating into the predominantly non-Jewish societies in which they live, adopting their values and culture. They live on the fringes of the Jewish community, or are almost completely alienated from it. Community decisionmakers and educators are searching for ways to increase affiliation and active involvement among the general Jewish public. One tactic entails outreach to increase participation in local Jewish community events. Another way of trying to solve this weighty problem is to bring Diaspora Jewry closer to Israel, making it an integral part of Jewish identity in the Diaspora for the next generation.

Each year, thousands of young Jews from around the world participate in educational group tours to Israel.[1] The name 'Israel Experience' has been widely adopted for this broad programme,[2] which began shortly after the founding of the modern State of Israel and whose alumni to date number over half a million. The tours are usually organized abroad by various bodies such as youth movements, religious or community organizations, Jewish schools, etc. in cooperation with a central Israeli entity, the largest of which is the Department of Education of the Jewish Agency for Israel.[3]

Beginning in 1999, a free 10-day tour to Israel has been offered through the Taglit-birthright israel programme. *Taglit* (from the Hebrew word for 'discovery') brought over 120,000 participants to Israel in the first seven years of the programme.[4] Israel Experience tours differ from the Taglit-birthright israel tours in several important ways. Most of the Israel Experience tours are linked with the Jewish Agency, the trips are longer in duration, they are targeted to a slightly younger population and participants pay a (sometimes subsidized) fee.

In 2004, the Government of Israel and the Jewish Agency for Israel, with the support of several major Jewish philanthropic institutions, founded yet another educational tour programme to Israel, this one offering long-term visits of between a semester and a year. Named MASA (from the Hebrew word for 'journey') the programme provides information, assistance and in some cases financial support for Diaspora youth interested in long-term programmes, as well as helping to develop and improve the programmes available. Through MASA, students may come to Israel for their post high school 'gap year' before continuing their studies at home, or they may study at an Israeli academic institution or may come to Israel after completing their university studies.[5] It may be said that both Taglit-birthright israel and MASA are the offspring of the Israel Experience tour programme.

While reference will be made to these newer phenomena in organized Jewish youth travel to Israel, the primary research for this book concerns the classic Israel Experience programmes. Despite differences between the programmes, as will be seen, the main results of the independent evaluations of the Israel Experience and Taglit-birthright israel programmes have revealed similar characteristics, highlighting the function of the visit to Israel as a larger phenomenon, over-riding particular differences in the specific programmes.

Among educators and community leaders, the youth tour to Israel is considered one of the central tools for preserving Jewish identity and Jewish solidarity into the future and for stemming the tide of assimilation. This view is increasingly shared by public figures both in Israel and among Jewish Diaspora communities. For example, former Member of the Israeli Parliament and Minister of Justice Yossi Beilin proposed bringing every Jewish youngster reaching the age of 18 to visit Israel, preferably free of cost, a campaign which he suggested should be part of Israeli policy with regard to Diaspora Jewry (Beilin, 1999, 2000; Steinhart Foundation, 2005). Private philanthropists and leaders in the North American Jewish community Charles Bronfman and Michael Steinhart actualized this vision by establishing and funding the Taglit-birthright israel programme, which offers free tours with the goal of bringing every Jew to Israel at least once during their formative years.

Why do so many see a visit to Israel as such a significant event? The educators and leaders who determine policy give different reasons why the visit to Israel is of value for contemporary Jewish identity, yet all agree that the visit represents an important crossroads for Jewish teenagers, a crossroads that enables them to formulate their identity and influences their path in life.

Shlomo Gravetz, former head of the Youth and Hechalutz (Pioneer) Department of the World Zionist Organization, thus summarized the importance of the Israel Experience in the life of a young Jew:

> In an age of free choice of identity, one meaningful tool, perhaps the most meaningful, for linking the individual Jew with the collective Jewish fate is the bond with the Land of Israel, the State of Israel and Israeli society. The Israel Experience is an educational tool, a hands-on experience, aimed first and foremost at bringing individuals closer to

the historic heritage, which has Israel as its centre, and in this way to tie them to Judaism, to Israel and to Zionism. The minimum that the programme must achieve is the involvement of these young people in the community in which they live. (Shlomo Gravetz, personal interview, April 1996)

Character of the Tours

The very name of the Israel Experience indicates that the visit is not merely a tour to see Israel, but also a process of active experience. Although the Israel Experience has undergone significant changes, many aspects have remained the same since the days of its inception. The Central Zionist Archive in Jerusalem has preserved the minutes of a meeting held in Jerusalem in 1947 (soon after the Israel War for Independence broke out), at which the first official Israel Experience tour was planned. At this meeting the executive board of the Department of Youth Affairs at the Jewish Agency passed a resolution, as follows:

> Minutes of the meeting held on Wednesday December 26, 1947, in the offices of the Youth Affairs Department.
>
> Present: Dr B. Benshalom, Y. Halevy-Levin, Y. Hochstein, Y. Meyuchas, A. Harman.
>
> The meeting was told that many requests had recently been received from Jewish educators in various countries wanting to arrange summer camps in *Eretz Yisrael* ['Land of Israel'] for Jewish students from the Diaspora.
>
> After discussion, it was agreed that:
>
> (A) Implementation of this enterprise would be the function of the Youth Affairs Department, the Zionist Tourism Information Bureau and the Youth Office of the National Authority's Education Department, which would cooperate with the department in carrying this out, and for this purpose a committee would be established, consisting of those present together with Messrs Z. Weinberg and A. Spector.
>
> (B) The practical programme should include: tours of the country, cultural activities and recreational activities.
>
> (C) Even if this cannot be carried out in the summer of 1948, it is to be hoped that it will be possible to carry it out in the summer of 1949, so it is necessary to start working out the programme right away.
>
> (D) In the first year arrangements must be made for three groups, each about thirty young people from the United States, Britain and France.

(E) These youngsters should be aged 13–17.

(F) The camp should be held between July 15 and the end of August, for a period of one month.

(G) A further meeting will be called to discuss the programme outlines.

In the summer of 1949, 45 young people took part in the first Israel Experience tour, as planned in this meeting, thus launching the programme that has continued each year and grown for over half a century. Today's programmes still fit the basic format envisioned on the eve of the founding of the State of Israel. The size of the groups ranges between 25 and 50 participants. When larger trips are organized they are split into groups of 30–40 students.

In general, the Israel Experience visit lasts between two to six weeks, although there are both longer study programmes of up to a year and the shorter 10-day Taglit-birthright israel programmes. Groups from more distant countries usually have longer tours, while those from countries closer to Israel who are more likely to visit more than once, often have shorter tours. Participants' ages range from 13 to 26 (junior high school to college students). Most Israel Experience participants are between the ages of 15 and 17. Taglit-birthright israel participants are aged between 18 and 26.

The cost of the visit varies with the length and nature of the stay, the participants' home country (cost of plane fare) and the component elements of the tour. In summer 2007 tours ranged from just under $5000 for a four-week tour of Israel to approximately $7000 for a six-week programme beginning with a week in Eastern Europe and continuing in Israel. Prices varied slightly between programmes sponsored by different organizations. Some offered subsidies or scholarships.[6] Since 1999, the Taglit-birthright israel programme, has offered free 10-day trips.

Counsellors from the participants' home country accompany the groups from abroad. Generally there is one male and one female counsellor. These counsellors are usually of college age and do not receive a salary for their work, other than the cost of the visit itself. During the time in Israel the group is also accompanied by Israeli counsellors. The roles of the teams of home-country and Israeli counsellors are explored in depth in Chapter 11.

In general terms the visit is structured according to an informal education model. Youth movements and summer camps have had considerable influence in shaping the educational concept of the visit. The early Zionist youth movements sent groups of their members to Israel, and the model they laid down has been preserved to a large extent to this day. Even when a school from abroad sends its students on a visit, the informal nature of the experience is still a crucial factor in the success of the programme.

Brochures marketing the Israel Experience highlight the combination of different components that the visit to Israel is intended to express, as typified by this sample of an advertising bulletin put out by the B'nai Brith Youth Organization (BBYO):

> BBYO summer programmes are specially designed to meet the needs of the Jewish youth of today. In a balanced combination of touring, study and encounter, hundreds of young people experience Israel, learn about its history and its culture and reinforce their Jewish identity. Experiencing Israel with BBYO will be the summer of your lives.

A brochure from the Masada movement advertising a special programme for high school graduates in Michigan says:

> From jeep tours in the desert to sleeping in a Bedouin tent to sailing kayaks down the River Jordan – you will find adventure while discovering your roots.

A typical visit includes a few days touring the country from north (Galilee and Golan Heights) to south (Negev desert), time in Jerusalem, and visits to various historic and cultural sites. Many take part in programmes such as a short stay on a kibbutz (collective farming community) or joint seminars with Israeli youth. Thus, the tour simultaneously covers a number of elements: recreational, social, religious/spiritual, educational, historical, cultural and personal. The nature of the tour will be a function of the balance between these components and will be influenced by the specific goals of the sponsoring organization and the wider context in which it takes place (for example, the current political situation in Israel). It will also be influenced by the group structure, division of time, sites visited, activities and the chronological order of the tour. There are differences not only in the tour route but also in the emphasis given and the explanations provided by the tour guides.

The planners' intentions influence the tour route itself and the choice of sites that are visited, and these, in turn, affect the entire experience. The local institutions that organize the trips are affiliated with a wide range of religious and political ideologies and therefore have different priorities in terms of which of the many faces of Israel to present to participants. The flexible curriculum, designed for each group from a menu of activity options (called 'modules') allows organizers to tailor the tour to meet their specific goals.

Sites may be differentiated into the following general categories:

- *national sites*: government buildings, memorials to national figures, events;
- *religious sites*: the Western Wall, synagogues;
- *sites of importance for Jewish identity*: Holocaust Memorial, Diaspora Museum;
- *historic sites*: antiquities, sites from early Zionist settlements, battlefields;
- *sites demonstrating the achievements of the State*: Tel Aviv, factories, kibbutz, Jewish National Fund tree nursery;
- *nature sites*: nature reserves around the country, Dead Sea, Sea of Galilee;
- *sites related to ethnic groups and minorities*: Bedouin encampments, Druze villages;
- *places of entertainment*: discotheques, rappelling,[7] swimming pools, the beach.

Some sites, of course, have multiple levels of meaning and may carry simultaneously recreational, religious, historical and cultural significance for Jewish identity.

The selection of sites gives a certain meaning to the visit, and emphasizes various aspects of Jewish identity. The activities and tour route chosen make an educational and ideological statement. Abraham Infeld, director for more than 30 years of the Melitz Centre for Jewish-Zionist Education, says that if it were necessary to choose only three sites, he would choose the Western Wall, as a symbol of Jewish memory, a kibbutz as an example of an alternative Jewish existence and the Knesset (Israeli Parliament) as a symbol of Jewish sovereignty. In fourth place he would choose Sheinkin Street (a trendy spot in Tel Aviv) and Bialik House (home of a famous Israeli poet, now transformed into a museum), as symbols of Israeli creativity. In fifth place, he would choose the Supreme Court. His selection emphasizes an encounter with the Jewish contemporary community living in the State of Israel. Only one of the sites, the Western Wall, is related to Jewish religion and ancient history. Infeld also emphasizes the importance of meeting Israelis during the tour.

Not all organizers share Infeld's priorities. Some tours focus more on visiting religious sites and emphasize the spiritual connection between Jews and Israel. Some explore the political situation through organized meetings with Israeli youth, visits to Bedouin villages or time on an army base. Some offer opportunities for volunteer work on a kibbutz or with a social programme. Still others start with visits to Holocaust sites in Europe and emphasize the connection between Jewish survival and the State of Israel. By design, most trips are intentionally non-religious, although each does include some religiously-oriented activities such as praying at the Western Wall, visiting synagogues and experiencing Shabbat with the group and/or Israeli families. Tours organized by religiously-traditional youth groups or synagogues may give more emphasis to religious sites and activities.

It is informative to see how tour routes have been altered to match the changes that have taken place in values. An archive document from 1951 records that young people who visited Israel that year were taken to the studio of the 'Voice of Zion calling the Diaspora' (an early radio programme from Israel aimed at an overseas audience), the 'Faluja Pocket' (a site in the south of the country where a key battle in Israel's War of Independence took place), newly-built Israeli factories, Mikve Israel (the first agricultural school, established in 1870 by the Alliance Israélite Universelle, to train Jewish pioneers) and a Bedouin desert encampment. They climbed the 'Scorpions' Ascent' in the Negev desert and swam off the beach at Ashkelon. The tour of Galilee included a visit to Degania, the first kibbutz established in 1907, and to the grave of a prominent early Hebrew poetess, Rachel (1890–1931). Some tours visited a transit camp and received a presentation about the absorption of immigrants. Other stops in early tours included a Jewish National Fund tree nursery, the *yeshiva* (religious school) of the B'nai Akiva youth movement, antiquity sites, the drained Hula Valley swamps and the ancient cities of Tiberias, Safed and, of course, Jerusalem.

The schedule of a programme for American youth held in the summer of 1963 included two and a half weeks touring the country, two weeks of seminars and activities in Jerusalem and a full two weeks on a kibbutz (Comet, 1965).

The visit to Israel in those days also included learning some Hebrew, a boat journey and landing at the Haifa port, and considerable time devoted to learning Israeli songs and dances. The country was presented as a place of activity, of building, renewal and creation. Many aspects of the new state were portrayed to show Diaspora Jews how Israelis live, with the aim (among others) of encouraging young people to consider personally joining the national cause by immigrating.

The tour route, naturally, has altered over time, although many of the same key sites are visited. Some of the changes are a result of the development of the tourism infrastructure and the establishment of new sites. For example, Masada, site of the last holdout of ancient Israelis against the Roman Empire, which ended in a mass suicide, was excavated and restored only in the 1960s. Access to the Western Wall became possible only after the 1967 Six Day War. The Diaspora Museum and the Israeli Holocaust Memorial *Yad Vashem* each opened in the 1970s. Since his assassination in 1995, the grave of former Israeli Prime Minister Yitzhak Rabin has become a site to visit. Each of these sites is a stop in many Israel Experience tours. Other changes came with the disappearance of sites such as the transit camps (*ma'abara*), where new immigrants were temporarily lodged or the 'Voice of Zion calling the Diaspora' studio.

Another type of change arose because of changes in the perception of the visit's meaning and aims. Presenting Israel's achievements in industry and settlement is seen as anachronistic and unnecessary. More time is devoted to sites relating to the history and religion of the Jewish people. At the same time, a number of the innovations in recent years are actually reminiscent of the old programmes. For example, although planes have replaced ships as the primary mode of transport, since 1994 there has been an option of completing the last leg of the journey from Europe to Israel by ship, simulating the illegal immigration of the pre-State days and provoking a nostalgic form of identification. Meetings of an informal nature between Israelis and Diaspora youth have also regained a central place in the programmes.

In recent years, some changes have been made in the Israel Experience programme because of the political situation. For example some sites, in or near the West Bank and Gaza, have been dropped, as they were considered too dangerous. Some tours include seminars addressing the ongoing conflict and the peace process.

In summary, the Israel Experience is a short-term, group tour organized co-operatively by the Israeli government, philanthropists and Diaspora community institutions to expose Jewish youth to a wide range of activities and sites in Israel. While they are meant to be enjoyable, the tours are not purely recreational, but have explicit educational and ideological goals, and these will be explored in the next section.

Objectives of the Israel Experience

The Israel Experience must strive to meet the objectives and expectations of numerous parties: the Israeli governmental and Diaspora community institutions that organize and sponsor the tours, the parents who send their children and of course the participants themselves. The goals of these interested parties overlap, and yet are not synonymous. It may be said that an educational tour to Israel represents a sort of crossroads of expectations of the Jewish people at the turn of the millennium. In this section we will look at the objectives of this educational, heritage tour programme from the perspective of the organizers, the participants, and their parents.

In the early years of the Israel Experience, a visit by young Jews from the Diaspora to Israel was seen as a preparatory step towards participants' eventual *aliya* (immigration).[8] A questionnaire from 1955, found in the Zionist Archives, clarifies this objective of the tour beyond any doubt: tour participants were asked whether they intend to settle in Israel and, if so, were asked to indicate in what type of settlement they would like to live. In the evaluation of a 1963 summer programme participants were asked whether or not they personally want to live in Israel and whether they believe that eventually all Jews must move to Israel (Comet, 1965). Today, there is little expectation that immigration to Israel will be an outcome of the programme.

Another goal of the founders of the programme was to reach Jewish youth at the periphery of the Jewish Diaspora communities, and to bring them back into the national collective through the trip to Israel. As will be seen, one of the perennial paradoxes of educational tourism to Israel is that the programmes consistently appeal to young Jews who are already affiliated and involved with Jewish communal life. Success in recruiting young Jews who have few or no prior connections to Jewish institutions and without at least some Jewish educational and religious background has been limited.

Over time, the objectives of the programme have evolved and expanded. General objectives include instilling a sense of affiliation with the Jewish collective, enhancing participants' personal Jewish identity, strengthening connection between the State of Israel and Diaspora Jewry, providing a personally enriching experience, and training future leadership for Jewish communities. Each of these objectives spans numerous dimensions: ideological, religious, educational, social, cultural, historical, personal and political.

General objectives

Ideological

The Israel Experience programme has a strongly ideological dimension, particularly for organizers and parents, but also for participants. The ideological objectives of the programme span a wide range of national and religious thought. Some parents and organizers expect that the trip may even establish or form Jewish identity and a connection with Israel where none previously existed, although this has been found to be generally unrealistic. In fact, for many the trip to Israel is an expression of an already-strong pride in Jewish heritage and solidarity with Israel. A more realistic expectation is that the trip to Israel, particularly for those visiting for the first time, will make ideals more tangible, and therefore strengthen commitment to them.

One way of creating this sense of affiliation is to encourage identification with Jews around the world. In the context of the Israel Experience tour, this aim may be achieved through imparting an understanding of the different lifestyles of communities and exposing the students to the problems of communities in distress. For example, tours may visit development towns or absorption centres for recent immigrants. The Diaspora Museum, with its exhibits related to Jewish communities around the world and from different time periods is another site included in the tour in order to achieve this goal of instilling a sense of collective Jewish peoplehood. The sense of Jewish peoplehood includes the desire to encourage youngsters to identify with Jews from difficult periods in the past such as the Holocaust, with the rich Jewish community life in Europe, North Africa and other Arab countries that has vanished, with various communities living in different parts of the world, and with the Jewish community living today in Israel.

Religious

A differentiation may be made between a general sense of affiliation with the Jewish people and Jewish heritage, and a more explicitly religious objective. Religious goals of a tour programme would include learning about the Jewish religion, increased ritual observance and strengthened religious faith. In general, the Israel Experience tours do not emphasize explicitly-religious goals, although there are tours organized by Orthodox youth groups.

Educational

There may be differences of opinion with regard to the particular content that each organization would like to teach its students, but there is widespread agreement that the visit also has a cognitive aim: to increase the student's knowledge of Israeli history and geography, the Hebrew language, and Jewish religion and culture. Given the nature of the tour, educational objectives tend to be experiential and informal, for example learning Jewish history by visiting sites of key events or participating in archeological digs.

On a practical level, the Israel Experience is seen as a preliminary step in the education and training of future leaders of local Jewish communities who are familiar with and committed to Israel. This, in turn has an ongoing impact on Jewish education in the Diaspora.

Social

The Israel Experience programmes include a number of social goals. On the part of the young people in particular, this is expressed in a desire to meet new friends and to have a fun, recreational experience with a group of peers. That they chose to spend their vacation on a tour of Israel with a Jewish youth organization indicates that the social component is not neutral, but is connected to the ideological goal of affiliation with the Jewish collective mentioned above.

On the part of parents and organizers, widespread concern over assimilation and intermarriage has created a need to encourage young Jewish people to take part in Jewish-oriented social activities, to make Jewish friends, and to marry Jewish partners, so that they too will bring up families with clear ties to Judaism. With an intermarriage rate of over 50% in the US and approaching (or even surpassing) this figure in some other Diaspora communities, exogamy has become a topic of particular concern in terms of Jewish continuity and group identification. Many of the parents and almost all of the Jewish leaders that we interviewed see the visit to Israel as something that can help to prevent exogamy. The tour is meant to achieve this goal both ideologically, by convincing participants of the importance of Jewish continuity through marriage and family, and practically through the intense social encounter with Jewish peers of the opposite sex. As will be discussed in more detail later, participant alumni often become more involved in their local Jewish communities after the trip, and this provides an ongoing milieu for meeting potential dating partners. Thus, the Israel Experience can be seen as a factor in matchmaking.

To have these social objectives reinforced by a visit to Israel, the programme must emphasize the feeling of belonging and group coherence. The sense of belonging operates on several levels: the specific youth organization, the local Jewish community, the Jewish people and the State of Israel.

Cultural

In general, international travel is considered to be a cultural experience. In the case of the Israel Experience, there are two faces to the cultural dimension: one is affiliation with a generalized Jewish culture, of which the Diaspora youth are considered to be a part, and the other is the specific Israeli culture, which may be quite foreign to the visitors. Learning Hebrew may be considered a cultural objective of a visit to Israel, although on short tours this would be limited to a few words, phrases or songs.

Personal

In addition to the specifically Jewish objectives, the tour is seen as a means of enriching participants' world in a general way. Overseas travel has long been considered an enriching educational experience, from the European tours of the 18th century to current study-abroad programmes. Visiting another culture, particularly at a young age, is eye opening – a formative experience that adds another layer to their personal identity. International travel can endow status and social capital (Skelton & Valentine, 1988). In fact, a website offering advice to Jewish students applying to competitive universities specifically suggests that alumni of Israel Experience or similar tours should include this in their personal statement of their application.[9] Personal growth and increased independence were found to be among the motivations and impacts of students (in this case, specifically, female students) taking part in year-long programmes in Israel, both at religious institutions and universities (Ohayon, 2004).

Political

The visit to Israel also brings participants into contact with Jewish nationalism and sovereignty, providing an opportunity to explore and interpret the bond that they as Diaspora Jews choose to have with Israel and Israelis. Given the intense controversy surrounding Israel as the Jewish State, the political objectives of the Israel Experience programme may be considered among the most sensitive. In general, it may be said that one of the purposes of the tour is to increase the support of Diaspora Jews for Israel, if not necessarily to espouse particular stances on specific issues. From the perspective of the Israeli organizers, strengthening the support of the international Jewish community for the State of Israel is a key objective. Specific activities may have explicit political messages, for example time spent on army bases or seminars on the peace accords. Again, tours organized by various organizations may impart different political messages, although none stray too far from the basic ideal of the State of Israel as a modern democracy with a Jewish character.[10]

Objectives of the organizers

The way the organizers see the aims of the visit dictates its character to a large extent. The directors recognize the importance of the tours they help organize in the education and development of Jewish identity of participants. To understand the fundamental objectives of the Israel Experience programme, we may look at what programme directors indicate are the most important messages to be imparted to tour participants.

In 1985 and again in 1992, as part of the comprehensive survey of the Israel Experience programme, directors were given a list of statements that addressed issues such as the relationship of Jews to Israel and the centrality of the Jewish religion and Jewish culture, and were asked to rate how important they think it is that the Israel Experience programme imparts each sentiment to participants. Table 1 shows the four statements that received the highest rating of importance, and compares the percentage of surveyed programme directors that answered 'very important' to each of these four statements.

The vast majority of directors stressed the importance of the programme imparting to participants a connection with Jewish culture as well as a connection to Israel. The Israel Experience tour is seen as a part of Jewish identity education as a whole. Additionally, the percentage of programme

What is the 'Israel Experience'?

Table 1 Sentiments to be imparted to Israel Experience participants as rated by programme directors (percentage answering 'very important')

Statement	1985	1992
Israel is a central factor in Jewish existence in the Diaspora	72%	85%
Jews must be familiar with Jewish culture	76%	70%
The young Jew is part of an ancient Jewish culture	76%	76%
Israel is the original homeland of all Jews	77%	68%

Source: data from 1985 (Shye, 1986); data from 1992 (Cohen, E.H., 1992a)

directors that see defining Israel as the central factor in Jewish Diaspora life as one of the goals of the Israel Experience increased between 1985 and 1992, while the percentage that include defining Israel as the original homeland of all Jews as a programme objective decreased. This could be interpreted as indicating a slight shift from a past-orientation to a present-orientation, that is, on Israel's role for the Jewish people today, not in ancient history. On the other hand, while the percentage of directors who see instilling in participants a feeling of being part of an ancient culture remained steady, the percentage who feel that Jews today must be familiar with Jewish culture declined. This seems to indicate an emphasis on an emotional feeling of belonging and identification rather than on knowledge and practice.

The increasing importance given to Israel's role in Jewish life in the Diaspora, and the declining importance given to the concept of the 'homeland' both show that explicit recognition of continued Jewish life outside Israel has become widely accepted among the programme's leadership, even though this sentiment contradicts classic Zionist ideology, which predicted the end of the Diaspora following the founding of the Jewish State.

In a structural analysis of the goals of the directors of 290 Israel Experience programmes, Shye (1986) found four general categories of objectives arranged as two sets of opposed concepts: encouraging *aliya* (immigration) as opposed to encouraging involvement in participants' home Jewish community, and universal values as opposed to specifically Jewish values.

To further investigate how the programme's leadership perceives the objectives and purpose of the tours, we looked at how several key figures involved in shaping and operating the programmes over the years have explained in their own words the purpose of a trip to Israel for Jewish youth from abroad.

Mordechai Bar-On, head of the Youth and Hechalutz Department of the

World Zionist Organization during the 1970s, describes how he sees the Israel Experience vision:

> Every hill and every valley is steeped in the continuity of Jewish culture. The encounter with the living Jewish reality and a country saturated with messages is how Jewish identity is transmitted during the visit to Israel. (Bar-On, 17 June 17, 1982, Zionist Archives)

In a letter sent to parents of tour participants in 1993 Dani More, Director of Israel Experience in the Youth and Hechalutz Department of the WZO, said:

> Through the Israel Experience every individual is exposed to a wide range of activities provoking thought, emotion and action. This combination ensures a positive Jewish experience, reflecting the modern components of Jewish identity, Jewish community and Israel. The programme aims to provide a better understanding of the history and culture of the State of Israel and the Jewish people.

Rabbi Paul Friedman, formerly one of the leaders of Conservative youth in the USA who has since immigrated to Israel, says:

> The assumption is that a person who has visited Israel carries something powerful with him. The Israel encounter is perceived as an inoculation against assimilation, with medium and long-term influences. The effect is like a vaccine that influences one's environment, that is, family, friends and synagogue. Today the Israel Experience is seen as the strongest educational resource available to Jews, as effective in the fight against assimilation. (Rabbi Paul Friedman, interview, April 1994)

Melitz director Avraham Infeld related to more detailed aspects of the significance of the Israel encounter. He noted that almost every Jewish community today has a new organization with a name that includes the phrase, 'Jewish continuity.' For Infeld:

> Jewish continuity depends on collective memory and therefore the significance of the Israel Experience is to re-connect the young person with the collective memories of the Jewish people as they are 'stored' in the land and people of Israel. Israel has the largest store of Jewish memories and this store is common to all Jews. (personal communication, 1998)

Zvi Bekerman, an anthropologist and former executive director of Melitz, is of the opinion that a Jewish tourist experience in Israel can bring to the surface aspects of identity that cannot be studied in books, but whose existence can be revealed through an encounter with the 'text' of Israel.

Dr Ron Kronish, director of the Inter-religious Coordinating Council in Israel (ICCI), indicates different models that are likely to dictate the character of the visit. One model views Israel as a museum where one can see, in a concentrated, organized way, all the important elements of contemporary Jewish identity (Kronish, 1983, 1984). A visit of this kind is essentially passive and is based mainly on sensory experiences and the learning of content. Another model views Israel as a laboratory in which different types of Jewish life can be observed and experienced. Israel has a concentration of institutions and people who are capable of expressing their opinions clearly on alternative forms of Jewish life. This is a more active experience, but fundamentally intellectual.

Bernard Reisman, Professor of Jewish Communal Studies at Brandeis University, believes what is missing from the usual visit to Israel is the contribution to the search for God, and there is a lack of understanding of the participants' need for spiritual elements (Reisman, 1990). However, some parents are concerned that the programme will be 'too religious'. The organizers must balance these ambiguous spiritual and religious goals with the other ideological, social and educational goals of the programme.

While there is room for difference of opinion and philosophy among the organizers of the programme, on a practical level co-ordination and compromise become necessary in planning a smoothly-run programme. Despite the difference between the priorities of the various organizers' positions (Israeli and Diaspora, different religious and political streams), there is general agreement on the main aims of the Israel Experience on the part of the organizers: to encourage young Jews to identify with their Jewish heritage and to increase their sense of commitment to Israel.

Goals of the participants

In addition to the range of expectations expressed by programme directors, there is a difference between the expectations of the organizers and the expectations of the young people. While the organizers want to reinforce Jewish identity and connection with Jewish heritage, the participants want first and foremost to have a good time and make new friends. The adults expect the youngsters to learn about Judaism and Israel while the teens are eager for freedom in what, for many, is a first trip without their parents.

Though motivations for joining an Israel Experience tour vary somewhat between sub-populations, there are some universal themes. Table 2 shows the results of responses to a list of motivations given to participants in the summer 1998 Israel Experience programmes.

Table 2 shows not only that the motivations of the participants differ somewhat from the objectives of the programme's organizers, but also that

Table 2 Motivations for visiting Israel, participants from USA, UK and France, summer 1998 (percentage of respondents answering 'yes')

	USA	UK	France
To have a good time	84%	87%	59%
Heard good things about the programme	74%	77%	50%
Israel is the Jewish homeland	71%	70%	68%
Israel is a beautiful country	70%	61%	76%
Israel strengthens Jewish identity	64%	61%	63%
I knew others who were enrolled	63%	69%	45%
I knew previous participants	60%	69%	43%
Israel is the Promised Land	55%	48%	75%
The programme content interested me	49%	35%	83%
To develop my spiritual identity	47%	35%	40%
It was a good break from my academic routine	45%	46%	24%
My parents encouraged me	43%	36%	13%
I wanted to visit a foreign country	37%	25%	27%
It is a *mitzvah* (religious commandment) for Jews to come to Israel	26%	17%	28%
Israel needs the support of Diaspora Jews	23%	21%	36%
I am considering *aliya* (emigration to Israel)	13%	9%	25%
Israel is a free, democratic country	9%	6%	9%
The tuition is inexpensive	8%	1%	5%
Israel is an international political centre	6%	4%	4%
To learn Torah	6%	3%	2%
Israel is advanced in arts and humanities	5%	2%	6%
Israel is advanced in science and technology	4%	2%	12%
Israel is inexpensive	3%	3%	1%
Number of respondents	792	494	75

Participants could provide multiple answers, so percentages do not total 100%.

Jewish youth from different Diaspora countries have different motivations for joining the tour. The highest-ranked motivation of American and British Jewish youth to participate in the Israel Experience is to have a good time. Their participation was also strongly motivated by their peers ('heard good things about the programme', 'knew others who were enrolled', 'knew previous participants'). The French participants, in contrast, were far more likely to say they joined the tour because the programme content interested them. Also, their feelings about Israel itself were more important than recreation; Israel is the Promised Land, a beautiful country, the Jewish homeland and a place that strengthens Jewish identity – these were stronger motivations for the French than having a good time. Overall, strengthening Jewish identity, one of the key goals of organizers, was a motivator for about two-thirds of all participants. Developing personal spiritual identity was cited as a reason for joining the tour by just under half the American participants and even fewer of the British and French. The theme of Israel–Diaspora relations ('Israel needs Diaspora support') motivated less than a quarter of participants, although it should be noted that the French were significantly more likely to say this was part of the reason they joined the tour than were the Americans or British. Similarly, the French were more likely to say they are considering immigrating to Israel (*aliya*), but even among this group only a quarter said it was a reason for joining the programme. As noted earlier, encouraging a move to Israel, one of the central goals of the tour in early years, has lately been de-emphasized. Learning Torah was a motivating factor for very few participants. It is likely that young people interested in coming to Israel for this reason would select other programmes, such as learning in a longer-term religious study programme such as a yeshiva.

There was a wide gap in the percentage of young people from these three major Diaspora communities who said that they joined the tour because they were encouraged to do so by their parents. As seen in Table 2, the American participants were most likely to say that the encouragement of their parents was a factor in their decision to come to Israel; the French were the least likely to say so. The next section explores why parents encourage their children to take part in Israel Experience tours.

The parents' expectations

Today's adults witnessed the start of mass tourism to the State of Israel. Many of the parents, organizers, teachers and chaperones of the groups visited Israel when they were in their teens. For parents who are Israel Experience alumni (or who visited Israel in other fora), their children's visit may have a nostalgic aura, sometimes even to an exaggerated degree. At the same time, parents who visited Israel as teenagers often have concerns and expectations for their children that they did not consider during their own tour. Parents who have never been to Israel themselves may be unsure of what to expect, or may have unrealistic expectations for the tour. Many parents see the visit to Israel as a turning point in their children's lives.

Naturally, parents expect appropriate supervision and precautions for their children's safety. In addition to general concerns related to teenagers travelling without their parents, there are concerns related to the ongoing political violence in the region.

In 1991, Levenberg and Isaacs surveyed the parents of Israel Experience participants in the United States. They found that parents are less concerned with the social aspect of the trip than their children tend to be. They are more interested in the educational message of the visit, and especially in reinforcing Jewish identity. Additionally, many parents assume that the significance of a visit to Israel is religious, and as a result some parents who are not religious felt that the programme would not be suitable for their children.

In 1995, I conducted a study of a special programme organized by the Detroit Jewish community in which data on parents' and participants' expectations were collected and compared (Cohen, E.H., 1996a). I found that the parents' expectations are similar to the expectations of the participants, but that their order of priorities is different, with the parents putting more emphasis on learning and identity development, and less emphasis on fun and recreation. In general it can be said that the parents have a longer, more detailed list of expectations and goals.

Many parents said that fostering pride in the Jewish people was the most important aim of the programme. Parents expect the visit to Israel to deepen or even form their children's Jewish identity, which was usually described in cultural rather than in religious terms. Parents want their children to establish a bond with Israel. These aims were more important to the parents than to their teenaged children. Most of the parents surveyed wanted their children to want to visit Israel again, but it is rare for them to hope their children will make *aliya*. In fact, there have been cases in which parents and school teachers made an effort to tone down enthusiasm of youth after their return from Israel, to 'calm them down' so they could return to everyday life. This expresses the extent to which parents consider the trip to Israel a means of enhancing Jewish identity in the Diaspora community, rather than a means of encouraging immigration to Israel.

Parents expressed a desire that their son or daughter come home with a sense of responsibility for the future of the Jewish people and will act accordingly. Parents also expected their children to develop greater confidence and maturity and to see the visit as an opportunity for growth and personal development.

Many of the parents surveyed in Detroit considered strengthening the belief in Judaism to be an important aim of the visit. The parents also expressed anxiety about their children marrying non-Jews and hoped that the experience would create a commitment to marrying within the faith.

In the social realm, while the parents put less emphasis on fun and pleasure, there was a prevalent desire that the child would meet new people and acquire friends, both American and Israeli. The parents expected that their son or daughter would learn to be part of a group and that the sense of belonging would be an integral part of an experience of this kind. The teenagers placed less emphasis on the group experience. They stressed the aspect of potential interpersonal relations, while the parents expected them to get a sense of the overall dynamic of the group.

Some of the parents expected the tour to introduce their children to the everyday life of Israelis so as to understand the rules and customs of Israeli culture. Parents also wanted their children to develop an interest in the Hebrew language, in the hope they would learn Hebrew in the future.

The parents expected their children to learn during the tour, for example acquiring knowledge about the history of the State of Israel and the Jewish people. They also expressed their hope that the visit would shed light on the political situation in Israel and the Middle East. Many said they wanted their children to understand the importance of Israel, not only for Judaism, but also for the world as a whole.

It must be stressed that this survey was conducted only among parents from a particular community. Those in other countries are likely to have different priorities. For example, a general survey of French Jewish heads of households found widespread support for the idea of their children moving to Israel (Cohen, E.H., 2002a), so it may be expected that a higher percentage of the parents of French participants in Israel Experience programmes would consider the tour as a preliminary step towards *aliya*. Additionally, a large percentage of French Jews make multiple trips to Israel and many have family living there, so French parents may stress learning Hebrew and being exposed to daily life in modern Israel as objectives of their children's visit. However, systematic surveys of parents of participants, along the model of the Detroit study, would be necessary to better understand the objectives of parents in other communities.

The Israel Experience tours are laden with symbolic meaning in which the Jewish community at large places great significance and hopes. In a few weeks of visiting historic and religious sites, brief encounters with Israelis, seminars and recreational activities, it is hoped that the teenage participants will take important steps towards being more strongly affiliated with Judaism and with Israel. Leadership and social skills, religious education, cross-cultural communication, political awareness, history, geography and language are all touched on, while simultaneously giving a group of youngsters an enjoyable trip during their school vacation. More than half a century after its inception, the programme is well established as an integral part of Jewish Diaspora education. In the next chapter we will look at the dynamics of participation in the programme.

Notes

1. There are also educational tour programmes to Israel aimed at different populations. For example, the Jewish Agency offers educational tours for adults, one aimed at those between the ages of 30 and 50 and one for those over the age of 50. The America-Israel Friendship League offers trips to Israel for non-Jewish youth as part of their Youth Ambassador Student Exchange. See http://www.aifl.org/html/web/people_edu_prog.html (accessed 11.11.07). Such programmes were not included in my survey of Israel Experience programmes, and are not included in the current analysis.
2. In its early years, it was variously known as Israel Tours, Israel Summer Institute, etc. Annette Hochstein first officially used the term 'Israel Experience' for the programme in 1986.
3. For years, this entity was the Youth and Hechalutz Department of the World Zionist Organization. This department has known several organizational changes, and is now fully integrated into the Department of Education of the Jewish Agency for Israel.
4. See www.birthrightisrael.com (accessed 11.11.07).
5. For information on MASA see http://www.masaisrael.org/masa/english/about+masa/what+is+masa (accessed 11.11.07).
6. See for example: http://www.israelexperience.com/JewishAgency/English/Jewish+Education/experiences+in+Israel/Short+term+Programs/Teen+Summer+Programs/(accessed 11.11.07).
7. Rappelling is descending a rock face or cliff with rope and harness.
8. The Hebrew term *aliya* literally means to 'go up'. Its ideological and religious connotations are much stronger than those of the word 'immigration'.
9. For more information, see http://www.jewishvirtuallibrary.org/jsource/personal.html. (accessed 11.11.07).
10. In 2005, an independent group launched a counter-tour, 'birthright unplugged', with the aim of imparting a very different political message, their itinerary including visits to Palestinian refugee camps and meetings with Palestinian leaders and Israeli peace activists. See http://www.birthrightunplugged.org/index.html (accessed 11.11.07).

Chapter 3
Participation in the Israel Experience

Rate of Participation

Table 3 shows the rate of participation in the Israel Experience over the years. The programme was well established by the late 1950s and participation was relatively steady until just after the Six Day War in 1967. The number of Israel Experience participants increased almost five-fold between 1966 and 1978. Pride in and connection with Israel among Diaspora Jews was notably strong following Israel's victory in the Six Day War (Lederhendler, 2000). Participation continued to climb relatively steadily until it reached a peak in 1978. In this year, subsidies to the programme were cut, significantly increasing the cost of the programme to participants' families, and participation declined by more than a third over the next few years. Participation levels recovered in the 1980s possibly as a result of the strong economy at that time in the US, home of the vast majority of the participants. In 1987 the first *intifada* (Palestinian uprising) broke out, and participation dropped sharply. Participation gradually recovered again during the 1990s as the political situation stabilized and the peace process seemed to be progressing, until the second *intifada* broke out in 2000 and participation in Israel Experience programmes (along with general tourism to Israel) plummeted.

At precisely this critical time, the Taglit-birthright israel free tours were established, and succeeded in bringing large numbers of young people to Israel, despite the political situation. With the decrease in attacks on Israeli civilians by 2003, participation levels in the Israel Experience programme began to recover, and the number who joined the Taglit-birthright israel tours almost doubled. Some Diaspora populations were quicker to resume sending their children to Israel. Participation rates from the UK, Mexico, Belgium and France in 2003 and 2004 actually surpassed pre-intifada numbers (Levran, 2004). Also in the case of the Taglit-birthright israel tours, the number of participants from the US fell from 8104 in 2001 to 3208 in 2002, whereas the number of participants from Argentina, Australia, and France rose. Most graphic was the increased participation from the former Soviet States and Eastern Europe. In 2001, young people from the USA made up 60% of the Taglit participants, while those from the former Soviet Union and Eastern Europe comprised only 11%. In 2002, the percentage of

Table 3 Number of participants in Israel Experience programmes

Year	Number of participants	Year	Number of participants	Year	Number of participants
1949	45	1972	8,419	1990	7,221
1950–52[a]	703	1973	6,894	1991	6,763
1953–56[b]	2,410	1974	7,215	1992	8,300
1957	1,060	1975	7,233	1993	9,564
1958	1,484	1976	6,743	1994	9,607
1959	1,220	1977	9,585	1995	10,831
1960	1,013	1978	11,348	1996	8,821
1961	1,787	1979	7,533	1997	13,213
1962	1,419	1980	5,921	1998	12,900
1963	2,058	1981	6,260	1999	13,355
1964[c]	2,000	1982	6,318	2000	13,705 (9,462)[d]
1965	2,437	1983	10,063	2001	3,629 (13,365)
1966	2,377	1984	8,581	2002	2,026 (11,397)
1967	4,193	1985	10,542	2003	6,106 (17,019)
1968	2,910	1986	11,475	2004	9,413 (21,138)
1969	4,431	1987	12,925	2005	11,128 (17,943)
1970	5,757	1988	7,269	2006	11,428 (23,834)
1971	8,619	1989	8,398	Total:	336,506 (114,158)[e]

The data were collected by the authors in the Zionist archives (Jerusalem). We also used the data delivered by Mittelberg (1994: 137–138) to assess our own data.
(a) data concern all three years;
(b) data concern all four years;
(c) estimate;
(d) figures in brackets are for Taglit-birthright Israel;
(e) total for 2000 to 2006.

US participants fell to only 28% of the total for that year, and participants from the CIS and Eastern Europe rose to 40%! By 2005 and 2006, however, the numbers of participants from Russia and the other former Soviet States had fallen to a few hundreds. This may be attributed to several factors. With continued migration from the former Soviet Union, the Jewish population in these countries has dwindled. Those who remained tended to be the least affiliated with Judaism or Israel (Trier, 1996). Additionally, marketing in other countries may have received more attention in the years that participation from the US and Canada fell so drastically. From these figures, we see that participation reflects the state of Israel–Diaspora relations, personal concerns (cost and safety) and possibly organizational and marketing issues.

Character of the Population

Country of origin

Israel Experience participants come from 37 different countries. Groups travelling together are usually uniform in terms of country of origin. The country of origin of the visitors and the character of the community from which they come represent important considerations in terms of how the programme is prepared and implemented. As will be discussed in subsequent sections of the book, nationality of participants has a great influence on the programme. The United States, home to the largest Diaspora population, sends the most participants in terms of sheer numbers, though it is not the best represented in terms of percentage of young Jews who join the tour. Table 4 shows the total Jewish population of the main countries from which Israel Experience participants come and the relative proportion of the targeted age cohort who took part in the tours in a sample year, 1998. The UK, Australia and Latin American countries (particularly Mexico) send far greater percentages of their youth to Israel on these tours, a situation with far-reaching implications for the local community. The countries of the former Soviet Union and Germany send the smallest percentage of their Jewish youth (Cohen, E.H., 2002b).

Of the over 100,000 participants in Taglit-birthright israel tours between 2000 and 2006, more than 70% were from North America (60% of the participants were from the US alone). There was very little participation from the other major Diaspora communities that are represented in the population of Israel Experience tours, such as France (fewer than 4000 participants, 3% of the total) and the UK (only 598 participants, 0.5% of the total), and this reflects the marketing and advertising focus of the Taglit programme.

Table 4 Market penetration of Israel Experience tours, 1998

Country	Number in targeted age cohort (15–19)	First timers in Israel Experience programme*	Market Penetration of IE programme[a]
USA	76,572	8,785	11.5%
CIS	1,796	287	15.9%
France	5,753	921	16.0%
Canada	5,228	1,138	21.8%
UK	3,287	1,442	43.7%
Argentina	2,486	643	25.9%
Brazil	1,050	395	37.6%
Australia/New Zealand	1,320	417	31.6%
South Africa	1,214	324	26.7%
Germany	672	39	5.8%
Hungary[b]	585	104	17.8%
Mexico	550	496	90.2%
Belgium[c]	337	50	14.8%
Total	100,850	15,041	14.9%

* The 'first-timers' in Israel Experience programmes may have previously visited Israel in other frameworks, such as family visits.
(a) The penetration of the Israel Experience programme is calculated by dividing the number of first timers in the programmes by the total relevant age cohort figure.
(b) Age cohort unknown: calculated here based on the percentage in the Former Soviet Union.
(c) Age cohort unknown: calculated here based on the percentage in France and Switzerland.

Age

The Israel Experience programme is usually intended for youngsters aged 15–18. This seems to be the age group for which the Israel Experience is most successful. On standard Israel Experience tours, there has been a considerably lower level of satisfaction among the 18–29 year olds than prevails among the younger group. Longer programmes with a study component, such as high school or university study abroad programmes, intensive Hebrew language programmes, religious study programmes at yeshivas (traditional Jewish study schools) and volunteer programmes such as Sherut La'am (Service to the People) are successful among older participants (Cohen, E.H., 1995a). The Taglit-birthright israel programme is open to participants between the ages of 18 and 26, although most participants are at the younger end of this range, between 18 and 20 (Saxe *et al.*, 2001: 2). The availability of this free tour for the older age group may encourage parents to wait several years before sending their children to Israel.

In many Western Jewish communities, young adults aged 15 to 29 tend to be alienated from Judaism and the Jewish community. In the years following the bar/bat mitzvah rite of passage (age 12 for girls, 13 for boys) participation in community life and their Jewish public involvement decreases considerably. Although this is the most significant age in terms of shaping identity, it is the stage when young Jews drop out of public and organized Jewish life. This phenomenon, which may be called the 'black hole of Jewish community life', has become very prevalent in the large Jewish centres in the West. The Israel Experience is aimed specifically at teenagers at the start of this period. 75% of the participants are aged 14 to17. The Israel Experience brings together relatively large numbers of young people at this stage of transition from childhood to adulthood.

Gender

A general characteristic of the Israel Experience groups is the relative preponderance of girls. Slightly over half (approximately 56%) of those who visit are girls. This figure remained relatively constant during the decade I conducted the ongoing survey of the programme, although between 2001 and 2003 (when security concerns were highest), the reverse was true, and more males came on tours to Israel. Recently, as the situation has stabilized, there have been near-equal ratios of males and females. Interestingly, in an early summer trip, conducted in 1963, a full 72% of the participants were female (Comet, 1965)!

This gender imbalance has implications for one of the aims of the programme namely, to encourage dating among young Jews (and by extension, to encourage endogamy). The male–female imbalance becomes even more pronounced among relatively older groups of participants. Even among groups of visiting students on longer programmes the proportion of girls is far greater, and it is in precisely these groups that participants have greater expectations of finding potential dating partners.

Participants' background in Jewish education and community involvement

As mentioned above, the Israel Experience does not usually appeal to organizationally unaffiliated Jews. Rather, it represents one part of a rich variety of Jewish educational and community activities in which they and their families participate. Young people who have not previously received a Jewish education and have not participated in related activities are far less likely to come to Israel, particularly in the framework of a group educational tour.

The participants arrive in Israel with some – and often with significant – Jewish background. Of more than 40,000 participants surveyed between 1993 and 1998, over half attended Jewish Day Schools and/or Sunday schools, 81% were members of a Jewish youth organization, 72% attended Jewish camps, and 72% were involved in Jewish community events at least once a month during the years prior to their trip to Israel. Most took part in these formal and informal educational settings over the course of a number of years. These figures were consistent for the years of the study, with little fluctuation. In the past few years, however, this has begun to shift slightly. For example, among French Jewish youth, there has been a decline in involvement with the political youth movements and an increase in involvement in non-political (cultural or religious) youth organizations (Ilanit Rozner, desk director of European Israel Experience programmes, personal communication June 28, 2007). A greater percentage of participants from the USA are recruited through Jewish Day Schools, and a smaller percentage through youth organizations (Dani More, general director of Israel Experience programmes, personal communication, June 28, 2007). These changes in the clientele may necessitate adaptation of the curriculum design.

The differences in educational background between participants from various Diaspora communities can be seen in Table 5. The questionnaire differentiated between various educational settings in order to determine whether formal education (such as Jewish Day Schools) or informal education (such as youth movements) was more strongly related to participation in Israel Experience tours. Overall, participation in informal settings such as summer camps and youth organizations was more widespread. However, almost all participants from South Africa and South America, for example, attend Jewish Day Schools, while virtually none from Eastern Europe do. In North America, the extra-curricular Sunday school education is more prevalent.

The parents of many Israel Experience participants also have significant experience with Jewish education and with Israel. Levenberg and Isaacs (1991) found that parents who had received a Jewish education themselves were three times as willing to send their children to Israel as those who had not. Of the Israel Experience participants surveyed, 78% said that at least one of their parents had been to Israel before, and 22% said at least one of their parents had come to Israel as part of a youth group tour. While these

Participation in the Israel Experience

Table 5 Jewish educational background of Israel Experience participants, by continent

	North America	South America	Western Europe	Eastern Europe	South Africa	Australia & New Zealand	Together
Studied in Jewish Day School	49%	86%	41%	14%	90%	78%	52%
Studied in Sunday school	73%	5%	56%	22%	6%	39%	58%
Attended Jewish camp	76%	69%	65%	76%	71%	80%	71%
Participated in Jewish activity during past three years – monthly or weekly	72%	78%	70%	68%	65%	75%	72%
Participated in Jewish youth organization	83%	73%	83%	74%	74%	87%	81%

statistics were also consistent over the course of the survey, they varied widely among participants from different countries, as seen in Table 6. The graphic difference between visitation rates of parents of participants from Western and Eastern European countries undoubtedly reflects the political and economic barriers that would have prevented travelling to Israel from Eastern Europe in past decades. While the percentage of North American participants whose parents had visited Israel is relatively low compared to most of the other populations, it is significant that only 40% of US Jews overall have visited Israel, while 70% of the parents of Israel Experience

Table 6 Visitation of participants' parents to Israel, by continent

	North America	South America	Western Europe	Eastern Europe	South Africa	Australia & New Zealand	Together
At least one parent visited Israel	70%	74%	91%	43%	88%	86%	78%
At least one parent visited Israel as part of a youth group tour	19%	23%	31%	7%	20%	25%	22%

participants have been to Israel. The impact of being the first generation in a family to visit Israel, compared to being the child of parents who have been to Israel, and particularly of IE alumni is a topic which deserves further investigation.

In offering their free tours, the Taglit-birthright israel programme organizers hoped to reach further into the periphery of the Jewish community than previous Israel Experience programmes succeeded in doing. Perhaps the greatest results of the Taglit-birthright israel's campaign to recruit outside of traditional youth movements and community institutions is that the Taglit groups are more internally diverse than those of the Israel Experience. As mentioned, Israel Experience tours are generally organized through a specific community institution and therefore participants tend to be from the same religious and ideological stream. Often they are from the same home town and many knew each other previously. This is not the case with Taglit-birthright israel tours, whose groups are made up of participants from different geographic areas (mostly within the US and Canada), and with relatively greater diversity in their level of previous Jewish educational background and community involvement. The programme has had to come to terms with this diversity, making the programme and activities understandable and meaningful for those with less background yet interesting and challenging for those with more.

Somewhat ironically, the political tension in Israel during the first years of the Taglit-birthright israel programme led to an unforeseen situation: a greater proportion of young people from Orthodox families joined the tours. Those without a previous strong commitment to Israel and Judaism were unlikely to come when the danger was the greatest (Saxe *et al.*, 2004).

In summary, participation in educational group tours to Israel among Diaspora youth has increased over the decades, with fluctuations due to political instability in the region. The vast majority of participants, numerically, come from the United States, although some smaller Diaspora communities send far greater proportions of their youth. Participants are adolescents, primarily high school students. They come with strong backgrounds in Jewish education, both formal and informal.

The personal backgrounds of participants must be considered in the larger social and cultural context of the programme, which will be discussed in the next chapter.

Chapter 4

The Historical and Sociological Background of Jewish Youth Tourism to Israel

The development of the Israel Experience as an educational tool over the past 60 years, its impact, significance and limitations, can be understood only against the background of some of the issues that characterize the Jewish world and the world as a whole in the second half of the 20th century. It is worth going into some detail about these issues:

(1) relations between Israel and the Jewish Diaspora;
(2) the State of Jewish education from 1945 to the present;
(3) the sociology of contemporary tourism;
(4) the nature of contemporary Jewish identity;
(5) adolescence as a formative period in shaping personal identity.

Changes Occurring in the Relations between Israel and the Jewish Diaspora

Barry Chazan (1993) sums up as follows the changes that have occurred over the last century in the place Israel occupies in Jewish identity: 'Once Israel was a dream, then it became a cause, now it is a living human reality and context'.

Relations between Israel and the Diaspora can be divided into a number of stages.

Stage 1 – from 'negation of the exile' to establishment of relations between the new State of Israel and the Diaspora.
Stage 2 – pride in Israel and Jewish identity: the end of the 1960s as a turning point.
Stage 3 – reciprocal relationship between Israel and the Diaspora: the 1980s–2000.
Stage 4 – after the *intifada*: renewed debate about the nature of the relationship.

Stage 1:
From 'negation of the exile' to establishment of relations between the new State of Israel and the Diaspora

Zionism is the Jewish nationalist movement for a homeland. The modern Zionist movement began in the mid-1800s, at which time the Turkish-Ottoman Empire controlled Palestine and the Jewish population, known as the Yishuv, numbered less than 10,000, primarily in Jerusalem. In response to recurrent anti-Semitism throughout the Diaspora, some Jewish philosophers, thinkers, rabbis and philanthropists[1] began advocating increased Jewish settlement in *Eretz Yisrael* – the Land of Israel, and the eventual establishment of an autonomous Jewish state. The First World Zionist Congress was held in Switzerland in 1897. Waves of Zionist immigrants from Europe and Russia began establishing new settlements in Palestine, with the support of Diaspora individuals and institutions. These were largely non-religious and influenced by socialist philosophy. The Kibbutz Movement was founded in 1908, and in 1920 the General Federation of Jewish Workers in Palestine (commonly known as the Histadrut) was established in Haifa. A number of Zionist youth movements and Labour Zionist movements were active in Europe, Russia and the United States. In 1917 the British issued the Balfour Declaration, which (in contradiction to the earlier Sykes–Picot Agreement with the Arabs and French) promised the Jews a national homeland in what was by this time British Palestine. In 1939 this promise was officially dropped, and the British restricted Jewish immigration to British Palestine. The Jewish population in British Palestine on the eve of World War II was approximately 400,000. Many Jews attempting to flee Europe during and immediately after the Holocaust were turned back by the British blockade. A nascent Jewish army (the Haganah and Palmach) began to fight for the establishment of a Jewish state. In 1947, the United Nations Special Committee on Palestine submitted their Partition Plan, ending the British Mandate and creating two independent states, one Jewish and one Arab, with Jerusalem in an international zone to be controlled by the United Nations. Between the time of the UN vote and the day it was to go into effect, fighting broke out between the Arabs (of Palestine and the neighbouring Arab countries) and the Jewish residents, now approximately 600,000. Some Zionist supporters in the Diaspora sent money and weapons; others attempted to influence the political process surrounding the conflict; some came themselves to join the struggle. On May 14, 1948 the day before the British Mandate was to end, David Ben-Gurion declared the establishment of an independent State of Israel. The surrounding Arab states immediately declared war. After a series of battles, truces and negotiations, an armistice was reached in 1949, establishing the borders between the new State of Israel, and Jordan, Egypt, Syria and Lebanon. In the next two decades, the population of the State of Israel swelled with Jewish migrants from Europe and Russia as well as from the Arab countries of the Middle East and North Africa (Blumberg, 1998; Halpern & Reinharz, 1998).

Classic Zionist ideology advocated and predicted the 'Negation of the Exile' and 'Ingathering of the Exiles' (Kornberg, 1983; Robertson, 1997). In other words, all the Jews would eventually move to Israel. The basic assumption was that a person who identifies with Zionism plans to personally fulfil this ideology. Members of Zionist youth movements were expected to immigrate to Israel at the age of 18, and those who did not do so were forced to leave the movement. According to this ideology, assimilation and anti-Semitism are dangers lying in wait for Diaspora Jews, so they would do well to move to Israel before it is too late.[2]

At the same time there were fears that the nation-building project of the Jews would not succeed, or that a new disaster would wipe out Israel. Therefore, there were some Jews who, while they supported the State of Israel, believed that the long-term survival of the Jewish people necessitated the continuation of Jewish populations in other parts of the world. The pre-State writer Ahad Ha-am became disillusioned with practical, political Zionism, and instead advocated cultivating national pride and cultural advancement among Jews both in the Yishuv settlements and throughout the Diaspora, as a means of strengthening the Jewish people as a whole (Kornberg, 1983).

On a practical level, the difficulty of life in the pre-State settlements and in the early days of the State prevented many Jews from moving there. Even among those who could not stay in their previous homes (refugees from the Holocaust or Muslim-Arab nationalist movements in North Africa and the Middle East), some chose instead to migrate elsewhere, most commonly to the United States, Canada, Australia or France, expanding some Diaspora communities.

Thus the early days of the State of Israel were characterized by the establishment of relations between the new Israeli society and the Diaspora communities which, despite ideology, did not disappear. These relations consisted largely of financial and political support for the State in the first difficult decades. Relatively few young Jews came on tour to Israel, and those who did were generally members of Zionist youth movements who were expected to be preparing for a permanent move.

Stage 2:
Pride in Israel and Jewish identity: The end of the 1960s as a turning point

The end of the 1960s marked a change in Israel–Diaspora relations for a combination of political and cultural reasons. The most dramatic event was Israel's victory in the 1967 Six Day War with Syria, Egypt and Jordan, in which Israel captured the Gaza Strip, Sinai Peninsula, Golan Heights and the West Bank including East Jerusalem. Throughout the Diaspora, pride in Israel and feelings of affiliation with the State blossomed in the years following the war (Lederhendler, 2000).

This political event coincided with a cultural movement, particularly among young people in the United States, which intensified its impact on Israel–Diaspora relations. The ideological crisis that swept the West following the students' revolution, the Vietnam War and the Watergate scandal exploded the myth of a single American identity. A trend emerged of emphasizing the culture of different ethnic groups: blacks, Spanish-speakers and even those from different European countries. For young Jews, ethnic identity largely found its expression through identification with Israel. Israel became a kind of pilgrimage destination for young people, a place of ideals and spirituality. In particular, the socialist utopian vision of the *kibbutz* was attractive to American Jews at this time. In general, Zionism offered an ideology in which young Jews could 'find themselves'.

These developments influenced the Zionist credo. The change in relations was given formal expression in the 'Jerusalem Plan,' accepted by the 27th Zionist Congress in 1968, redefining who is a Zionist. According to this definition, a Jew could live in the Diaspora and still be considered a Zionist on condition that he or she works for the good of Israel and supports it. This included working to strengthen an Israeli society based on the prophetic vision of justice and peace, opening the door for people from the ranks of the New Left to join the Zionist movement.

Following this recognition that the Diaspora was not ending, the Zionist movement began to take greater responsibility for Jewish education in Diaspora communities. Israelis were sent as emissaries to Diaspora communities to work in Jewish educational settings as experts in the fields of religion, Hebrew language and Jewish culture. As seen in the previous chapter, participation in Israel Experience tours began to increase exponentially. Tours were seen less as a first step towards *aliya* and more as a personal spiritual journey or an expression of affiliation with Judaism and Israel.

Stage 3:
Reciprocal relationship between Israel and the Diaspora: The 1980s–2000

By the 1980s, it was generally assumed that both the Diaspora and the State of Israel would continue to exist for the foreseeable future, and a reciprocal relationship came to be established. Israel came to function not only as a physical refuge for Jews fleeing anti-Semitism (i.e. the mass immigration of Jews after the collapse of the Soviet Union and of Ethiopian Jews), but also as a spiritual refuge from assimilation. Not only was legitimacy granted to the continuation of the Diaspora, but Israel found itself enlisted to help ensure the continued existence of the Jewish people in the Diaspora by discouraging or even reversing assimilation. This new perception, in which Israel plays a role in the continued existence of the Diaspora, has come to represent the Zionist mainstream. It unites Israel and Diaspora Jewry in terms of history, culture and identity, and gives the two communities common objectives.

One of the interesting changes taking place as a result of these developments is the change in patterns of donation to Israel. While Israel has faced difficult times recently, the State is well established and there is not the same sense of urgency among Diaspora Jewry to send money to ensure Israel's survival. Diaspora Jews continue to contribute money to Israel, but they also express opinions about what is happening there. As one way of trying to influence Israeli society, Diaspora Jews contribute directly to specific programmes rather than to the general fund of the United Jewish Agency. For example, in Project Renewal programmes, a Jewish Diaspora community may adopt a development town, neighbourhood or school. The New Israel Fund invests in projects promoting democratic values, pluralism and social justice.

Thus, a reciprocal relationship formed, in which Israel is involved in what is going on in the Diaspora and the Diaspora is involved in what is going on in Israel. Generally, the Diaspora provides political and financial support for Israel, while Israel provides content and symbolic support to Diaspora communities and their educational systems. In such a relationship, the problems of Israel and the Diaspora may be, to a considerable degree, viewed as shared problems.

During this phase, Israel Experience tours became common among more strongly affiliated Diaspora young people, some of whom were children of previous programme alumni. Increased interest in meeting young Israelis during the tour illustrates the emerging reciprocal relationship. It is worth noting that, although participation rates dropped after the outbreak of the first *intifada*, the decrease was not nearly as dramatic as in 2001.

Stage 4:
After the intifada: Renewed debate about the nature of the Israel–Diaspora relationship

Despite the formation of this reciprocal relationship, recent years have seen new tensions arise between the Israeli and Diaspora communities. Some Israeli leaders claim that whereas once Diaspora Jewry maintained Israel, now it is Israel that maintains Diaspora Jewry, financially as well as spiritually. In raising money for Israel, local Jewish institutions take a share and thus maintain themselves financially and organizationally, whereas the total sum of Jewish donations from the United States per year is negligible in the Israeli economy (Beilin, 1999).[3]

By this time, a close relationship with the US government and ongoing military support seemed to have replaced the need for political support on the part of local Jewish organizations.[4] In the 1990s, when the Oslo peace accords were moving forward, there also seemed to be less need for volunteers from overseas or for moral and ethical support from Diaspora Jews.

The outbreak of the second *intifada* in September 2000 raised serious questions about the reciprocal relationship between Diaspora Jewry and Israel. The dramatic drop in tourism, and particularly the cancellation of many Israel Experience tours, were perceived as abandonment of Israel by the Diaspora in a time of crisis and an illustration of a gap between Diaspora Jewry and Israel (Anti-Defamation League, 2001). The economic and security crisis in some ways reversed the trend towards perceiving Israel as a spiritual centre to serve a rapidly assimilating Diaspora population, and returned to a more classic Zionist view of an embattled Israel in need of support by Diaspora Jews.

In the face of international criticism of Israel, many Diaspora Jewish communities did hold rallies in support of Israel and a few sent 'missions' to physically show their support. However, some Jews were openly critical of Israel, bringing to the forefront the issue of Diaspora participation in Israeli politics. Many Israelis felt resentment that Jews who are afraid to come to Israel in times of political instability would attempt to dictate from afar how Israel should respond to the uprising. An editorial in the 12 June 2001 edition of the popular Israeli paper *Ma'ariv* bluntly expressed this feeling:

> The next time Diaspora Jews tell us to either withdraw from this or that hill or not withdraw from this or that hill, or advise to either go to war, or not go to war, we should remember that they are not really part of the State of Israel and that therefore, their right to determine our fate borders on nil. (*Ma'ariv*, 12 June 2001)

Nevertheless, during the fighting between Israel and Lebanon in the summer of 2006, most Diaspora Jews supported Israel, holding rallies, raising money and responding to the anti-Israel bias and anti-Semitism that some perceived in the media coverage of the war (Berkman, 2006). During the war with Lebanon, increased numbers of anti-Semitic acts were reported in many Diaspora communities around the world (Bekker, 2006). During the same time period, Holocaust denial was highly publicized owing to a cartoon contest and conference on this issue sponsored by the President of Iran. Thus, while there was some criticism of the policy of the Israeli government during the war, these coinciding events seemed to solidify Diaspora support for Israel, at least during the crisis. Additionally, following the war with Lebanon, there seemed to be greater tolerance for Diaspora critique, at least of specific policies of the Israeli government (Barkat, 2007), perhaps because the Israeli population itself was highly critical of the government at this time.

Another facet of the changing relationship is expressed in the desire of some Diaspora leaders to limit the direct involvement of Israeli emissaries in the affairs of their community (Cohen, E.H., 1997a). Such emissaries may represent a certain religious stream and thus influence from outside the dynamic within the community. Additionally, given the rise in anti-Semitism linked with attitudes towards Israel, some Diaspora Jews wish to make clear the distinction between Jews and Israelis, in opposition to the idea that Diaspora and Israeli Jews are part of a single people with shared concerns.

In the face of this difficult scenario, some Jewish leaders envision a paradigm shift in Diaspora–Israel relations. Until now, those who belong to the community have felt a normative obligation, as part of their Jewish educational process, to come to Israel. Those who have distanced themselves from the community do not feel this sense of obligation. Michael Steinhart, one of the founders of the Taglit-birthright israel Foundation, frequently speaks of the visit to Israel as a right, not an obligation; a 'right of passage' as opposed to a 'rite of passage'. The shift in perception of the Israel visit from 'rite' to 'right' is in its early stages and it will be interesting to track this change over time.

A typology of Israel–Diaspora relations

In order to better understand the dynamic of the Israel–Diaspora relationship, my colleague Gabriel Horenczyk and I developed a typology of attitudes towards Israel-Diaspora relations (Cohen, E.H. & Horenczyk, 2003). The typology is based on the results of a survey conducted in 2000 of 416 Jewish youth leaders visiting Israel from the USA, UK, Canada and

France. Respondents were given a list of nine statements about the Israel–Diaspora relationship and asked to rate the extent to which they agree with each on a scale from 1 (definitely disagree) to 5 (definitely agree).

After analyzing the results using the Smallest Space Analysis technique (see Chapter 1), we created a schematic diagram, shown in Figure 1. Israel, Diaspora Jewry or the Jewish people may be perceived as the centre of the relationship. Each of these attitudes could then reflect a Zionist or non-Zionist view. The statement in the Diaspora-centred Zionist view negates traditional Zionist ideology of all Jews eventually moving to Israel and stresses the utilitarian role of Diaspora Jewry in supporting Israel. There are no statements expressing a Diaspora-centred non-Zionist, attitude, as such a view would seem to be beyond the scope of Israel–Diaspora relations. The statements in the Israel-centred Zionist category emphasize the role of Israel as a haven against anti-Semitism and assimilation. The statement in the Israel-centred non-Zionist category is a vision of Israel as a democracy, not as the Jewish State or Jewish homeland. The statement in the Jewish

	Zionist view	**Non-Zionist view**
Diaspora-centred	The continued existence of a Diaspora is important for the existence of Israel.	
Jewish people-centred	Jews in the Diaspora and in Israel are brothers/sisters that live separately. Israel is the world centre for Jewish life. Israel must be a 'light unto the nations' from a moral standpoint. We (all Jews) are one people.	True Judaism does not require a state.
Israel-centred	Jews in the Diaspora want Israel as an 'insurance policy'. Non-orthodox Jews in the Diaspora will eventually assimilate.	Israel does not have to be a Jewish state, but should be a state for all its citizens (Israeli Jews and Arabs).

Figure 1 Schematic diagram of attitudes towards Israel–Diaspora relations
Source: Cohen, E.H. & Horenczyk (2003)

people-centred non-Zionist category doesn't recognize the need for a Jewish State, although it leaves open the possibility for Israel as a spiritual pilgrimage site. The majority of the statements fall into the Jewish people-centred Zionist category.

This typology may provide a theoretical basis for understanding Israel–Diaspora relations. For example, when the four Diaspora populations included in the study were compared using this typology, we found that, despite the many differences between them, all of the four national sub-populations were most closely correlated with the statements in the Jewish people-centred Zionist category. In other words, they see the collective entity of the Jewish people as the heart of the relationship, yet consider Israel to be the spiritual centre for the Jewish people. This is in line with the general observations regarding the Israel Experience and Diaspora tourism to Israel, which emphasizes the importance of a visit to Israel as a part of the ongoing relationship between Jews living around the world. It may be said that the approach expressed by Ahad Ha'Am (Simon, 1922), advocating the common development of the Jewish people and Jewish culture, with Israel serving as a spiritual centre, is more widespread within this study population.

The State of Jewish Education from 1945 to the Present

General background

As mentioned earlier, the Israel Experience is part of the larger Jewish educational context. Additionally, differences between various Diaspora populations in terms of attitudes towards Israel and towards Jewish identity have been linked, in part, to the nature of the Jewish education they receive in their home community. For these reasons, in order to understand the Israel Experience it is necessary to understand the history and current state of Jewish education throughout the Diaspora.

The aims of Jewish education in the Diaspora are complex. For the most part, Jews want to maintain their identity as Jews while being successfully involved in the predominantly non-Jewish societies in which they live. Jewish school systems must struggle with the quandary of how to educate towards involvement in an exclusive, separate minority culture without causing feelings of alienation from the surrounding society (Rosenak, 1987; Cohen, E.H., 1997b, 2006a, in press-a). This educational quandary has not yet been resolved, and has impacts on the Israel Experience programme. As discussed in the section on expectations and objectives, there is a fear among some parents and some Diaspora organizers that too powerful an experience in Israel will make youth 'too Jewish' and distance them from their home society. Therefore, programmes tend to emphasize solidarity within the group, with Israel functioning as a sort of spiritual summer camp.

In the second half of the 20th century, changes took place in the educational, religious and cultural perceptions of the Western world, which naturally also influenced the Jews, who were in the vanguard of such changes.[5]

In most Western countries, general education became inclusive, free and secular. This trend towards de-segregation of public schools was tied to movements for social equality for minorities. The other side of the coin was that voluntary separation such as private Jewish schooling was perceived as a declaration that the Jews wished to remain a distinct minority. For the most part this separation was viewed as undesirable and as a disincentive to sending children to exclusively Jewish schools. Most Jewish families sent their children to public schools, which were seen as necessary for successful integration (Steinberg, 1979, 1984).

Mass migration from Third World countries has generated a change in attitude towards ethnic minorities in developed countries. For example, in the United States multiculturalism has gradually replaced the concept of the melting pot. In France, a large influx of immigrants from former colonies has challenged the concept of a homogeneous, secular culture in which loyalties to specific ethnic or religious groups must be relegated to the private sphere. The role for parochial, religious and ethnic educational systems in a multicultural society has re-emerged as a critical, if controversial, topic.

In addition to these changes in the educational system at large, after World War II the Jewish people underwent radical changes that affected the nature of Jewish education. The most traumatic cause of change, of course, was the Holocaust, a national-cultural disaster during which entire communities and entire networks of schools in Europe were wiped out. Many of the students and teachers who were saved from extermination fled to other countries, primarily to Israel, the US, Canada and Australia, though some relocated within Europe after the defeat of the Nazis.

As well as the obvious physical and demographic changes, the Holocaust had a profound and lasting impact on Jewish identity, which then affected the content of Jewish education. The Holocaust is taught in virtually all Jewish educational settings, and the many Holocaust memorials and museums serve as powerful informal educational settings. *Yad Vashem*, the Holocaust memorial in Israel, is a stop on the vast majority of Israel Experience programmes. Some Israel Experience programmes focus on the Holocaust, and spend the first days of the trip in Europe visiting concentration camps, graveyards, memorials, etc. In such programmes, the connection between the Holocaust and the creation of State of Israel is emphasized.

Jewish education has had to deal with another important change: the weakening of the most important informal educational tools, the Jewish family and the Jewish community. Though obviously less violent than the Holocaust, this can also be seen as a trauma in Jewish identity with far-reaching consequences. The phenomena of weakening of families and communities are not unique to Jews, but are trends throughout Western societies. Geographic dispersal from extended family and ethnically-homogeneous neighbourhoods, stratification of the community structure, permissive education, the demanding careers of both parents, the increase in the divorce rate, and greater separation between place of residence and place of work are only some of the many and complex causes of the breakdown of family and community. Even among cohesive families with community connections, the impact of individualism, materialism, rationalism (that is, distance from faith-based values and distrust of revolutionary ideologies) and the busy modern lifestyle all tend to limit deep involvement in Jewish life or in activities related to Israel.

For Jews, who constitute a tiny minority in all Diaspora countries, the impact of this social trend has been particularly strong. As Jews assimilate into the larger society and less Jewish tradition is observed in the home, the family becomes less able to impart Jewish knowledge, rituals and values to its children. In addition, many parents see Jewish content as being of secondary importance to a general education that will allow their children to succeed in the larger society. Jewish subjects are seen as part of a sense of identification, not as something requiring special attention.

We find an early analysis of this change, and its relationship with programmes such as the Israel Experience, in some writings prepared by Mordechai Bar-On for the Zionist Executive Committee of 1969:

> On the assumption that the Jewish family has lost its educational character and its role as a factor in the continuity of Jewish tradition and identity, and on the assumption that Jewish schools are not comprehensive and are also limited in their ability to correct this distortion, is it possible to go back and establish Jewish identity during adolescence or at university age? Do the State of Israel and Zionism as an idea assume not only the centrality of Israel but also the duty of young people to immigrate to Israel in order to ensure its existence and future ... a key role in rehabilitating the Jewish awareness of Jewish youth, and what actions are required as a result?[6] (Mordechai Bar-On)

The community, too, has lost the binding impact it once had. As social boundaries have become more permeable, members of ethnic minorities are increasingly able to leave their communities and integrate into the general society. Particularly in the United States, home to the largest Jewish

Diaspora population, ethnicity has become largely symbolic (Gans, 1979, 1994). Thus, while the ideal of multiculturalism permits pride in affiliating with a minority group, that affiliation no longer affects every aspect of daily life as it once did. The traditional Jewish community served to provide economic, social, cultural and religious support for its members. The lifestyle of many modern Jews does not leave a lot of room for community life in general, and for the Jewish community in particular. The loss of the community's role in central spheres of the individual's life turns the community into a place of entertainment for leisure activities.

An additional change in the Jewish world that had an impact on the nature of Jewish education, of course, was the founding of the State of Israel. Since 1948 Israel has played an increasingly important role in Jewish education throughout the Diaspora, even beyond the specific case of educational visits to Israel. For example, a large number of Jewish educators have been to Israel as part of their own education. In his book on informal Jewish education, Reisman (1990) describes the typical profile of the Jewish teacher today. One of the significant differences between today's Jewish educators and those of the past is that the typical Jewish teacher of today has usually studied in Israel, often for a year or longer.

My 1992 study of staff members in informal Jewish educational settings in seven countries (Argentina, Brazil, Britain, Canada, France, South Africa and Uruguay), found that a visit to Israel is perhaps the broadest common denominator uniting the over 10,000 people employed in various positions in this field: 71% have visited Israel.

Changes in Jewish education

The innovations and changes taking place in the field of Jewish education over the past half century are expressed both in terms of organization and content. New umbrella organizations have been created to deal with Jewish education and there has been a significant increase in Jewish schools providing a full day's education. It is worth noting that enrolment in Jewish Day Schools varies widely in different countries, and this affects the character of the target population for the Israel Experience programmes. Throughout Latin America, home to approximately half a million Jews, enrolment in Jewish Day Schools is high: 60% in Argentina, 71% in Brazil, 85% in Mexico, 90% in Venezuela and 98% in Panama. In South Africa, virtually all school-aged Jewish children, especially those in the urban centre of Johannesburg, are enrolled in day schools (World Jewish Congress, 2001). In sharp contrast, just under a quarter of Jewish students in the US (2004) and just under 30% of those in France (Cohen, E.H., 2002a, in press-a) attend Jewish Day Schools, though these figures represent significant increases in recent decades.

There are educational institutes that are not full schools, such as the Sunday school network, extra-curricular Hebrew school programmes, synagogue youth movements that have educational activities (especially during school vacations), the summer camps network, classes for Jewish studies in regular schools in parallel with Christian religious studies lessons, and many departments and courses at colleges and universities on subjects relating to Judaism. These part-time options make it possible for a connection with Judaism to be preserved without over-emphasizing the separation from the general population. Another option is community leisure activity frameworks, such as sports and culture centres, which not only focus on Jewish content but provide a place for friendship among Jews and help to shape their identities.

The curricular content of the Jewish school has also undergone significant change. First, unlike the traditional *yeshiva*, which aims to train the child to function in a religious Jewish environment, Jewish Day Schools are expected to prepare students to function as Jews in the framework of society at large. This is expressed in the massive introduction of secular studies in the curriculum, and the predominance of part-time Jewish education.

Second, Israel as a modern society plays an important role in the educational programmes of each of the educational frameworks. Israeli teachers, school principals and educators work in Jewish schools, youth movements, summer camps, community centres, and synagogues throughout the Diaspora. Many Diaspora educators receive part of their training in Israel. For example, every year the Department of Education of the Jewish Agency implements programmes that bring teachers from Jewish schools in the Diaspora to Israel in order to improve the level of teaching about Israel and Israel-related subjects.

An increasing number of Jewish children learn Hebrew as a modern language, not only as the holy tongue of prayer and study. (The study of other Jewish languages, such as Yiddish and Ladino, has virtually ceased.) Students learn about Israeli history and follow current events. Israel is a source of pride and identification. It creates fashion and symbols. Israel plays an important role in virtually all Jewish schools.

The centrality of Israel in Jewish education in the Diaspora represents a key point in understanding the place of the Israel Experience as an educational tool, on which many today pin great hopes. In the widely diverse world of the Jewish Diaspora, Israel may be the only fixed issue on which there is widespread agreement.

The Israel Experience was created in part to address the educational challenges faced by Diaspora Jews. Like summer camps, the tour provides a time during which the pressure to assimilate into a non-Jewish society is temporarily suspended, and at the end of which youngsters return to their previous social and educational milieu. The intense experience of being in Israel is expected to fill gaps in the Diaspora educational systems and community structures. Participants see a society in which Jews are the majority, where Judaism can be expressed openly and in many various forms. The comments of thousands of programme alumni attest to the emotional impact of the trip. Such feelings of being connected to Israel, Jewish history and the Jewish people are difficult to impart in classroom settings.

These are some broad, general changes in Jewish education. But the Diaspora is not homogeneous. The countries where Jews live are different from one another, and as a result their Jewish organizations and educational frameworks also differ. These differences are reflected in the nature of the Israel Experience tours from the various countries. Some particulars of the educational systems in the largest Diaspora communities, and their impact on the Israel Experience programme are described below.

The United States

Following World War II, the United States became the largest Jewish Diaspora community. The Jewish community in the United States had to deal with the question of why there should be segregated Jewish education in a society whose ideal is the melting pot. Attending public schools was seen as important to successful integration into society.

Horace Kallen, a well-known Jewish philosopher with a fierce belief in the concept of the melting pot, wrote that the purpose of Jewish education in the US was 'To promote cultural pluralism in which democracy of the spirit can take place: never to teach Jewish issues without their dynamic connection to non-Jewish issues' and 'To present pluralism within the community in Jewish education, in that equal status is given to religious studies, secular Judaism, Hebrew and Yiddish,' (Kallen, 1954: 178). This attitude, which attempts to bridge the gap between the desire to stand apart and the desire to integrate, expressed the dominant aspiration of the generation of immigrants, who wanted to preserve Jewish tradition and yet wanted their children to be successful in America. The next generation (children of the immigrants) rejected their origins and accelerated the process of assimilation. The third generation (grandchildren of the immigrants) spans a spectrum from those who are almost completely assimilated and alienated from Judaism, to those who want to return to their roots, and have become active leaders working to revitalize Jewish Diaspora communities. Many of the latter are alumni of the Israel Experience programmes and cite the visit to Israel as a turning point in their lives, directing them towards greater involvement in Jewish communal life.

The Jewish educational system in the US is based mainly on the religious streams (Reform, Conservative, Orthodox and, to a lesser extent, Reconstructionist).[7] The secular, Yiddish-based socialist option, like that of the Bund common among Eastern European Jews before World War II, never took hold in the United States. Neither did the Zionist movement produce a network of schools in the US, but rather operated within the framework of youth movements. This reflects the political culture of the United States. Freedom of religion is protected, and Jewish schools can operate parallel to Catholic, Protestant and Muslim schools. However, strong ethnic affiliations, particularly those with nationalistic aspirations, are less accepted.

After World War II the scope of activities of Jewish schools began to increase. The several hundred thousand Jews who migrated to the US from Eastern Europe after World War II tended to settle in concentrated areas and send their children to Jewish schools. In 1962 there were 60,000 students in Jewish Day Schools. By 1977 there were 92,000. In the 2003–2004 school year there were 205,000 students enrolled in 759 Jewish Day Schools (elementary and secondary) in the United States (Schick, 2004). The number of both elementary schools and secondary (high) schools increased during these decades. As the Jewish population dispersed throughout the country, the number of schools outside traditional Jewish population centres increased proportionately.

In the 1970s, a number of overlapping factors spurred the expansion of the Jewish education system in the United States.

(1) There was a decline in the standard of public schools, while the standard and reputation of the Jewish schools was high.
(2) There was a general awakening of ethnic pride among America's minorities. The discovery of anti-Semitism among some ethnic minorities and anti-Israel sentiment in some elements of the Left impelled Jews away from a larger, liberal multicultural movement and back to their own community.
(3) Young people were engaged in a search for new spiritual ideologies. American Jews participated in this non-assimilationist counter-movement, and looked for new meaning for their Jewish existence. The counter-culture allowed Jewish students to stand up against the educational establishment.
(4) Israel's wars in 1967 and 1973 and the struggle on behalf of the Jews of the Soviet Union contributed to the search for Jewish identity, and highlighted the importance of education.

The changes in awareness and identity among the American Jewish community led to dissatisfaction with traditional forms of Jewish education and prompted a pedagogic and organizational response. In particular, the opinion that afternoon schools were not successful in transmitting Jewish content or instilling feelings of identity with the Jewish people and tradition became widespread. Furthermore, there was increased recognition that Jewish education should not end at a child's bar/bat mitzvah, and thus there was an increased tendency to concentrate on educating young adults, high school and college students and families (Mandel, 1991). The establishment of Conservative and Reform Day Schools provided an option for non-Orthodox families who wanted Jewish education for their children, although even today more than 80% of students in US Jewish Day Schools are enrolled in Orthodox schools (Schick, 2004).

While previous generations were eager for their children to successfully integrate into American society, today America's Jews are worried that they have integrated too successfully, to the detriment of Jewish continuity and identity. Therefore, support for Jewish education has grown and Day Schools have been portrayed as a bastion against assimilation. However, private Jewish education in the US remains expensive. While religious schools in Canada and Europe receive significant government subsidies, most Jewish community leaders objected in principle to government support for private religious schools, as the separation of Church and State was perceived as protecting Jews from the official discrimination they suffered in other countries.[8] The Jewish education budget, today more than two billion dollars,[9] comes mainly from tuition fees, funds and charity, with a smaller part coming from Jewish federations.

Group youth tours to Israel are similarly promoted as an antidote to assimilation. In many ways the tour to Israel fits well with the lifestyle of American Jewish youth. It fills the need for an exploration of one's roots. It promises fun and adventure. Scheduled during school vacation, it does not unduly interfere with participation in the wider American society. The structure of the group allows boys and girls in early adolescence to enjoy close companionship without pressure to form couples. Participants can have a personally satisfying experience without much pressure to make significant lifestyle changes.

Europe

After World War II the Jewish education system in Europe was in ruins. Its rehabilitation has been carried out gradually, and the rebuilt system differs in many ways from the one that was destroyed. Many Jews left Europe for Israel, the US, Canada or Australia. Of those who remained, many moved from Central and Eastern to Western Europe. During the first ten years after the War, the economic situation was difficult. During this time there also began to be a complete separation between Eastern and Western Europe. The countries of the West developed and flourished, as did the Jews living there, while in the East the Jewish community and its education system deteriorated.

Western European society in general, during this time, became increasingly secular and modernized. In the Jewish community, the birth rate declined and the number of intermarriages increased. Most Jews in Western Europe were no longer affiliated with a particular synagogue. Many families no longer bore characteristically Jewish names, so that many of them were almost 'underground' and could conceal their Judaism with ease. This hyper-assimilation may be seen as a response to the trauma of the Holocaust, after which many of the Jews who remained in Europe wished to completely distance themselves from Judaism. In any event Judaism was a very marginal factor in their lives. Among other reasons, the disappearance of Jewish geographic concentrations caused problems in getting children to the schools and an increase in cost.

In their analysis of the situation facing European Jews, Elazar and Trigano (1995) suggest that the small and scattered communities need to work together to create stronger educational and institutional systems, noting that:

> possibly (but not likely) excepting France and Britain ... they do not have the resources to train their own rabbis or teachers, Jewish communal professionals, or other needed personnel. They cannot sustain more than the simplest Jewish educational experiences for their children and even those depend upon importing teachers and *shlichim* (emissaries) from Israel. (Elazar & Trigano, 1995)

France

After the Holocaust, during which more than a quarter of French Jews were killed or deported, including many of their leaders, the French Jewish community, along with all its institutions and educational structure, had to be rebuilt. In the 1950s and 1960s, waves of Jewish migrants moved to France from the former colonies and annexed territories in North Africa, predominantly Algeria, Morocco and Tunisia. Today over 70% of French Jews are of North African origin (migrants or their descendents). This demographic shift has had far-reaching consequences for French Jewry and the community's educational system (Bensimon & Della Pergola, 1986). The Jewish community in France has taken on a more conspicuous, public character. North African Jews display a somewhat more publicly open form of Jewish identity – by wearing Stars of David or skullcaps, for example. However, the French Republican value of laity restricts religion to the private sphere, for example prohibiting students in public schools from wearing conspicuous religious symbols. In some cases, open signs of affiliation have made French Jews vulnerable to verbal and physical attacks; in 2003, after an attack on a Jewish school, Chief Rabbi of France Joseph Sitruk advised Jewish boys to wear baseball caps in public instead of the traditional skullcap (McClintock & Sutherland, 2004; CRIF, 2003). Jews of North African origin are largely acculturated into French society but, at the same time, they feel close to Israel and visit frequently, both in the framework of group tours and as private family vacations. In fact, many French Jews have bought vacation homes in Israel, and bring their families each year. Thus, many French Jewish high school students prefer to spend their vacations with their families and friends (either friends who travel with them, or friends they re-meet each year during their common vacations in Israel), and enrolment in Israel Experience tours has dropped among this population (Ilanit Rozner, desk director for European Israel Experience programmes, personal communication, 2007; Cohen, E.H., 2005b).

French public schools play a strong role in transmitting values of citizenship, universalism and public *laïcité* (secularism). While a system of private, parochial schools does exist, sending one's children to private school is viewed by some as unpatriotic or 'communitarian.' The term communitarian refers to affiliation with a specific ethnic or religious community rather than with the nation, a concept with strongly negative connotations in French society, and an accusation sometimes made against Jews. Nevertheless, enrolment in French Jewish Day Schools has increased dramatically, for several reasons:

(1) a desire, particularly among the traditional Sephardi population, to preserve Jewish religion and culture. In this regard the public school system poses several problems for religiously observant families because of restrictions against wearing religious apparel (such as *kipa* or *tzitzit*) and the meeting of classes on Saturdays;
(2) government support for and recognition of private schools has enabled an improvement in the general academic standards of religious schools;
(3) an increase in drugs, violence and anti-Semitic incidents in public schools has motivated some Jewish families, even those who are not very religious, to move their children out of the public school system (Cohen, E.H., 1991, in press-a).

In a recent survey of French Jews, I found that almost a third of French

Jewish students are enrolled in non-Jewish (predominantly Catholic) private schools.

United Kingdom

British Jews have long been socially and economically integrated. In the mid-1800s, England's chief rabbi emphasized Jewish education and the establishment of Jewish Day Schools (Schmidt, 1962: 302). However, there was widespread concern that separate schooling would impede social and career opportunities. Jewish schools were largely concerned with Anglicizing Jewish immigrants from other European countries, for example by teaching English and discouraging the use of Yiddish (Finestein, 1986). Increasingly, British Jewish families sent their children to public schools. At the end of World War II, only a handful of Jewish Day Schools were in operation and in 1967, less than a quarter of British Jewish children attended Jewish Day Schools. Since then, Jewish education has experienced a renaissance (Miller, 2001). The multicultural movement catalysed by immigration from Asia, Africa and the Caribbean has legitimized public Jewish identity. The most recent figures (Della Pergola *et al.*, 2005) show that in the greater London area over 60% of Jewish children are enrolled in Day Schools, which do not have the facilities to accept all the students who apply. Enrolment in outlying areas is significantly lower.

The majority of Jewish schools in the UK are Orthodox. Indeed, most synagogues and Jewish community organizations in the UK are Orthodox, although most British Jews are not strict in their observance of Jewish law and could be described as either traditional or secular. According to Valins *et al.* (2001), while half the students in British Jewish Day Schools come from families that are not religiously observant, only 7% of secular British Jewish families send their children to Jewish Day Schools. Taken together, these two findings indicate that Jewish learning in the UK may be expanded by providing formal and informal education that emphasizes Jewish culture, Hebrew language, Israeli studies and non-Orthodox religious studies. The Israel Experience is one such available programme, and for many young British Jews, the trip to Israel has become a widely practiced rite of passage (Kosmin *et al.*, 1998; Grant, 2006).

Eastern-Central Europe and the former Soviet Union

For many centuries, Eastern Europe and Russia were home to numerous Jewish communities.[10] The Jewish communities of Eastern Europe were diverse; some Jews were highly educated in secular studies and the arts, others emphasized traditional religious learning. These communities and their educational systems were decimated during the Holocaust. Immediately following World War II, many surviving Jews left for Western Europe, the United States, Canada, South America, Australia or Israel. Those who remained lived under the Communist regimes which, for many decades, prohibited any religious education. In addition, many of the heads of the Jewish communities in these countries themselves were Communist. In Jewish schools the students were not given a Jewish education at all, and in the ORT schools,[11] which continued to function throughout the Communist era, there were many non-Jewish students. During the years of the Cold War, the Jewish communities of Eastern Europe and the Soviet Union were very isolated. Only after the fall of the Soviet empire was connection with world Jewry, including Israel, re-established. Many Jews who lived in Eastern Europe and the Soviet Union during the Communist era emigrated to Western Europe, Israel or the US when given the opportunity. Those who remained are in the process of re-building a Jewish educational system; a challenging endeavour. The communities are small, and most of the potential teachers, that is those with an interest in and understanding of Jewish tradition and texts, have left. Also, some of the international Jewish groups and institutions supporting the revitalization of Jewish education in Eastern Europe and the former Soviet states are Orthodox, and the style of education and religious outlook they espouse is not understood or accepted by Jews raised in a thoroughly atheist society (Gitelman *et al.*, 2003).

The number of Israel Experience participants from Eastern European countries is very low. However, as mentioned earlier, some tours spend time in Eastern Europe touring historical sites related to the Holocaust and meet with members of the Jewish communities in these countries. In this way, the Israel Experience reaches young Jews who do not themselves take part in the tour. Such programmes establish links between groups of Diaspora Jews from very different circumstances and give them an opportunity to discuss the various issues their respective communities are facing.

Latin America

Jewish identity in predominantly Catholic Latin America tends to emphasize ethnic components such as family, language and culture rather than religion. Affiliation with Jewish community centres and institutions is high, while religious ritual practice is low. In recent years, economic instability spurred a wave of *aliya*, but this levelled off as the economy recovered.

The region's economic crisis has had a detrimental impact on local Jewish educational systems. For example, between 1992 and 2004 the number of students enrolled in Jewish educational settings in Argentina dropped from 21,000 to under 15,000 (Jewish Information and Referral Service, 2006). Families are less able to afford private school, and schools are unable to offer sufficient aid. Enrolment in Jewish Day Schools fell, schools were closed, hundreds of Jewish studies teachers were dismissed and the number of hours of Hebrew and Jewish studies was cut. The ORT schools established in the Soviet Union and Eastern Europe spread to Latin America in the 1940s and became an important part of the Jewish educational system in the region. International organizational and financial support for the ORT schools has allowed the schools to weather the regional economic problems (ORT, 2006).

Elazar (1999) says that Latin American Jews never felt quite at home in the countries where they lived and that they feel a spiritual connection to Israel as a homeland even if they don't intend to move there. Raanan Rein (2004), an expert on Latin American Jewry, expresses a similar sentiment:

> Being Zionist in Argentina, for example, often has had little to do with the State of Israel. More often, it has been one of the strategies espoused by Jews in order to become Argentines. Like every other immigrant community, Jews in Argentina needed to have their own Madre Patria (mother fatherland). Just as the Italians had Italy and the Spaniards had Spain, so Jews had their own imagined Zion, or Israel. This brand of Zionism was about becoming Argentine while staying Jewish, and not moving to Palestine. (Rein, 2004: 3)

The Israel Experience tours fit well with the goals of an educational system rooted in this type of Zionism. Indeed, the Latin American communities, while small, send a high percentage of their youth on Israel Experience or other organized trips to Israel.

South Africa

The South African Jewish community, established in the 1800s by Jewish emigrants from Europe drawn by the country's wealth, was historically strongly religious and Zionist, with high levels of enrolment in Jewish Day Schools. The vast majority of South African Jews call themselves Orthodox, and there has been a trend towards affiliation with Chabad and other religious movements. 'This increase in religiosity has been attributed to a desire for stability in an otherwise unstable society' (Weiner, 2005).

South Africa has relatively lower exogamy rates than other Diaspora communities, only about 20% (Della Pergola *et al.*, 2005). Nevertheless, the Jewish population has been in steady decline since the 1970s. In the years following the collapse of the apartheid regime, many South African Jews left, particularly those of the younger generation, primarily because of a fear of rising crime and economic insecurity. Some Jewish Day Schools, faced with falling enrolment, opened their doors to non-Jews seeking a higher level of education than is offered in the public schools (Goodman,

1994). In the past few years, the flow of emigration has slowed. The Jewish community has become concentrated in Johannesburg (55,000 of the country's approximately 80,000 Jews). About 60% of Jewish children are enrolled in day schools overall; this figure reaches 80% in Cape Town.

Because of the school schedule in the southern hemisphere, Israel Experience tours from South Africa most often take place during the Israeli winter months, a slower time in the tourism season. South African groups, therefore, may not be able to participate in some of the 'mega-events' during which multiple groups converge for certain ceremonies or presentations.

Australia

Jews have lived in Australia since the first days of European settlement. Like other Diaspora populations, they attempted to balance between integration and preservation of Jewish identity and tradition. There has been relatively little overt anti-Semitism in Australia, and the Jews living there are generally considered part of the white majority.[12] Many Jews sought refuge in Australia before and after World War II. Between 1938 and 1961 the Australian Jewish population almost tripled in number. Jews comprise less than 0.5% of the Australian population. The approximately 100,000-120,000 Australian Jews are concentrated in Melbourne (50,000) and Sydney (45,000), each of which has a number of synagogues, Jewish schools, etc. Much like the British model, almost all of Australia's synagogues are Orthodox and the majority of affiliated Australian Jews describe themselves as Orthodox, regardless of their level of ritual practice. About half the Jewish children in Sydney and Melbourne attend Jewish Day Schools (Shyovitz, 2007). Jewish youth movements are also active in Australia, and there is a relatively high level of participation of youth in local Jewish community activities (Cohen, E.H., 2004a).

Towards the future of Jewish education in the Diaspora

In summary, Jewish education in the Diaspora faces a number of challenges. Many communities are still in the process of rebuilding their leadership and structural institutions following the trauma of World War II and the Holocaust; some (particularly in Eastern Europe) will probably never return to their pre-war status. Holocaust education has become a major feature of Jewish education programmes around the world.

Most young Jews throughout the Diaspora are highly assimilated into the dominant society. Jewish educators (many of whom are culturally assimilated and not strongly religiously observant) must struggle to make the tradition relevant to these youth (Kohn, 1999; Schoem, 1982; Rosenak, 1987). Jewish Day Schools are experiencing a revitalization, partially in reaction to a perceived decline in the public school systems throughout the West. This system is in a period of transformation to adapt to non-Orthodox students (and parents). Informal Jewish education, such as summer camps, plays an important role in Jewish identity education, with a wide variety of options available around the world (Lorge & Zola, 2006). The educational tour to Israel, as we shall see in subsequent chapters, has become a central element in contemporary Jewish education for Diaspora Jews.

The Sociology of Contemporary Tourism

Leisure activities in general, and travel in specific, have become increasingly important in the way individuals explore and express their identity. Studies of tourism as a sociological phenomenon are helpful in interpreting the case of the Israel Experience.

Boorstin (1964) analysed the difference between travellers interested in seeing and learning in-depth about the reality of the places they visit and tourists who seek only superficial 'pseudo-events'. The social relations between host and guest are reduced to economic relations of staff or merchant and consumer. Additionally, tourists are outside the social codes both of their own society and that of the society they are visiting, resulting in a lack of social restraint (i.e. in clothing, sexual conduct, photographing) (Reisinger & Turner, 2003).

MacCannell (1976, 1992), one of the pioneers of the sociology of tourism, holds that tourism is a type of modern pilgrimage undertaken in an attempt to seek authenticity and to overcome feelings of alienation. He writes that tourism is a cognitive activity undertaken in an attempt to create a uniform world ideology:

> After considerable inductive labour, I discovered that sightseeing is a ritual performed to the differentiation of the society. Sightseeing is a kind of collective striving for a transcendence of the modern totality, a way of attempting to overcome the discontinuity of modernity, of incorporating its fragments into unified experience. (MacCannell, 1976: 13)

In applying MacCannell's thesis to the specific case of Jewish travellers to Israel, I would suggest that the visit to Israel provides an opportunity to experiment with and experience a Jewish wholeness not available for most Jews living as minorities in their home countries.

The quest for authenticity, for an integrated sense of Self, or for a spiritual centre that tourists seek in the exotic Other or in nature, is generally frustrated by the contrived encounters and barriers set up by the tourist industry and by the sometimes unromantic realities of the destination. In recent years specialized branches of tourism have developed to try to provide more authentic experiences for visitors, including heritage tourism, eco-tourism and tours to sites of tragedies.

The concept of sustainability has received much attention in recent years. Sustainable forms of tourism would take into account the tourists' relationship with and impact on the natural environment, the economy and the social structure of the destination, and make an effort to establish types of tours that are not exploitive (Bramwell & Lane, 2000; Hall & Lew, 1998). Significantly, although it is a heavily visited area with delicate ecosystems, irreplaceable archaeological and historic sites, and a wide variety of religious communities living in close proximity, the subject of sustainability in tourism to Israel has barely been broached, and has not yet become widely considered in the Israel Experience tours, although recently some programmes have begun to include seminars and discussions of issues such as the environment and inter-faith relations.

Building on the approaches of Boorstin (1964) and MacCannell (1976, 1992), Cohen, E. (1979, 1984, 1985, 2007)[13] developed a typology of tourism according to degrees of alienation from the tourists' spiritual centre, from the most superficial type of tourism through the most meaningful: recreational or pleasure-seeking tourists; diversionary tourists seeking stress relief; experiential tourists searching for meaning in the exotic; experimental tourists looking for an alternative to their everyday life; and existential tourists visiting a spiritual centre away from home. These are archetypes. In applying Cohen's model, I have found that in practice the same individual may span several of these categories, even within a single trip.

Smith (1977) emphasized the importance of differentiating among the mass of tourists by their personal background (gender, class, nationality, etc.), their motivations for travel and their chosen destination. The Jewish traveller to Israel may be understood as a particular case. The same Jewish traveller on another vacation to, for example, India or Jamaica, would have significantly different motivations and expectations and thus a different type of experience than they would while travelling in Israel. While non-Jews also make religious pilgrimages to Israel, their experience, too, will differ from that of the Jewish tourist in the modern State of Israel. In their study of visitors to the Wailing Wall in Jerusalem, Poria *et al.* (2003) found that the tourists' perceptions of a site and the degree to which they consider that site part of their own heritage has a significant impact on the visit, and heritage tourist sites must be understood in the context of the perceptions that visitors have of the sites.

Given the rapid rate of change in the local destination cultures, the tourists' home cultures and the global framework with which both interact, it is

Historical and Sociological Background

increasingly difficult to isolate the impacts of tourism on travellers or hosts. Rather, in the age of globalization and post modernity, it may be more accurate to speak of the role tourism plays within the larger context of social, political, ecological and economic flux (Burns, 2005).

In the case addressed in this book, Jewish youth travel to Israel, it must be recognized that both Diaspora Jewry and Israeli society are undergoing periods of major upheaval. Hollinshead (1998, Hollinshead & de Burlo, in press) insists on considering the ambiguities and hybrid identities within both the tourist population and the host population. Thus, the impact of the tours must be analyzed within the larger framework, considering such issues as exogamy, secularization, the political situation in Israel and the surrounding region, resurgent anti-Semitism in Europe, the exodus of Jews from the former Soviet Union to Israel, and more.

In a similar vein, the type of travel traditionally called tourism may be considered only one example of mobility in a spectrum from daily travel to migration (Coles *et al.*, 2005). In the specific case of Jewish youth travel to Israel, then, the summer trip may be considered one example of interrelated Jewish travel ranging from visits to local Jewish community centres through *aliya*.

The scope of the Israel Experience programme began to expand in the late 1960s, at the same time that tourism as a phenomenon began to grow all around the world. While in general mass tourism tourists play no social role in the society they are visiting, this is not the case for Jews visiting Israel. It is more similar to types of heritage tourism in which descendants of immigrants return to their ancestors' homeland, even though the families of most Jewish tourists lived in various Diaspora countries for centuries. Nevertheless, by virtue of the religious and cultural tradition, Jews have an emotional tie to Israel as their homeland. In addition, many do have extended or even immediate family who live in Israel, due to the various routes of migration following the creation of the modern State. Nevertheless, it would be erroneous to romanticize or over-simply the relationship Jewish tourists have with Israel and Israelis. Jews have a wide variety of motivations and expectations for their trip to Israel. The visit to Israel is simultaneously a pilgrimage to sites within the traveler's own culture and a journey to a foreign country.

Jewish tourists to Israel in general, and Israel Experience participants in specific, display characteristics of each of the types of tourists in the Cohen model (Cohen, E., 1979, 1984, 1985). For example, they may exhibit traits of recreational tourists while spending the day at the beach, of experiential tourists while visiting historic synagogues in a Hasidic neighbourhood and of existential tourists while praying at the Western Wall. There is a wide range of options available to Jewish youth who wish to visit Israel, and different programmes are likely to attract participants with varying expectations and goals, as found in a comparison of students at a religious women's school and a university in Israel (Ohayon, 2004). These young tourists must navigate between the ideal of visiting the Jewish Homeland and the reality of being in a country in which they don't speak the language and don't understand many of the norms and values. When young Jews from the Diaspora meet their Israeli peers, they are simultaneously meeting an 'Other' and searching for themselves, the selves they could be if they lived in Israel.

Diaspora tourism is gaining recognition as a type of heritage or cultural tourism. The Israel Experience is undoubtedly the longest running, most consciously planned, and most thoroughly researched example of Diaspora tourism. The information on these young travellers yields valuable information about a type of tourist who may not precisely fit into earlier typologies.

The Nature of Contemporary Jewish Identity

The psycho-social concept of 'identity' is a modern one. The study of identity as we understand it today was pioneered by social researchers such as Weber (1922/1991), Mead (1934), Goffman (1959, 1961) and Erikson (1968, 1974), who looked at how individuals understand their place in society and Barth (1969), Geertz (1973) and Dashefsky (1976) who studied how groups see themselves. (This brief list of pioneers in the field is only indicative, and not meant to be exhaustive.)

Beginning in early childhood, people develop a system of dispositions, tastes, values and preferences, *habitus* in Bourdieu's terminology (1979), absorbed from the surrounding society. For members of the majority or those living in a homogeneous community, these tastes and dispositions may be considered natural, not even questioned on a conscious level. Members of a minority, or migrants, may hold tastes and values that differ from those of the dominant or host society. Minority adolescents must navigate between the two systems to develop their own identity, which is often a hybrid or hyphenated identity (Cohen, E.H., 2004b; Jensen, 2003; McLoyd & Steinberg, 1998).

Until relatively recently, for most people, ethnic and religious identity were determined at birth, with little chance to change. The possibility – or responsibility – of choosing one's identity, what Berger (1979) calls the 'heretical imperative', is a hallmark of post-modern society. In the post-modern world, identity has become fragmented. Maintaining a sense of belonging to one distinct group has become increasingly difficult. This surfeit of choices can undermine the very idea of a personal identity, transforming identity from a coherent concept to a perpetually unfinished 'subject in process' (Sarup, 1996: 47).

Identity can be imposed from without or embraced from within, and may be positive, negative or neutral. Additionally, identity may operate at cognitive, affective and behavioural levels.

It may be noted that issues of group identity and assimilation have been recognized in Jewish society since ancient times.[14] Indeed, many Biblical stories may be understood as struggling with questions of individual and national identity (Askénazi, 1984/ 2005; Gordin, 1995; Magonet, 1995; Gold, 2003). Nevertheless, when Jews were more segregated from non-Jewish society and the Jewish community was all-embracing, Jews had far fewer options in terms of lifestyle, and their identity was largely assumed. The current issues of identity with which the Jewish world is pre-occupied are recent developments, which mirror similar issues faced by people around the world today. Jewish identity may be said to include

> ... *Jewish consciousness* – how strongly Jews feel about Judaism and/or Jewishness, and how much space these feelings occupy in their lives; and *Jewish meaning* – how Jews define the Judaism to which they subscribe and how they define their Jewishness, how they relate to the organized Jewish community, what are the implicit or explicit boundaries of Jewishness, and so on. (Gitelman *et al.*, 2003: 342)

Israel–Diaspora relations, anti-Semitism and the Holocaust, education (formal and informal, Jewish and general) and heritage tourism each have an impact on the nature of contemporary Jewish identity. However, discussions of Jewish identity in the Diaspora today tend to focus primarily on the issue of assimilation versus continuity.

In early studies of migration and ethnicity studies, sociologists assumed that among migrant and minority populations, ethnic identity unavoidably diminished and groups eventually assimilated into the larger society, but gradually recognized that there are a number of possible routes of adaptation (see, among many others, Gordon, 1964; Gans, 1979, 1994; Bochner, 1982, Furnham & Bochner, 1986; Jiobu, 1988; Featherstone, 1990; Appadurai, 1996; Guibernau & Rex, 1997; Ben-Shalom & Horenczyk, 2003).

Berry (1997, 1990, 1984, 1976; Berry *et al.*, 2002) developed a typology of four potential responses of migrant groups to their host society: integration, separation, assimilation or marginalization. Berry's model also applies from the point of view of the host society. The four comparable types of responses are multiculturalism, melting pot, segregation and exclusion.

Throughout Jewish history, we can find examples of all of these types of acculturation. Even today, in different parts of the Diaspora, Jews have various responses to their role as an ethnic-religious minority population.

In the West today, there is little segregation or exclusion of Jews. With the exception of some small groups of ultra-Orthodox and Hasidic Jews, who have opted for segregation, Jews are either integrated or assimilated into the societies in which they live. Those who are integrated function in the wider society, but maintain ties to Jewish religion and culture. Those who are assimilated have severed all but the most symbolic ties to their religious or cultural heritage, and have fully adopted the values and culture of the surrounding society. However, periodic resurgences of anti-Semitism may prompt feelings of marginalization or seclusion among otherwise integrated or assimilated Jewish populations.

As America has moved from a melting pot model in which all groups meld into a single culture with many influences to a multi-cultural model in which groups maintain their distinctive cultures while living in an integrated society and most overt forms of segregation have ended, it has become easier for minority groups to integrate, and maintaining ties to one's heritage has fewer negative social costs. French society, too, is struggling with the question of multiculturalism. Although with rising anti-Semitism and the secular nature of French culture, public affiliation with Judaism may be more difficult, the strongly traditional Sephardi majority also tends more towards integration, rather than the fuller assimilation that was common among French Jews of previous generations. In other countries too, larger questions of national identity, the status of minorities and multiculturalism all influence how the Jews within their borders express their own identities.

As mentioned, the Israel Experience programmes have had little success in reaching the most fully assimilated Jews. The tours also have few participants among the segregated ultra-Orthodox (who send their children to Israel through other study programmes). Therefore, we may say that most Israel Experience participants come from families who are integrated into the societies in which they live; that is, they have adopted the core values and behavioural patterns of the surrounding society, yet maintain significant ties to the Jewish culture, religion and community. Since the participants come from many different countries, the cultures into which they have integrated differ, and this affects the character and impact of the tours from various origins. The encounter with Israel may offer alternatives to the forms of Jewish identity expressed in participants' home communities.

In addition to changes in the nature of Jewish identity, the way in which identity is transmitted has changed in recent generations. The influence of the family, which was the main vehicle for passing on Jewish identity in traditional society, has been considerably weakened as a result of changes in how the role of the family is perceived. One result of this weakening of the framework is a high divorce rate among Jews; another is the search for external elements to take on one of the roles of handing Jewish identity to the next generation.

Jewish identity is simultaneously religious, national, cultural and personal/familial. Additionally, it touches on spheres such as differentiation from non-Jews, a sense of group affiliation, values, and psychology (Reisman, 1993).

Aspects of Jewish identity

Differentiation from non-Jews

The Jews' perception of themselves as the Chosen People, found throughout Jewish texts, is a central feature of the traditional religion, but one that modern, liberal Jews may find uncomfortable. Many, if not all social groups, define clear boundaries between group members (insiders) and non-members (outsiders). Spicer (1980) cites it as one of the common criteria among 'enduring peoples' that are necessary for ethnic survival. Today, in most parts of the world, Jews can completely blend in to non-Jewish society. Jews have few, if any, physical characteristics to distinguish them. Assimilated Jews may be culturally indistinguishable from their non-Jewish neighbours. Identification has become voluntary. And yet, to maintain identity as a Jew, some differentiation from non-Jews must be maintained. This differentiation may be religious, cultural or, as Gans (1979, 1994) claims, largely symbolic. A reactive or negative type of identity, in which being Jewish is almost exclusively defined in opposition to being gentile, was found among suburban American Jews, for example (Schoem, 1982), and in particular among Jewish youth raised in the strongly Christian environment of Texas (Cohen, E.H. & Bar-Shalom, 2006; Bar-Shalom, 2002), who tended to define themselves as 'not Christian'.

Affiliation

Identification with Judaism can be manifested in four areas of life – religious, national, community, and family. The national definition is problematic in some contexts because of questions of dual loyalty to the country where the Jews live and their affiliation with the Jewish nation.

Identification with values

In the field of identification with the values seen as Jewish, there is the greatest disagreement between different groups and streams. For example,

David Forman, director of the Israel Experience programmes for the Reform movement in the US, defines Jewish values as equality and justice, while ultra-Orthodox Jews hold that the highest value is to keep the commandments as written in the Jewish code of law. Moreover, there are cases in which the values that are considered to be Jewish conflict with each other, and each side feels that its Judaism requires fighting the perception of Judaism of the other.

Sense of commitment

In contrast, feeling of commitment towards the Jewish people has the widest consensus. This feeling is awakened particularly during times of hardship and physical or spiritual danger. The feeling of commitment can be towards other Jews who are in distress, such as the Jews of the Soviet Union before its collapse, or a sense of commitment of Diaspora Jewry towards Israel in times of war. It can be related to a desire for continuity with the past and the traditions of parents and grandparents, and sometimes it can arise from anxiety over the future of Jewish existence. A sense of commitment can cross other ideological borders because the specific content is left undefined, beyond a generalized commitment to the Jewish people. According to Rosenak (1987: 262), a sense of loyalty can co-exist with, and in fact enable, diversity of opinion, belief and practice within the larger community: 'The more one can take for granted in terms of loyalty, the larger the scope for spontaneity and individuality within the parameters of religious education and life'.

Psychological

In this type of identification, Judaism is associated with specific character traits, tastes, and patterns of behaviour. It varies in different social contexts. For example, in Russia and the Ukraine non-religious Jews differentiated themselves from their gentile neighbours because they (the Jewish men) did not get drunk or beat their wives (McKee, 1999; Liebman, 2003). American comedians such as Woody Allen and Jerry Seinfeld parody stereotypically Jewish traits such as a need to achieve, the overbearing Jewish mother, and even neuroticism.

The Israel Experience and Jewish identity

During the Israel Experience, participants are exposed to all the areas of identity discussed above. It gives participants a chance to explore and experiment with aspects of identity that may be less readily available to them in their home communities, for example by spending Shabbat with religious families, volunteering on an army base, learning Hebrew, etc.

Cognitive learning takes place as guides explain the meaning of sites and teach about periods in Israeli and Jewish history. The information is presented as part of the tour's goal of instilling or intensifying participants' feelings of identification with Jewish history, the Jewish people and the nation of Israel. However, some critics have charged that the tours over-exploit the participants' emotions, particularly the emotion of guilt, and do not appeal enough to young people's critical sense (Forman, 1989).

A typology of Jewish identity

Each year for a decade, the questionnaire my research team distributed to Israel Experience participants included an item related to the nature of Jewish identity (Cohen, E.H., 2004b). Included in the list are those concepts that appear repeatedly, and that were borne out by years of research in the field. These components are birth, culture, choice, commitment, religion, education, hope, language, family, reaction to prejudice and relationship to a national homeland. Participants were asked to indicate all of the components that they felt describe their relationship to Judaism. The question was formulated:

> I consider myself Jewish: by birth, by family, by culture, by choice, by language, by commitment, by loyalty, by hope, in reaction to anti-Semitism, in reaction to the Holocaust, in relation to other Jews, in relation to Israel.

While over the course of the 10-year international research the formulation and wording of the question varied slightly, every effort was made to keep the phrasing of the question similar in order to enable comparison.

Based on this database of tens of thousands of responses from the years 1993 to 2003, I developed a typology of the components of Jewish identity (Figure 2). This graphic representation of the components of identity was created using the Smallest Space Analysis procedure described in Chapter 1. The items are plotted based on their inter-correlation, with strongly correlated items close together and weakly (or negatively) correlated items far apart. This basic typology may then be used as a basis for comparison between sub-populations of Israel Experience participants (i.e. nationality, gender, denomination, etc.).

This procedure enables us to see the structural relationship between the components of identity, as perceived by the participants in Israel Experience tours. The structure consists of four categories arranged around a central item. The central item is 'Jewish by culture.' Culture is a kind of meeting point of many components: public and personal, familial and national, received and chosen, biological and historical. As expressed by Bekerman (1997), 'culture is not "out" nor "in" but in-between'.

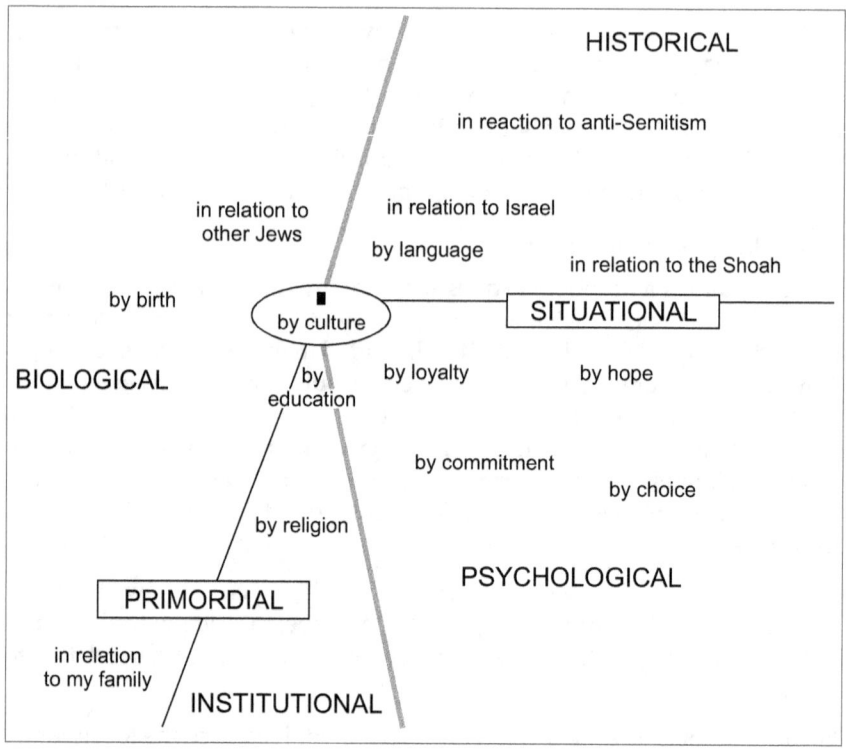

Figure 2 Typology of components of Jewish identity, participants of Israel Experience programmes 1993–2003

The four regions surrounding this central concept are:

(1) *biological*, consisting of the items: Jewish by birth, in relation to other Jews and in relation to my family. This region represents kinship, the most basic and widely recognized means of identification with an ethnic group;
(2) *historical*, consisting of the items: Jewish in reaction to anti-Semitism, in reaction to the Shoah, in relation to Israel, and by connection to Jewish languages;
(3) *psychological*, consisting of the items: Jewish by loyalty, by commitment, by hope and by choice;
(4) *institutional*, consisting of the items: Jewish by education and by religion.

The four regions are arranged as two sets of opposed concepts. The biological–psychological opposition represents personal aspects of identity, while the historical–institutional opposition represents communal aspects of identity. The thick border shows an additional division in the structure. The biological and institutional regions together form a larger region of 'given' or primordial aspects of identity. The historical and psychological regions form a larger region of 'chosen' or situational aspects. While the realities of political situations such as the existence or lack of an ethnic homeland or of prejudice may appear to be givens, reaction or relationship to them is a matter of choice, like the components in the psychology region.

In some cases, language may be a primordial or institutional aspect of identity, learned at home and spoken in school. However, few if any of these respondents speak Hebrew, Yiddish or Ladino as their mother tongue, and therefore 'Jewish languages' are more closely related to historical events than to family.

Into this basic structure of identity, four sub-groups of Israel Experience participants were introduced as external variables, as shown in Figure 3. Their placement in the map shows the aspects of identity with which each group was most strongly correlated, though all of the components play a role in the identity of each.

The variant Jewish identity expressed by the various Diaspora populations is important for several reasons. It tells us something of the social context in which these Jewish youth are educated and socialized. Western European participants (primarily British and French) were located in the biological region. For them, the connection to their immediate and extended families and the larger 'family' of the Jewish people is the primary focus of identification. Eastern European and South American participants were located in the historical region. They are most likely to link their Jewish identity with anti-Semitism, the Holocaust and events in Israel. North American participants were located in the psychology region. For these youth, identification with Judaism is a matter of choice and personal development.

The types of Jewish identity emphasized among the various Diaspora populations also impact the Israel Experience tour itself. As noted, one of the primary goals of the tour is to enhance Jewish identity. But Jewish identity, as clearly shown in this analysis, is a complex, multi-faceted concept, and different facets are more or less important to different groups of Jews. The planners and organizers of the trips need to be aware of this in order to make critical educational decisions. Once the 'flavour' of Jewish identity among a group of participants is understood, the curriculum can then be

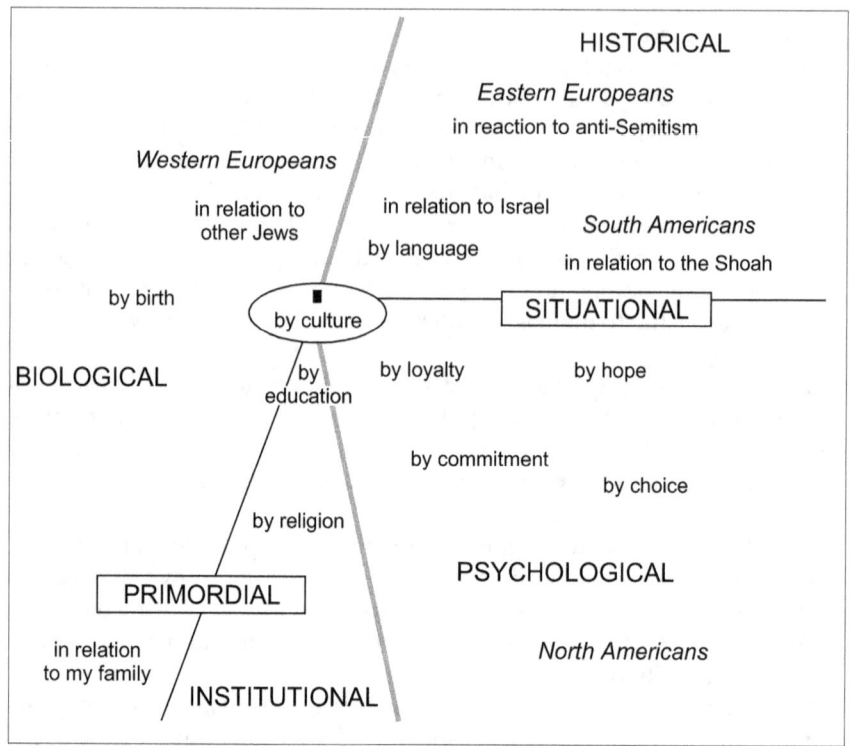

Figure 3 Typology of components of Jewish identity with major Diaspora subpopulations as external variables

designed either to further enhance already strong aspects of identity, or to attempt to address aspects that receive little attention in the Jewish educational systems of the participants' home countries.

Symbols of Jewish identity

Symbols are central to ethnic and religious identity. Geertz (1973: 89) defines culture as '... an historically transmitted pattern of meanings embodied in symbols, a system of inherited conceptions expressed in symbolic forms by means of which men communicate, perpetuate and develop their knowledge about and attitudes towards life,' and religion as '... a system of symbols which acts to establish powerful, pervasive, and long-lasting moods and motivations ... ' (Geertz, 1973:90). In his study of 'enduring peoples' Spicer (1980: 346) said, ' ...we find in every case of an enduring people, common understandings concerning the meaning of a set of symbols.' Gans (1979) asserts that in American culture, identity has become primarily symbolic.

In order to explore the symbols of Jewish identity, I included in the questionnaires distributed to Israel Experience participants a list of 20 possible symbols related to different spheres of Jewish identity and asked them to indicate which symbols represent their personal Jewish identity. The results were analysed using the SSA procedure. Figure 4 shows the resulting typology of symbols.

At the core of the structure are symbols related to the struggle of the weak against the strong: the Biblical story of the young King David's battle with the giant Goliath, and the plight of Soviet Jewry. The recurrent theme of the weak triumphing over the strong may be considered central to Jewish identity. Surrounding this centre are six regions of semantically related symbols, each representing a facet of Jewish identity:

(1) *Contributors to world culture.* These figures are Jews who made significant contributions to the fields of science, art, music and humour. Although the success of Jews in general society may be a source of pride for minority youth, these were selected by only a minority of participants as central to their Jewish identity, and the Israel Experience tours have few activities, if any, related to the contributions of Jews to general society.

(2) *Justice.* Social justice is a concept key both to religious Judaism, with its numerous laws related to caring for the poor and setting up courts, and to non-religious Jewish culture, for whom the struggle for societal justice has been called a type of 'secular Jewish messianism' (Weisberger, 1997: 112). Israel Experience tours relate to this aspect of Jewish identity through the inclusion of volunteer work in social programmes.

(3) *Shoah* (Holocaust). Preservation of the memory of the Shoah has become a central point in Jewish education and in Israel Experience tours. Memory of the Shoah is ideologically linked to the justification for the creation of the State of Israel, as expressed in the Israel Experience tours beginning in Europe. Virtually all Israel Experience tours visit the Holocaust museum, Yad Vashem. In the map, this region is located between the region related to Justice and the region related to Israel.

(4) *Israel.* Until the creation of the modern State, Israel and Jerusalem played only symbolic–spiritual roles in Jewish identity, representative of a sort of utopian dream. Today, a relationship with the physical reality of the land, the State and the people of Israel forms a key

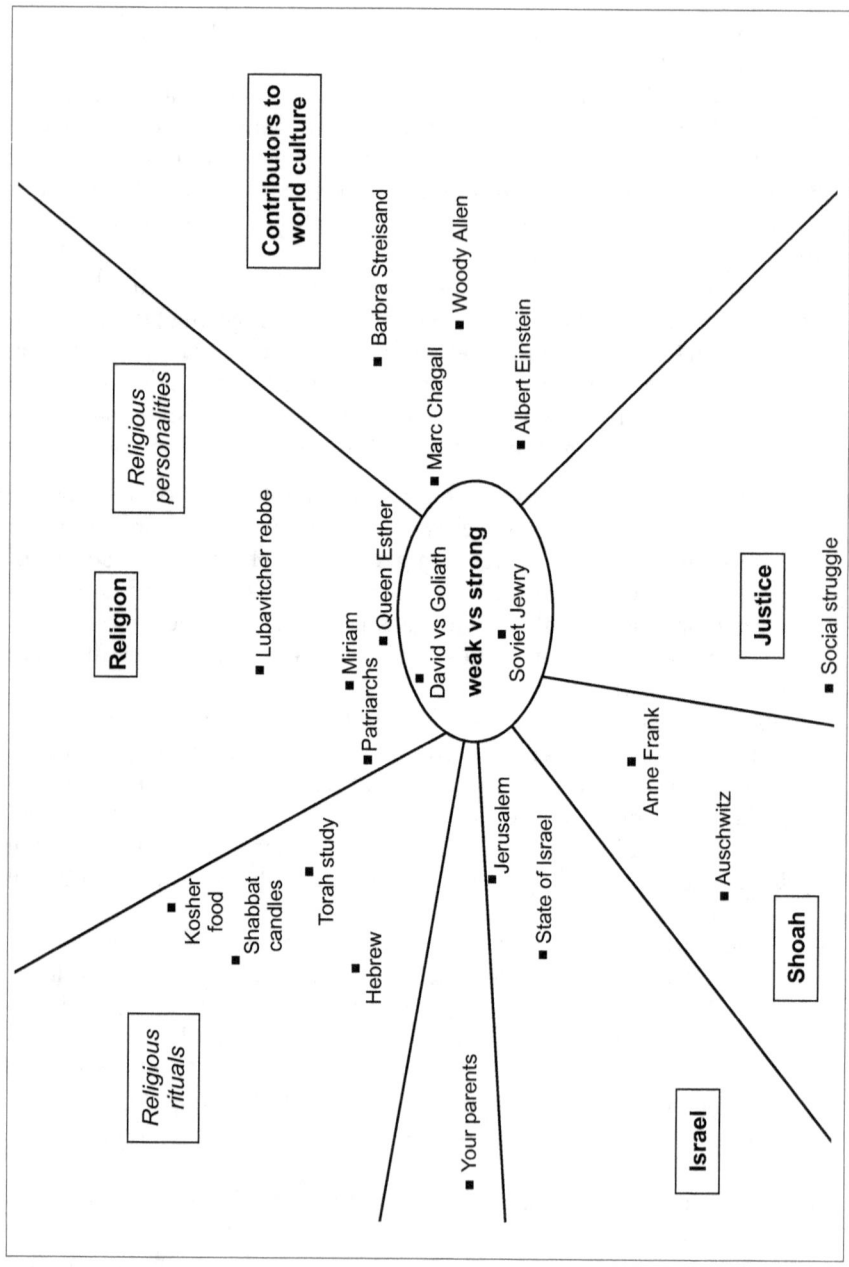

Figure 4 Typology of symbols of Jewish identity

component of Jewish identity. Of course, it is with this aspect of identity that the Israel Experience is most intensively involved.
(5) *Your parents*. Judaism is passed from parent to child, and family is a key aspect of identity. Parental support, financially and emotionally, enables many young people to travel to Israel. At the same time, the trip is often the participants' first major trip without their parents, itself an important aspect of the experience.
(6) *Religion*. This region is divided into two sub-regions: religious rituals and religious personalities. Although Israel Experience tours are not overtly religious, many include visits to religious sites such as graves of Biblical figures, and also some sort of Shabbat celebration.

As yet another indicator of Jewish identity, we posed a hypothetical question to participants: we asked them, what religion and nationality they would choose if they could be born again. This enables respondents to answer without taking into account practical considerations such as family obligations or career concerns. This question was also used as an indicator of Jewish identity in a study of international Jewish volunteers to Israel after the Six Day War (Horowitz et al., 1971) and in studies I conducted of French volunteers to Israel during the Yom Kippur War (Cohen, E.H., 1986) and of Jewish-French heads of households (Cohen, E.H., 2002a). Although the populations are not identical in terms of age or the type of programme that brought them to Israel, a comparison of the data across years and countries is nevertheless an interesting comment on contemporary Jewish identity.

During the years of the Israel Experience survey, there was little change in response to this question. But when we compared the data collected in 1967 (Table 7) with that of the Israel Experience survey (Table 8), we saw a decline in the percentage of respondents from almost every country who said they would wish to have been born Israeli. This is in line with the heightened enthusiasm for Israel that followed the victory of the Six Day War.

The single exception was South Africa. The political upheaval that South Africa experienced during the years of the Israel Experience survey may account for their drop in desire to be born in that country, if given a choice. South Africa, too, has the largest percentage who selected the choice 'Jewish in another country'. Indeed, a large percentage of the Jewish community of South Africa has emigrated over the past decade, to Israel and to other destinations.

A comparison of the Israel Experience participants from different countries (Table 8) shows that the participants from North America and Australia/New Zealand were the most content with being Jews in their home country, Eastern Europeans were the least. South Africans and

Table 7 'If you could be born again, would you wish to be ...' Responses of volunteers to Israel in 1967, by country of residence

	USA	Western Europe	United Kingdom	South America	South Africa
Jew in home country	47%	30%	29%	23%	50%
Jew in another country	5%	5%	10%	12%	5%
Jew in Israel	30%	47%	39%	43%	25%
Non-Jew	2%	2%	3%	3%	5%
No answer	16%	16%	19%	19%	15%
Total	100%	100%	100%	100%	100%

Source: Horowitz et al. (1971)

Eastern Europeans were the most likely to say they would prefer to be born as Israeli Jews, closely followed by Western Europeans. Eastern European participants were most likely to say that religion and nationality were unimportant to them. Virtually no respondents said they would prefer to be born as a non-Jew, indicating the strong pride in their Jewish identity.

Table 8 'If you could be born again, would you wish to be ...' percentage by continent, Israel Experience participants, cumulative data 1993–2001

	North America	Western Europe	South America	Eastern Europe	South Africa	Australia & New Zealand	Together*
Jew in home country	61%	48%	57%	30%	42%	64%	56%
Jew in another country	3%	6%	8%	8%	14%	4%	5%
Non-Jew	1%	1%	0%	2%	0%	0%	<1%
Jew in Israel	26%	37%	27%	41%	40%	27%	30%
Religion and place not important/other	8%	7%	8%	18%	4%	5%	8%

* Total survey population Israel Experience participants, cumulative data 1993–2001 in all continents (North America, Western Europe, South America, Eastern Europe, South Africa and Australia/NewZealand).

Adolescence as a Formative Period in Shaping Personal Identity

Adolescence is a period of intensive exploration and experimentation in formulating a sense of personal and social identity (Erikson, 1963, 1968). Personal and social identities are formed in parallel processes. Adolescents experiment with the various roles and identity options offered by society. Many teenagers adopt styles expressed through clothing, music and recreational activities (including drugs). They may also experiment with different value systems. The media is a strong force in creating and perpetuating these styles. Failure to formulate a suitable identity results in a sense of alienation and confusion. Adolescence is often a time of rebellion against parents and other authority figures.

Post-modernism has challenged the basic assumptions of identity theory. 'Erikson saw society as being relatively static and what an adolescent had to do was identify an appropriate niche in it. By comparison, the task for the adolescent today is to find a way of joining something which itself is changing' (Head, 1997: 20). Identity development for teens that are members of ethnic or religious minorities may be even more complex. They must adapt both to the dominant society and to their particular community. They must balance their desire to assert their independence from their parents with an exploration of their cultural roots.

There does not seem to be a radical gap between this generation of Jewish adolescents and their parents. In my studies of Jewish youth in France, for example (Cohen, E.H., 2002a) I found that young Jews tend to share the core values of their parents.

While most youth travel to exotic locations involves a search for identity in cultures totally different than the one in which they were raised, young Jews visiting Israel do not seem to be looking for a way of life that is radically different from that of their parents, but rather they are trying to assert their own identity within the culture inherited from their families. The trip to Israel does not represent a rebellion against their parents' values. In fact, most are encouraged and supported by their parents in taking this trip. Rather than being an act of rebellion, a visit to Israel with peers at this age is gradually becoming accepted as a rite of passage, similar to the bar/bat mitzvah.

Three main elements of the Israel Experience are particularly important in the process of participants' identity development: role models, the group, and values.

Role models

Young people look for role models with whom to identify. Effective role models may help adolescents work through and eventually overcome the difficulties of this stage of life. It has been found that one of the most important functions of the counsellors of the Israel Experience is to serve as role models for the teenagers on the programme. The counsellors are generally only a few years older than the participants, which reduces teenager's suspicions and resistance to adopting the values they embody. The counsellors may help address the many issues and questions inevitably raised during the intense experience of the programme in Israel, questions with which they themselves wrestled only a few years previously.

The counsellors from the home country provide examples of young adults strongly identified with Judaism and Israel and working in Jewish education, yet also fully integrated into the same home society as the participants. The Israeli counsellors provide a slightly different type of role model. They serve as the primary translators, not only in terms of language, but also in terms of culture, explaining and interpreting Israeli society to the visitors. Naturally, their experiences, attitudes and values are more foreign to the participants. Yet they provide important models of the types of young adult raised in Israel. For example, almost all have served in the Israeli army. Most are less religious than the counsellors from the home countries.

During the many activities of the tour, participants may meet other individuals who provide role models for them, for example, on army bases, at a kibbutz, working in social programmes and leading hikes in the desert. Though these encounters are short, perhaps lasting only a few hours, they offer examples of various paths taken by adults.

Professor Moshe Halberthal of Hebrew University (personal communication) points out that many of the Israeli adults encountered by young visitors may seem to behave to some extent like teenagers – the culture of public singing and folk dancing, the ongoing relationship with the army, the hikes in the desert, casual dress and so forth. Israel Experience participants find themselves presented with different types of adults from those they know at home.

The group

Intensive interaction with a peer group is also important in the process of adolescent identity formation (Skirball, 1988; Moss, 1988). As young people experiment with various roles, their peer group provides feedback. It is within the context of the peer group that young people learn many of their social skills, such as considering other people's needs, taking responsibility for their actions and ways of giving and receiving attention (Conger & Petersen, 1984).

Bonding among members of the Israel Experience group has been found to be another of the major factors influencing the success of the trip. Similarly, in the evaluation of the Taglit-birthright israel tours the 'bus community' is noted as one of the key factors (along with the guides and the interaction with Israeli youth) in the success of the short trip (Saxe *et al.*, 2006: 2).

During the visit to Israel, the youngsters are immersed in communal life. The members of the group are all dealing with similar confusions and issues of concern, and therefore can identify with one another. Their mutual dependence is increased as a result of being far from home.

The group has been found to be especially important to participants from France. The political culture of France discourages affiliation with ethnic or religious groups. The travellers create a community, albeit temporary, not available at home.

The encounter of the youngsters with the group during their time in Israel is all-embracing. The programme may be considered a type of 'total institution' as defined by Goffman (1961), with all aspects of daily life taking place in the company of a group, and all activities coordinated in order to fulfil an official goal. The Israel Experience may more accurately be described as a 'temporary total institution' (Cohen, E.H. & Bar-Shalom, 2006). Summer camps may also be considered an example of temporary total institutions, and there, too, the role of the group is of outmost importance (Zeldin, 2006).

Values

The temporary community, far from participants' home and family, enables young people to try out values within the context of the group, to receive feedback and to evaluate to what degree these values suit their individual personalities.

Table 9 shows the values expressed by Israel Experience participants from several of the largest national sub-populations. Values expressing personal development received the strongest response. Values such as honesty, honoring parents and helping others received stronger responses from all groups than did materialistic values such as earning money or buying a car.

Although the Israel Experience tours for youth from the various countries have similar structure and objectives, the different values of the participants have an impact on the nature of the group and the policies of the

Table 9 Values of Israel Experience participants in summer 2000, compared by nationality (percentage who answered 'very important' to each)

	US	Canada	UK	France	Together
Making the most of life	88%	85%	86%	70%	81%
Being an honest person	69%	69%	70%	70%	68%
Finding myself	64%	66%	55%	75%	63%
Honouring one's parents	60%	63%	58%	76%	62%
Having a good time with friends	66%	67%	63%	48%	61%
Helping other people	65%	66%	53%	58%	60%
Free to do what one wants	64%	62%	52%	41%	58%
Feeling part of the Jewish people	55%	56%	51%	76%	56%
Getting married	57%	55%	52%	65%	55%
Excelling in studies	57%	55%	46%	74%	53%
Realizing my talents in whatever field	56%	55%	48%	29%	51%
Marrying only a Jew	38%	39%	43%	68%	41%
Contributing to society and country	44%	40%	28%	30%	38%
Travelling abroad	34%	33%	26%	22%	30%
Being active in sports	28%	27%	24%	13%	26%
Being religious (keeping mitzvoth)	26%	20%	17%	37%	24%
Having a nice appearance	25%	21%	24%	20%	24%
Studying Torah and/or Talmud	19%	20%	12%	33%	18%
Making a lot of money	15%	15%	16%	24%	16%
Buying a car	16%	13%	16%	10%	15%

* Israel Experience participants in summer 2000, all countries

planners. For example, the programmes for young North American Jews, who value individual freedom, actually have almost no free time because parents and organizers are particularly concerned about alcohol, drugs and sex during the trip. Tours for French youngsters, who express more religious values, allow for more free time.

Dating patterns and attitudes towards religious exogamy

The period of adolescence is naturally also a period of shaping sexual identity and looking for contact with members of the opposite sex. The Israel Experience offers youngsters the opportunity to spend time with and get to know their peers, boys and girls alike, in a framework free of the pressures of everyday life. In fact, over a third of the surveyed participants said that finding a girl/boyfriend was one of the reasons they joined the tour! However, the emphasis on unity of the group as a whole places limits on serious pairing off of couples within the touring groups (Goldberg, 2002; Heilman, 2002).

Although a desire to stem the tide of exogamy has been a compelling reason for parents to encourage their teenagers to take part in Jewish organizations, camps and tours to Israel, the results have been, at best, ambiguous. We cannot yet document the marriage statistics for this group of adolescents, but their general attitudes towards intermarriage with non-Jews are indicative. We can see in Table 10, that even in the course of six years, there has been a steady decline in the percentage of Israel Experience participants who say they would be 'vehemently opposed' to intermarriage within their immediate family, and a corresponding increase in the percentage who say they see 'nothing wrong with it.' This finding is particularly striking in contrast to the stability of demographics and attitudes towards other issues during the same time period.

By cross-tabulating and calculating correlation matrices of these results with other demographic data, I found that religious denomination, representing the participants' family's outlook, is more strongly related to views on intermarriage than participation in Jewish community life (Cohen, E.H., 2003a). Participants from Reform and Conservative families are far more accepting of inter-faith marriage than those from Orthodox families. This result shows the uncertain impact of Jewish youth movements, camps or Israel trips in preventing intermarriage, despite the great faith put in these by many community leaders.

Table 10 If a close member of your family expressed the intention of marrying a non-Jew, what would your reaction be?

Year	1993	1994	1995	1996	1997	1998	1999	2000	*Together*
Nothing wrong with it	11%	15%	19%	20%	25%	24%	29%	27%	22%
Ambivalent to this	9%	11%	12%	16%	17%	14%	14%	16%	14%
Slightly opposed to it	41%	42%	40%	35%	32%	33%	28%	31%	35%
Vehemently opposed to it	39%	31%	29%	29%	27%	28%	29%	26%	29%
Total	100%	100%	100%	100%	100%	100%	100%	100%	100%

Source: Cohen, E.H. (2003a)

In this chapter we have looked at the phenomenon of Jewish youth travel to Israel in the context of Israel–Diaspora relations, Jewish education, tourism, contemporary Jewish identity and adolescence. These background factors interact. The objectives and style of the tour changed with the evolution of the relationship between Israel and Diaspora communities. The patterns of Jewish education in the home communities affect the way participants perceive Israel and Judaism. The psychological and sociological impact of travel to a foreign country distinguishes the Israel Experience from other informal Jewish educational programmes such as summer camps. The 'Jewish identity' that the tour intends to enhance and impact is itself a fluid concept, influenced by overarching issues such as the values of the participants' home community, anti-Semitism, the memory of the Shoah and intermarriage rates. Finally, the psychological and sociological processes distinctive of adolescence influence the tour, differentiating it from family tours or group tours for adults.

Notes

1. For example, Rabbis Yehuda Alkalai, Zvi Hirsch Kalischer, Azriel Hildesheimer, and Joseph Natonek, philanthropists Moses Montefiore and Baron Edmond de Rothschild, and philosophers and thinkers Leon Pinsker, Theodor Herzl, Ahad ha-Am and Eliezer ben-Yehuda.
2. Even today, after far-reaching changes in the perception of the Diaspora and the reality of the lives of Jews around the world, this idea is still hinted at or openly stated by Israeli leaders. For example, in July 2005 Israeli Prime Minister Ariel Sharon called for France's Jews to move to Israel to escape growing anti-Semitism in that country.
3. Former member of the Knesset Yossi Beilin said the total yearly donations of Diaspora Jews to Israel would be sufficient to finance only one week of a teacher's strike.
4. For example, during the negotiations of the Oslo Accords, then Prime Minister Yitzhak Rabin told the America Israel Public Affairs Committee that the Israeli government, not AIPAC, would represent Israeli interests to the American government.
5. For example, Émile Durkheim, who influenced reform of the French school system (Strenski, 1997), Emma Goldman, who helped found the Ferrer Modern Schools in the US (Goldman, 1911), and the many who were involved in desegregation, education for women, and other progressive educational reforms. See for example: Brettschneider, 1996; Freidenreich, 2002.
6. The speech is to be found in the Zionist Archives in a file of outgoing letters, April to November 1969. The original is in English.
7. *Orthodox* is the most traditional and religiously observant branch of Judaism; Orthodox Jews hold most scrupulously to Jewish traditional law and ritual. Orthodox Judaism may be further subdivided into 'ultra-Orthodox' (which includes various Hasidic sects) and 'modern Orthodox' who observe Jewish religious law but are more integrated into modern society.

Conservative: a branch of Judaism that advocates a less fundamentalist approach to Jewish traditional law than does Orthodox Judaism, combining traditional and modern sources in their approach.
Reform: a branch of Judaism that advocates a liberal approach to interpretation of Jewish tradition and law.
8. While state and federal governments in the US do not fund religious studies, some support is given to private religious schools, for example in the form of transportation and school lunch programmes.
9. Statement by Harman, D., former General Director of the Authority for Jewish Education, in a lecture at Kfar Hamaccabia, Israel in 1993.
10. On the eve of World War II, the Jewish population of Europe was about 9.5 million: over 60% of the world's Jewish population at that time (estimated at 15.3 million). The majority lived in Central and Eastern Europe and the Soviet Union. The Jewish populations of the various Central-Eastern European countries in 1933 were: Poland about 3 million, the Soviet Union and Baltic states about 3 million; Romania just under 1 million, Germany about 0.5 million, Hungary 0.4 million, Czechoslovakia about 0.3 million, and Austria 0.25 million (United States Holocaust Memorial Museum, 2007).
11. Established in Tsarist Russia, ORT is an acronym for the Russian name of the organization, roughly translatable as Organization for Educational Resources and Technology. 'ORT's mission is to work for the advancement of Jewish people through training and education; to provide communities wherever they are, with the skills and knowledge necessary to cope with the complexities and uncertainties of their environment; to foster economic self-sufficiency, mobility and a sense of identity through use of state-of-the-art technology. Through International Cooperation programmemes, ORT supports non-sectarian economic and social development in under-developed parts of the world, with vocational training and the provision of technical assistance' (http://www.ort.org/asp/article.asp?id=309; accessed 11.11.07).
12. Between 80% and 90% of Australian Jews are Ashkenazi. Sephardi Jews have experienced some more discrimination, including from Ashkenazi Jews, primarily due to being 'non-white', rather than to being Jewish (Gale, 1997, 1999).
13. Not the author of this book, but a Hebrew University of Jerusalem sociologist by the same name.
14. As can be seen, for example, in the Hannukah story, in which large numbers of Jews became Hellenized or the Purim story, in which many Jews preferred the pleasures of the non-Jewish society in which they lived.

Chapter 5
Survey of Research on the Israel Experience

Early Studies

Since young Diaspora Jews began coming to Israel, researchers have monitored this phenomenon, making it the best-documented case of heritage tourism. While I cannot possibly cover every study conducted on the subject, in this section I summarize the results of some of the most important studies conducted by my colleagues. The aim of this chapter is to present a number of noteworthy studies and detail their main findings, which are likely to help in making decisions and shaping policy with regard to the major issues under dispute and in formulating a position in principle as to the objectives of this educational enterprise. Additionally, these studies have influenced my own research by providing a context for analysing the results and comparison of data over the course of several decades. The studies are varied and cover a wide range of aims and research methods. They examine the influence of the visit to Israel on different components of Jewish identity, on the make-up of the groups, on the degree of closeness to the community, on changes taking place in the participants' attitudes towards Israel and so forth.

Comet (1965) surveyed 332 young American Jews who came to Israel for seven weeks in the summer of 1963. This early study also underlines the general stability of basic features of the tour such as the previous educational background of participants. Among the most interesting findings of this survey was that the pre-trip and post-trip questionnaires indicated an increase in participants' Jewish identity and awareness of their *American* identity, but little change in identification with Israel. For these American Jews, religious identity was more important than national-ethnic identity, which reinforces my own observations of American Jews today.

The first comprehensive study of the Israel Experience project was carried out by social psychologist Shimon Herman (1970, 1977a, 1977b). His pioneering study played a considerable role in determining the views of many researchers who came after him. Herman's study looked at groups of American students who came to the Hebrew University of Jerusalem on one-year programmes in the 1960s and 1970s. He used various research methods: questionnaires, interviews, focus groups, personal diaries and observations. Herman proposed a theoretical framework for examining the process of change undergone by these students that focused on four psychological areas in which change was likely to take place: the new psychological experience; the effect of the student being a foreigner on the periphery of the host society; the student being subject to the influence of both the host society and his/her society of origin; and the specific influence of this time on the student's perception. Herman examined the change occurring in the perception of Self, the perception of Israel and Israelis, and the perception of United States Jewry. Herman checked these attitudes at different periods of time: before the programme, at the start of the programme, during the stay in Israel and one year after the programme.

In 1975 Bubis and Marks carried out an in-depth study in which they compared groups of young people who had participated in different Jewish summer activities. One of the programmes they examined took place in Israel, while others took place in summer camps in the US. The aim of the study was to discover what kind of 'Jewish experience' will ensure a strong, positive Jewish identity; whether the visit to Israel strengthens Jewish identity in a way that is different from similar activities taking place in the United States; and, especially, to test the truth of the assumption that a stay in Israel strengthens young people's identification with Jewish attitudes and thus causes them to more emphatically choose Jewish behaviour. The study compared the participants' responses at the start of the programme, at the end of the programme and nine months after their return home. Various characteristics of Jewish identity were examined, including observance of the festivals, choosing a Jewish partner, knowledge of Jewish culture, Jewish education and tendency to universalism. Bubis and Marks used a scale of indices of identity (the Masaryk Scale) that compares strengths of identification while cancelling out the effect of differences in content between different world outlooks, and which helps distinguish between elements relating to the private life of the respondent and those that reflect public commitment.

The young people who went to Israel expressed stronger Jewish identity before the visit as well as after, emphasizing the self-selected nature of the population of young Jews who visit Israel. On some indicators (such as participation in Jewish festivals), stronger improvement was found among those who went to Israel, on others, (such as willingness to do further reading on Jewish subjects and attitudes towards intermarriage), a larger positive change was measured among those who took part in the US camp. For many indicators the two populations were very close. A follow-up survey nine months after the programmes found that attitudes had returned to those held prior to the respective programmes.

In the mid-1980s the Jewish Education Committee of the Jewish Agency initiated a series of research studies on the subject of the Israel Experience, coordinated by the Nativ consultancy company headed by Annette Hochstein (Hochstein, 1986; Cohen, S., 1986a, 1986b, Shye 1986). The studies examined the Israel Experience from the viewpoints of both the organizers and the participants.

Shye's survey of programme directors gathered general data on the participants, the programme itself and its success, in addition to directors' attitudes with regard to the aims of the visit, already discussed in the chapter on programme objectives.

Steve Cohen surveyed Israel Experience participants and their attitudes toward their visit. He also conducted a study in Canada comparing young Jews who have gone to Israel several times, those who have gone only once, those who had not been but intend to go, and those with no intention of going. He thus developed a typology of Jewish youth ranging from 'indifferent' through 'curious tourists' to 'committed Zionists' (Cohen, S., 1991). He concluded that it is difficult to differentiate between prior enthusiasm and the impact of a trip to Israel, but that impact increases with the number of trips.

Steve Cohen also surveyed United Jewish Agency 'missions' to Israel for adults (Cohen, S., 1996a). This study found many similarities with youth trips, such as the importance of past participants as recruiters, the goal of enhancing Jewish identity and commitment to Israel, and the importance of preparation and follow-up.

Another survey of adult educational tourism to Israel (Abrams et al., 1996; Klein-Katz, 1990, 1991) looked at a programme for Jewish teachers. Again, many of the goals were the same as for teenage participants, with the additional goal of gaining professional experience, knowledge and enthusiasm for the task of teaching their students about Israel. Also, the adult participants expected much more autonomy and freedom to pursue topics of personal and professional interest.

Goldfarb Consultants (1992) carried out another study that examined attitudes to the visit to Israel held by a large sample of Jewish families in Canada (adults and young people). The emphasis was on attitudes toward Israel and the visit there, the ways in which the youngsters get information about these programmes, and the reasons encouraging their desire to visit Israel.

In 1991, 20 years after the Herman study, Friedlander et al. carried out another study among students participating in the one-year programme at the Hebrew University. They examined the social background of the students, their motives for visiting and elements of Jewish identity that were strengthened by the visit. This study also went back and checked some of the factors examined by Herman. The research was carried out in five stages: the first questionnaire was given out one month before the students' arrival and the last one six months after their return to the United States and Canada.

In 1991 Mittelberg and Lev-Ari conducted a study on the Oren kibbutz intensive- language study programme (*ulpan*). They examined the special conditions relating to the kibbutz and made a comparison between the National Religious kibbutz experience and the non-religious kibbutz experience. They also examined how the Jewish background and the expectations of the participants affected their degree of satisfaction, their sense of Jewish fulfilment as a result of the visit and their intentions of changing their behaviour in their countries of origin. Mittelberg and Lev-Ari stressed the importance of kibbutz programmes having a clearly-defined educational aim and being staffed by dedicated and enthusiastic kibbutz members who understand the needs and expectations of the visitors from outside Israel.

In 1994, social anthropologists Harvey Goldberg and Samuel Heilman accompanied Israel Experience tours (Goldberg, 2002; Heilman, 2002). Their in-depth studies of a few groups personalize and flesh out the quantitative data compiled from the questionnaire-based surveys.

Another study on long-term programmes was conducted by Ohayon (2004) who surveyed participants in Machon Gold (a year-long programme for girls from religious Jewish families) and compared them with a control group of female students in university programmes in Israel. Ohayon used questionnaires and interviews to study participants' motivations for joining the respective programmes, and their attitudes to Judaism, Israel and their specific programmes. He found that religious belief and national identification were strengthened among both groups, but particularly among the Machon Gold students. University students gained much in terms of cognitive knowledge related to Jewish studies as well as secular studies; the impact of their studies on their religious beliefs and national identification was less pronounced than among the Machon Gold students

The Taglit-birthright Israel Survey

The Taglit-birthright israel programme has been tracked since its inception (Kelner *et al.*, 2000; Saxe *et al.*, 2001, 2002, 2004, 2006). These studies of the programme addressed issues such as the characteristics of participants, return visits to Israel, creation of community among alumni, religious behaviour, participation in local community and continued Jewish learning after the trip, as well as attitudes of the alumni towards Israel and Judaism.

The ongoing study of the Taglit-birthright israel programme has several important features: large numbers of participants are surveyed, and the study also included a control group of applicants who did not eventually join a tour. This control group is extremely valuable when analysing the results of the survey. The comprehensive analysis of the programme also includes post-trip follow-up surveys – another valuable feature that enriched the results and allowed us to track the long-term impact on attitudes towards Judaism and Israel.

The Saxe *et al.* studies consider only groups from the US and Canada, although Taglit-birthright israel groups come from all over the world. Even between the relatively similar contexts of the USA and Canada, differences were found between participants from the two countries. For example, Canadian participants had more Jewish educational background, but were less likely to have joined campus Jewish organizations after the trip (Saxe *et al.*, 2002: 46). In 2003, I conducted a parallel survey of 1146 participants from France, Australia/New Zealand, Argentina and Brazil. As in the case of my international studies of the Israel Experience programme, I found significant differences in the evaluations, expectations and base Jewish identity of the groups from the various Diaspora countries.

Table 11 compares a few key results of the Saxe *et al.* study with my study of Taglit-birthright israel participants from other home countries.

The findings of these various studies, and my own, overwhelmingly confirm one another. The participants do not come from the periphery or from unaffiliated families. They have Jewish education and were previously involved in their local Jewish communities. They feel a sense of attachment to Israel, but are not intending to move there. They are hoping for a fun tour that will help them in their personal search for identity.

Table 11 Taglit-birthright israel study; comparison of participants from USA and four other home countries. Respondents answering 'absolutely' or 'very much'

	USA and Canada	Australia & New Zealand	France	Argentina	Brazil
Trip was fun	86%	80%	96%	45%	68%
Trip was meaningful	80%	85%	62%	39%	76%
Trip was educational	75%	45%	80%	28%	68%

Source: USA and Canada, Saxe *et al.* (2004); other countries Cohen, E.H. (2004a)

The Ongoing Survey of the Israel Experience Programme

I first began to study the Israel Experience programme in 1974, with a survey of the summer programmes for French-speaking participants. As director of educational programmes for French speakers, I initiated a survey of over 500 students in order to gather data on the basic characteristics of the programmes' 'clientele' (Cohen, E.H., 1974). While working on my PhD, I examined the phenomenon of French-Jewish volunteers during the Yom Kippur War (Cohen, E.H., 1986). Beginning in 1989, I directed a research team that carried out ongoing evaluation studies of youth groups who came to Israel on tours co-sponsored and organized by the Israeli government, Diaspora community organizations and international Jewish institutions (specifically the Youth and Hechalutz Department of the World Zionist Organization, which later re-organized as the Department of Education of the Jewish Agency for Israel).

The research had two aims. One aim was to offer recommendations to the Department about the best way to organize its actions in terms of the technical aspects of the visitor programmes. The second aim was to examine in more general terms young people's attitudes towards Judaism and Zionism and changes resulting from the visit.

The ongoing survey was discontinued in 2000 for a number of reasons. After the outbreak of the *intifada* (Palestinian uprisings against Israel), many tours were cancelled. In fact, the Israel Experience programme almost came to a halt for several years and only small-scale internal surveys were commissioned for the small number of groups which did come in the framework of the Israel Experience.

The ongoing evaluation began with an examination of a small number of groups from the USA, and was gradually expanded over the years. Between 1993 and 2000, almost all participants in all visiting groups filled out a questionnaire at the beginning and/or at the end of their programme. The questionnaire has been translated into eight languages, including languages appropriate to large groups (such as French, Spanish and Portuguese) and languages spoken by smaller groups, such as Russian, Hungarian and Serbo-Croatian. Since the youngsters come in groups, it is relatively easy to distribute the questionnaires, and there are many advantages to surveying the entire population. The questionnaires contain closed questions on participants' background, attitudes and evaluation of various aspects of the programme, etc. In particular their attitude to Jewish identity and Israel are examined. The questionnaires also include an open question in which participants can add comments in their own words. In 1994, a compilation of the participants' comments written in response to this open question were compiled in 13 volumes of quotes (Cohen, E.H., 1994a).

As often as possible, groups were given questionnaires both at the beginning and the end of the tour, in order to obtain an accurate picture of the changes that take place as a result of the programme. Some of the same questions were included in both questionnaires, and consistent wording of these questionnaires enables us to track changes from year to year. Demographic background on respondents allows us to compare subpopulations according to nationality, age, gender, religious affiliation, membership in various youth organizations, etc.

In addition to the questionnaire, the research included observation of groups engaged in certain activities and in-depth interviews. Follow-up surveys have also been conducted. In 1994, a follow-up survey was conducted to monitor changes in the attitudes of the participants who visited Israel in the summer of 1993 one year after their return home. In 1995, special follow-ups of alumni were conducted in two communities in New Jersey (Cohen, E.H., 1996b). In addition to the ongoing evaluation, each year the research focused on specific aspects of the programme. The main results of the follow-up surveys and special studies are discussed in greater depth in subsequent chapters.

In 1994, the first of the studies on specific aspects of the Israel Experience programme looked at the kibbutz-stay, during which participants volunteer for several days on a kibbutz. In 1995 there was an in-depth investigation of programmes in which groups of youngsters from the Diaspora spent time with groups of Israeli youth (*mifgashim*). In this case, questionnaires were given both to the visitors from abroad and the Israelis. Additional information on the Israeli–Diaspora youth interactions was collected through observations and questionnaires given to the counsellors to assess their attitudes (Cohen, E.H., 2000).

In 1995, we conducted a special marketing study, in which we investigated how participants learn about the programme, why they chose to join tours, and what prevented their non-participating friends from joining tours (Cohen, E.H., 1995b). In 1996 we studied the level of services and the programme in Jerusalem. That same year, we conducted a survey of a special summer camp for adolescents and students from the former Soviet Union. In 1997, we looked at a special programme that brought participants to Prague before coming to Israel and also conducted a special study on the counsellors of the Israel Experience programme (Cohen, E.H., 1997c, 1997d, 1997e, 1997f).

My research has also included studies of longer-term visits to Israel. A follow-up study was conducted among alumni of the *Sherut La'Am* ('service to the people') programme, in which young people volunteer in Israel for a few months. A sample of programme alumni who had volunteered with *Sherut La'Am* between 1987 and 1992 filled out questionnaires at least one year after their return home. Another research study carried out as part of the evaluation of the programmes organized through the Youth and Hechalutz Department of the WZO was an evaluation of the one-year programme for overseas students at Israeli universities. This programme has expanded since it was surveyed by Shimon Herman and today operates in all the major universities in Israel, as well as in a number of local colleges.

In 1995 my research team was invited to monitor a pioneer programme launched by the Detroit Jewish community, in which the community organized and subsidized the journeys of 250 youngsters to Israel.[1] The programme was accompanied both by preparatory activities and by follow-up activities after the youngsters return home. The programme benefited from previous research and started out by offering what had been identified as conditions for success: sending a cohesive group of youngsters from the heart of the community, who had received training and would continue to work as a group after their return. This study benefited from the foresight of the community in having the programme monitored at all stages from its first preparatory stages through the trip itself to a follow-up nine months after the participants returned home. This provided ideal conditions for tracking the programme. The Detroit programme offered a model appropriate for the style of contemporary Jewish education in the US, particularly given the decline of youth movements there as a widespread organizing force within Jewish education.

Beginning the research with the preliminary stages enabled the researchers to examine expectations of the programme held by the programme directors, the counsellors, and the participants. The advance knowledge of the identity of the participants offered us the possibility of also studying the Israel Experience from an important perspective that had not been sufficiently examined previously, that of the parents. For the first time we could examine the expectations of the parents and see how they evaluated the visit. Tracking the implementation of the programme in all its aspects right from the preparatory stages also enabled us to understand in greater detail what takes place in other groups. The study began with a preliminary questionnaire. Each future participant was sent a questionnaire with a number of both closed and open questions. The questionnaires showed us how the participants came to the programme and enabled us to learn about their Jewish identity and the Jewish education they had received. The open questions allowed respondents to express themselves freely.

The rich database collected through this ongoing survey and through special studies form the basis for the findings and analysis presented in this book.

Note

1. The 'Miracle Mission for Teens' was sponsored by the Jewish Federation of Metropolitan Detroit and its Michigan/Israel Connection, the Agency for Jewish Education, the Ben Teitel Charitable Trust and the Jewish News, in cooperation with Detroit congregations and the Department for Jewish Zionist Education, JAFI.

Chapter 6
Perceptions of Israel

A visit to Israel may have many aspects: a vacation to beautiful natural areas and recreational spots, a cultural and historical tour of the birthplace of Judaism, a pilgrimage to the spiritual centre of one's own religion, visits to religious sites of other religions. Indeed, there are tours of Israel available based on each of these outlooks and motivations. Each type of visit, clearly, would take on a different character, expressed through the sites chosen, the information provided by the guides and the way the guiding is expressed. The character of the tour also depends, to a great extent, on the perceptions of Israel held by the visitors at the outset of the tour. Even within the framework of the Israel Experience, participants' ideas about Israel and their expectations of the trip are not uniform.

The presentation of Israel does not follow an organized, consistent pattern. Within the space of a few kilometres, and sometimes even on the very same spot, the participants may learn about ancient history, the early Zionist pioneers, and modern events. Few leave Israel with a clear perception of the chronological order of Israeli history. Similarly, the tour itinerary is usually based on logistical rather than didactic–educational considerations, and the visitors' conceptions of the geography of Israel are often confused by the circuitous routes of the tour.

The emotional presentation of the country is also complex and multi-layered. Many Israel Experience organizers are convinced that the sight of the landscapes of Israel and the encounter with the Israeli people are sufficient to cause a change in the visitor, and that a sense of belonging and identification are natural. Sometimes this is the case. As one participant wrote in the open section of the questionnaire, 'The minute I stepped off the plane I felt that this was my country.' This sentiment is voiced by many participants.

However, the organizers and educators of the tour present Israel in various ways to instil in participants the knowledge and feelings that fulfil the goals of the programme. Israel may be seen as the Holy Land, as the Jewish Homeland and as a national cause to be fought for, or as a modern state in which Jews from around the world have come together. Israel Experience participants are exposed to all three of these images. The relative emphasis placed on each reflects the ideology and goals of each programme. The different components of the visit and the way they are

Table 12 Images of Israel, positive answers from participants summer 2000

	USA	Canada	UK	France	Together
Religion	95%	80%	89%	79%	91%
Jerusalem	90%	82%	78%	87%	86%
Holy places	88%	72%	75%	69%	81%
Hebrew	88%	83%	67%	73%	80%
History	80%	71%	61%	54%	72%
Tradition	81%	67%	58%	50%	71%
Kibbutz	68%	66%	57%	50%	63%
Roots	67%	61%	52%	64%	62%
Tel Aviv	67%	63%	48%	50%	60%
Spirituality	72%	66%	42%	34%	59%
Israeli army	56%	60%	39%	68%	52%
Tourism	60%	50%	42%	34%	52%
Hope	55%	54%	40%	55%	51%
Masada	61%	55%	34%	34%	50%
Identity	51%	54%	51%	43%	50%
Peace	48%	44%	39%	41%	45%
Aliyah	45%	40%	39%	48%	44%
Freedom	47%	46%	37%	32%	43%
Family	47%	41%	36%	40%	43%
Yitzhak Rabin	48%	46%	32%	41%	42%
Eilat	42%	36%	38%	39%	40%
Home	46%	38%	27%	49%	40%
Yad Vashem (Holocaust museum)	38%	40%	40%	47%	39%
Future	43%	38%	32%	40%	39%
Security	41%	37%	34%	29%	38%
Studies	43%	37%	23%	22%	35%
Pilgrimage	43%	30%	17%	32%	34%
Moral	39%	34%	20%	34%	33%
Immigration	30%	27%	18%	25%	26%
Danger	30%	26%	21%	16%	26%

Table 12 – *continued*

Shelter	27%	25%	14%	14%	22%
Success	20%	17%	13%	19%	18%
Democracy	19%	22%	11%	19%	17%
Solidarity	13%	28%	12%	45%	16%
High tech	16%	21%	9%	23%	15%
Discrimination	17%	14%	13%	2%	14%
Western country	19%	9%	10%	12%	13%
Disorder	12%	12%	10%	3%	11%
Bureaucracy	6%	6%	4%	2%	5%
Oriental country	3%	4%	4%	20%	5%
Number of respondents	3444	374	1371	459	5648

Source: previously published in Cohen, E.H. (2003b)

presented determine the educational message. Sometimes this message is explicitly formulated by the organizers, and sometimes it is based on successful past trips but is not made explicit.

It is also important to recognize that there is not a uniform or homogeneous perception of Israel among the participants at the outset of the trip. Examining the different ways in which Diaspora communities view Israel gives an insight into the culture and educational system of each community. A better understanding of the images that Diaspora teenagers have of Israel will also provide tools and directions to strengthen educational approaches in the home communities and the curriculum of the tour programme.[1]

A survey questionnaire distributed to Israel Experience groups in the summer 2000 programme shortly after their arrival in Israel included a list of 40 places, names and symbols related to Israel. The items in the list were chosen to represent the many faces of Israel. They fit into various different ideological, social, spiritual, historical and cultural perspectives as well as dealing with places in Israel, tourism and issues of Jewish identity. The participants were asked to indicate all of the aspects that they felt reflected their perception of Israel. 5648 participants from the United Kingdom, the USA, Canada and France completed this section of the questionnaire. The results are shown in Table 12.

An understanding of the overall, predominant images of Israel held by participants, as well as differences between sub-populations, is important in understanding educational, heritage tourism to Israel. Some items received wide agreement from all the national sub-groups, especially those related to the religious aspects of the country. Differences in the images of Israel held by young people from these countries reflect attitudes and socio-economic realities as well as the type of educational content related to Israel that is being provided by the Jewish school systems in each of these countries. For example, more than twice as many American as French youngsters associate 'spirituality' with Israel, whereas more than three times as many French as American youngsters associate 'solidarity' with Israel. As noted by Zvi Levran, (director of the Jewish Experience of Israel, JAFI, personal communication) 'American Jewish life focuses on significant and meaningful personal religious experiences and does not emphasize a Zionist concept of Jewish peoplehood and shared fate with the people and State of Israel'.

The results related to the items 'danger' and 'solidarity' from the last groups who came before the outbreak of the al-Aqsa *intifada* in September 2000 are a telling indicator of the actual responses of the Jewish communities in the various countries during the subsequent difficult years. During the political crisis of 2001 and 2002, American tourism to Israel almost ceased. Many American Israel Experience groups cancelled their tours, including all the groups associated with the Reform movement. Tourism from France declined less drastically and recovered faster. Interestingly, 60% of American participants associate Israel with tourism, compared with only 34% of French participants, suggesting that the visit to Israel is something other than a 'tour' for French Jews, and perhaps partially explaining the different reactions during years of political instability.

Pilgrimage, Shelter, Immigration and *Aliya*

A clearer picture of the participants' image of Israel can be seen by considering the relationships between their responses to the 40 items. The correlation data are plotted using the Smallest Space Analysis (SSA) procedure, detailed in Chapter 1. The resulting graphic representation of the images of Israel is shown in Figure 5. Four distinct regions are visible:

- *The Spiritual Region,* comprising the elements of a more traditional, and spiritual manner. These elements create an esoteric image of Israel as a place to come closer to the religious spiritual nature of being a Jew.
- *The Zionism Region.* These are images that are commonplace in the paradigm of Zionist ideology. It contains all of the physical places in Israel, from the Roman Empire-era stronghold of Masada to the Holocaust memorial to the kibbutz and the modern city of Tel Aviv.

Perceptions of Israel

- *The Home Region* contains elements that create an image of Israel as a place that provides opportunities for building a home and for the future.
- *The Pragmatic/mundane Region* characterizes the more practical elements of Israeli society, including the harsher realities.

The two regions on the left side of the map are instrumental, in that they focus on functional needs for living. The two on the right-hand side are affective-cognitive regions, which are more emotional and ideological.

Each of the four regions contains one item closest to the centre of the map

Figure 5 Images of Israel

Source: originally published in Cohen, E.H. (2003b)

that can be said to epitomize the regions. Significantly, for each region the central item represents a way of coming to Israel. In the spirituality region it is 'Pilgrimage', in the symbolic region it is *'Aliya'*, in the home region it is 'Shelter' and in the pragmatic region it is 'Immigration'. All four regions and their central item have distinct cultural perspectives that support them and display a distinct logic. Immigration is the social-economic action of moving to Israel in order to make one's life more viable. Generally it is a non-ideological desire to improve one's lot in life by integrating into the daily reality of modern Israel. *Aliya* (literally 'going up') on the other hand is an ideologically charged action of settling in the Land of Israel. It is a political-spiritual concept that combines contemporary Zionism with the Biblical ideal of settling in *Eretz Yisrael*. The concept of pilgrimage to Israel is that of a temporary visit undertaken to discover and connect to religious/cultural/spiritual heritage. The notion of shelter relates to the idea of Israel as a refuge: a place for all Jews to live, prosper and be safe.

In order to further explore the images of Israel held by the various subgroups of Israel Experience participants, external variables representing nationality, gender and religious denomination were introduced into the map (see Chapter 1). Participants from Canada, France and the UK fell into the middle of the map, between the Pragmatic/mundane and Home regions. Placement near the centre of the map indicates a balanced image of Israel. In contrast the American participants fell at the periphery of the spirituality region. The American perspective definitely emphasizes the aspect of Israel as the Holy Land, a land of spiritual searching, religion, history and tradition and a place for fostering Jewish identity, but not as a place to live. Cross-cultural studies have found that American Jews tend to think of Judaism primarily as a religion, rather than as an ethnicity or nationality (Cohen, E.H., 1992b, 1997b; Cohen, S. & Horenczyk, 1999). This reflects the political culture of the USA, tolerant of religious diversity but less tolerant of minorities with strong ethnic identity and nationalist aspirations. Jewish education in the US emphasizes religion over nationality and de-emphasizes contemporary Israel as a potential home (Chazan, 2000; Grauer, 2001).

In contrast, a major survey of the potential clients of the Jewish Day Schools in France found that one of the main incentives for them to take part in the Jewish educational system is the chance to have a warm and realistic contact with Israel (Cohen, E.H., 1991, 2002a). The political culture of France, while granting equal human rights to its minority residents, does not allow for the formation of ethnic sub-cultures (Hertzberg, 1968; Laborde, 2001; Shurkin, 2000; Szajkowski, 1970; Wieviorka, 1999), and during the tours the French groups form a community that they are not able create at home.

External variables representing the major denominations within Judaism were also introduced into the map. The Conservative and Reform participants are located at the periphery of the spirituality region. The Orthodox participants are closest to the centre of the map, between the spirituality and home regions. Those who defined themselves as 'Just Jewish' are in the periphery of the pragmatic/mundane region. This result gives us additional insight into the ways in which Israel is portrayed in various educational settings. The Conservative and Reform school systems, particularly strong in the US, tend to portray Israel in the idealized way described above, focusing on its religious significance and its role as a spiritual pilgrimage site. The Orthodox portrayal of Israel balances the images of the Holy Land as a spiritual centre with images of it as the homeland of the Jews. As noted in the section on participation rates, Orthodox participants continued to visit Israel during the years of the *intifada*, when Conservative and Reform groups cancelled their tours. It seems that, during times of potential danger, people will visit a place they think of as home and with which they feel solidarity, whereas those who are seeking a personal, spiritual encounter are more likely to stay away.

Similarly, in 2000, the first year of the Taglit-birthright israel tours, only 5% of North American participants came from Orthodox families. In 2001–2002, the percentage had risen to 18% and in 2002–2003 it was 21%. During the same years, the percentage of participants from Reform families fell from 31% the year before the *intifada* to 17% in 2001–2002 and then to 15% in 2002–2003.

Participants who defined themselves as Just Jewish and as Secular were located at the opposite side of the map, at the periphery of the pragmatic/mundane region, most strongly connected with images of daily life in modern Israel. Again, referring back to the section on participation rates during the *intifada*, we saw that the young people who thought of themselves as Just Jewish followed a different logic from those in the Conservative and Reform movements. They, too, continued to come to Israel between 2001 and 2003 on both Israel Experience and Taglit-birthright israel tours.

Male and female participants are at opposite corners of the map, indicating different, even diametrically opposed, images of Israel. The young men are located in the Pragmatic region, with images of Israel related to the political realities of the day, such as the Israeli Defense Forces (*Zahal*), danger, disorder and discrimination. The young women are in the Spiritual region with spiritual and religious images of Israel such as holy places, roots, identity and tradition.

In a study of the relationship between age, gender and tourism Gibson and Yiannakis (2002) found that many young male tourists are motivated by a desire for adventure and even danger, while young female tourists are more interested in learning about the culture and people of the places they visit. The thrill-seeking tendency in young Jewish men may be manifest as a desire to experience personally the struggle for Israel and identification with Israeli soldiers. (Even though both men and women serve in the Israeli army, men are more likely to be in combat units.) The young Jewish women coming to Israel anticipate exploring Jewish culture and spirituality.

The results of this analysis of the images of Israel emphasize the need for programme organizers to take into account the 'destination image' of participants. Whether organizers hope to strengthen an existing association with Israel or to change visitors' perception of Israel (a much harder task) they must understand how visitors view Israel at the outset of the trip. The participants' cultural and educational backgrounds have created an underlying attitude towards Israel that will colour the trip. Trips organized for participants from various countries and from various religious streams must take this into account. As educational tourism to Israel moves away from a format of trips organized in conjunction with various youth movements or community organizations, and towards larger programmes such as Taglit-birthright israel, this point must be emphasized. A universally applied template programme is likely to disappoint or confuse participants whose underlying attitudes towards Israel differ from the organizers' assumptions.

Note

1. A more detailed analysis of the perceptions of Israel held by Israel Experience participants may be found in Cohen, E.H. (2003b).

Chapter 7
Satisfaction with the Tour, and Elements of a Successful Visit

As we have seen, in order to plan a successful Israel Experience, it is necessary to take into account participants' level of Jewish education and community involvement and the character of their home community. Additionally, success may be defined differently by the various parties involved: the participants, their parents, the counsellors, the organizers in the participants' home community, the Israeli organizers, etc.

Nevertheless, it is possible to make some generalizations about what type of visit will reinforce the educational aims of the programme and will be satisfying for participants. In general, alumni of a successful programme will wish to return to Israel themselves, will recommend the programme to others and will feel that the trip positively affected their lives after their return home (i.e. in terms of participation in local Jewish community, maintenance of friendships from the tour, etc).

According to Reisman and Chazan (1978), the factors that ensure a successful visit to Israel can be measured in the motivation and interest shown by the participants, the aims and planning of the programme and the skill of programme personnel.

Chazan (1992, 1994) proposes that a successful tour is a holistic experience, centred on the individual participant and guided by a philosophy or ideology that is translated into an educational programme. The visit is enjoyable and is conducted by educators of a high standard and an excellent team of counsellors and tour guides. It makes maximum use of the group dynamic as an educational resource and creates meaningful interaction with Israelis. A successful visit is one that is preceded by a well-planned curriculum.

Cohen, S. and Wall (1994) asked programme directors what they considered to be a successful programme, and on this basis developed a set of criteria for determining programme quality from the perspective of the organizers:

(1) a programme that successfully draws in participants, using regular educational resources such as lectures, reading and so forth;

(2) a programme that succeeds in creating group unity right from the start;
(3) a programme in which participants develop group pride in their particular programme;
(4) a programme that projects and reinforces a sense of partnership and mission;
(5) a programme that takes advantage of the special qualities of adolescents and presents the teenagers with challenges that enable them to participate, grow and mature, intellectually, physically, socially and emotionally;
(6) a programme in which the staff regularly checks to see that each participant is involved in the activities and can make an evaluation.

The success of the programme may be defined either by identifying discrete elements of the programme and assessing each individually, or by looking at the programme as a whole. Each approach has its advantages. It is possible to have poorly-run activities disguised in a generally successful programme. Similarly, poor-quality lodging or food may have a significant impact on a programme, even if it does not lead to overall dissatisfaction with the tour. At the same time, the Israel Experience is a holistic experience, and the tour must be viewed as more than the sum of its individual parts. In a study of the educational modules of the Israel Experience tours (Cohen, E.H., 2006b) I examined the subject of satisfaction as an important index for determining the quality of the programme and identifying its weak points. Satisfaction is the only measure of the participant's sense of well-being. If the organization bringing the group chooses to emphasize social goals such as creating a sense of community, satisfaction is certainly an important measure of success, but even if the organization chooses to emphasize educational content and aims the participant's satisfaction is a necessary condition for the success of the programme as a whole.

Overwhelmingly, participants are satisfied with the visit and say they will recommend it to their friends and acquaintances. The youngsters say they have learned a lot about Judaism, about Israel and about themselves, and that the experience was unforgettable. As shown in Table 13, virtually no participants are dissatisfied with the trip. Therefore, the differentiation between the satisfied and very satisfied becomes the most significant in terms of evaluating the programme.

Naturally, satisfaction cannot be the only measure of a programme's success. It would be possible for the youngsters to enjoy themselves, dance at discotheques, swim, develop social relationships and be very satisfied with the programme, while the program's organizers achieve few of their educational aims. However, as discussed earlier, the participants expect the

Satisfaction with the Tour

Table 13 When you take into consideration all the different components of your programme in Israel how satisfied are you? (responses for years 1993–2001)

	1993	1994	1995	1996	1997	1998	2001	*Together*
Not satisfied at all	1%	1%	1%	1%	1%	1%	1%	1%
Not satisfied	5%	4%	4%	3%	4%	5%	4%	4%
Satisfied	44%	46%	47%	42%	43%	44%	44%	44%
Very satisfied	51%	49%	48%	54%	52%	51%	51%	51%
Number of respondents	7042	7097	6603	6279	5620	6495	6394	45,530

programme to be an enjoyable experience that also enriches their understanding of Judaism and Israel, as expressed in the following quotes,[1] which typify commonly-voiced sentiments of participants:

'The trip was everything I expected and more. I felt that I learned a lot and enjoyed learning. I feel close to Israel as a result of the visit.'

'I had a great time, now I understand a lot more about Judaism.'

The questionnaires included participants' ratings of specific programme components over the course of a number of years. Table 14 compares the evaluations of participants from the major Diaspora communities.

A key planning decision, particularly on short tours, is depth versus breadth; that is, whether to attempt to visit as many sites as possible or to spend more time at a few powerful and important sites. By including many sites, organizers hope to give participants an overview of the many important sites and subjects, and to convince them to return for subsequent visits. Nevertheless, there is also a phenomenon of cumulative physical and emotional exhaustion resulting in decreased attention.

The question of allocation of time is very important. Young people today are used to choice, and some resented the restrictions imposed by the tight schedule. Common frustrations with the schedule concerned not enough time at certain sites (particularly not enough time for personal reflection and exploration), too much time at others, too many activities packed into the short trip.

'We only had five minutes in a place we loved, and in a boring place we spent days.'

'There should be more options. Personally I am interested in learning about things like the peace process. There should be a choice, so that those who are not interested don't disturb those who want to go into greater depth.'

Table 14 Satisfaction with various elements of Israel Experience tours, by continent, percentage answering excellent or good (1993–2001 combined data)

	North America	Western Europe	South America	Eastern Europe	South Africa	Australia & New Zealand	Together
Tours	78%	80%	84%	79%	91%	89%	80%
Seminars	59%	59%	60%	61%	72%	64%	59%
Services	44%	35%	41%	47%	50%	35%	41%
Leisure activities	78%	64%	72%	55%	74%	80%	73%
Guides	75%	77%	72%	71%	83%	79%	76%
Home counsellors	84%	85%	84%	71%	88%	88%	84%
Israeli counsellors	88%	85%	85%	80%	91%	94%	87%
Accommodation	58%	47%	68%	56%	67%	58%	55%
Food	27%	28%	42%	51%	37%	19%	30%
Overall organization	66%	69%	62%	64%	83%	73%	67%
Balance of fun and learning	70%	69%	68%	54%	73%	67%	70%
Sufficient free time	54%	51%	53%	33%	42%	37%	53%

'We did everything in one week: jeeps, bikes, hiking; everything was squeezed into the week that we spent in the desert, and these experiences and physical activities should be spread out more over the rest of the time too.'

Another subject that comes up frequently in the participants' evaluations is the matter of free time. Many complained that they did not have enough time to wander around on their own.

'There was never enough free time to experience the country for ourselves or to go and just spend time with friends in this amazing country.'

'On the first evening we went to the promenade in Jerusalem and looked out over the Old City. I wanted to stay a while and soak up the view, but the guides hurried us back onto the bus. I would have liked us to have had more time in different places to sit and look at the view.'

'Masada is a very special place, and we wanted to wander around on our own. Instead, we were given lectures and stories. I wanted to have a personal experience there.'

It can be understood that from the point of view of the organizers the allocation of free time poses a problem because it gives the teenagers time to do things that are not permitted (drinking, drugs, sex). The security concerns in Israel may also limit the organizers' ability to allow participants to spend much time away from the group. At the same time, giving free time can have important advantages, such as providing the opportunity for private, direct experiences and encounters with life in Israel, and for giving the group a break, releasing them from the social pressure that is created in this type of context in the natural course of events.

It is not uncommon for the older participants in the Taglit-birthright israel tours to extend their stay in Israel for several weeks after the group tour, allowing them to re-visit at their leisure the places that they most enjoyed, or to explore aspects of the country they did not get to see during the tour. This, however, was much less common among the high-school-aged Israel Experience participants.

By comparing the correlations between the degrees of satisfaction regarding each of the various elements of the tour, we were able to create a 'macro-scope' of the Israel Experience. The Smallest Space Analysis map shown in Figure 6 is a graphic representation of the correlations between participants' level of satisfaction with each of the aspects of the tour.

Figure 6 shows the fields that comprise the overall visit: the various programmes, content related to Israel, content related to Judaism, the group, staff, and services. At the centre of the map we see the evaluation of general components such as the balance between learning and pleasure, overall organization, and willingness to recommend the programme. Tours, leisure and seminars are the central items for their corresponding regions (i.e. tours for the programmes region, seminars for the content region and leisure for the group region). It is notable that satisfaction with the Jerusalem programme and the Shabbat programme in Jerusalem were more closely related to Jewish content than to the tours and programmes in other parts of the country, highlighting the distinctive flavour of the activities in Jerusalem. It is also important to note that satisfaction with the *madrichim* (counsellor-guides; see Cohen, E.H. *et al.*, 2002) was much more central to the overall experience than was satisfaction with the tour guides.

In order to better understand what distinguishes participants who were 'very satisfied' with the programme from those who were only 'satisfied', subgroups of respondents were introduced into the map as external variables. This enabled us to compare levels of satisfaction in relation to each of the fields which make up the participants' perception of the Israel Experience. The external variables were introduced into Figure 6 with all the programme components, therefore the structure of the maps in Figures 6, 7

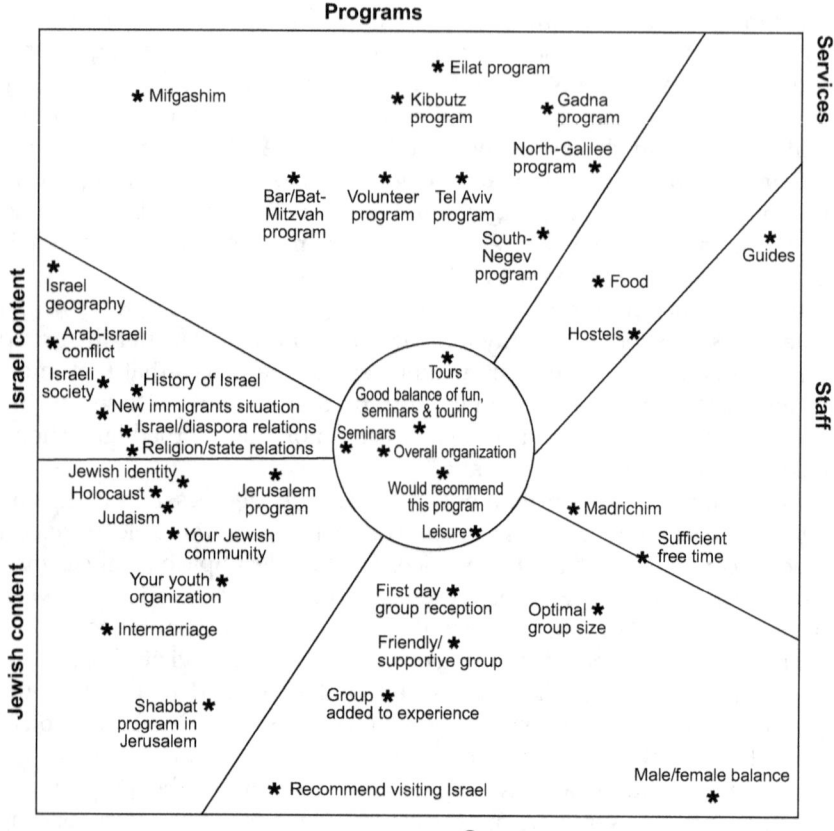

Figure 6 Satisfaction with components of the Israel Experience Programme as expressed by participants in summer 1993–2000*

* Throughout the years of the research, this basic similar structure has been repeatedly found.

Source: Cohen, E.H. (1994b, 1995c)

and 8 are identical. For greater readability, in Figures 7 and 8 the individual items were deleted, leaving only the schematic structure of the regions and the external variables.

Figure 7 shows the very satisfied and the satisfied participants for the whole population. The very satisfied participants are closer to the centre of the map than the satisfied participants. The region in the centre of the map indicates a balance of all elements. For the overall population, we see that

Satisfaction with the Tour

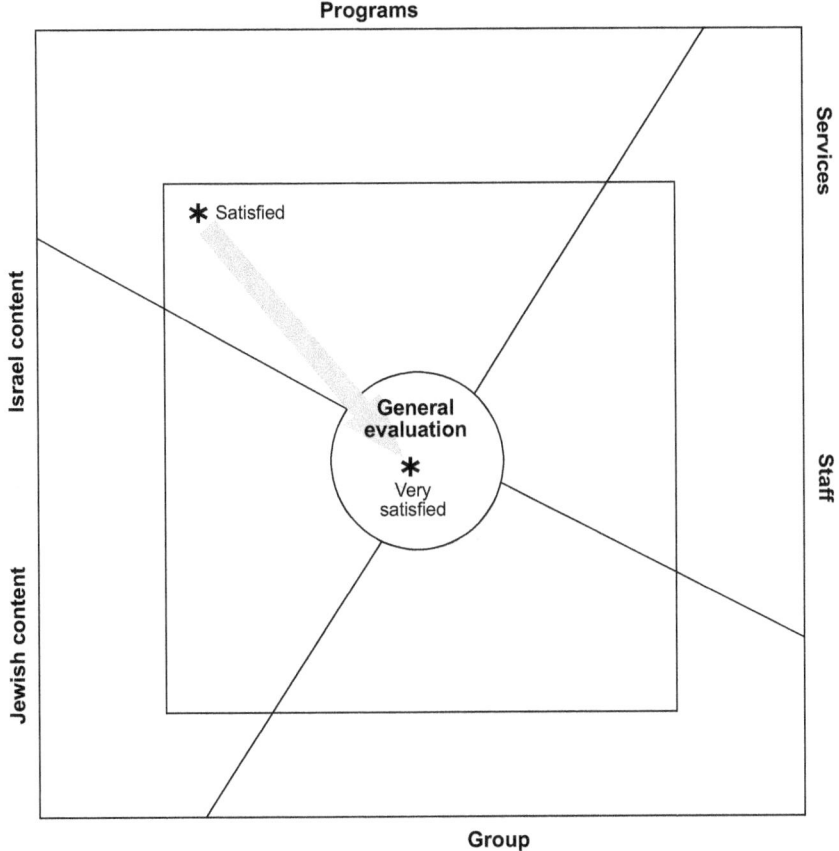

Figure 7 Comparison by level of satisfaction, whole population 1993–2000

the satisfied participants were located in the Programmes region, opposite the Group and Staff regions. The very satisfied participants were located in the centre of the map. From this we may learn that, in order to turn improve participants' satisfaction with the visit it is necessary to improve the way the group functions and the quality of the counsellors and guides.

Also for every national subpopulation, the 'very satisfied' participants are closer to the centre of the map than the 'satisfied' participants. In other words, despite the various emphases that groups from different home countries may have, in every case an excellent tour provides a balance of all the elements and good overall organization.

In looking at the distance and direction that separate each pair of

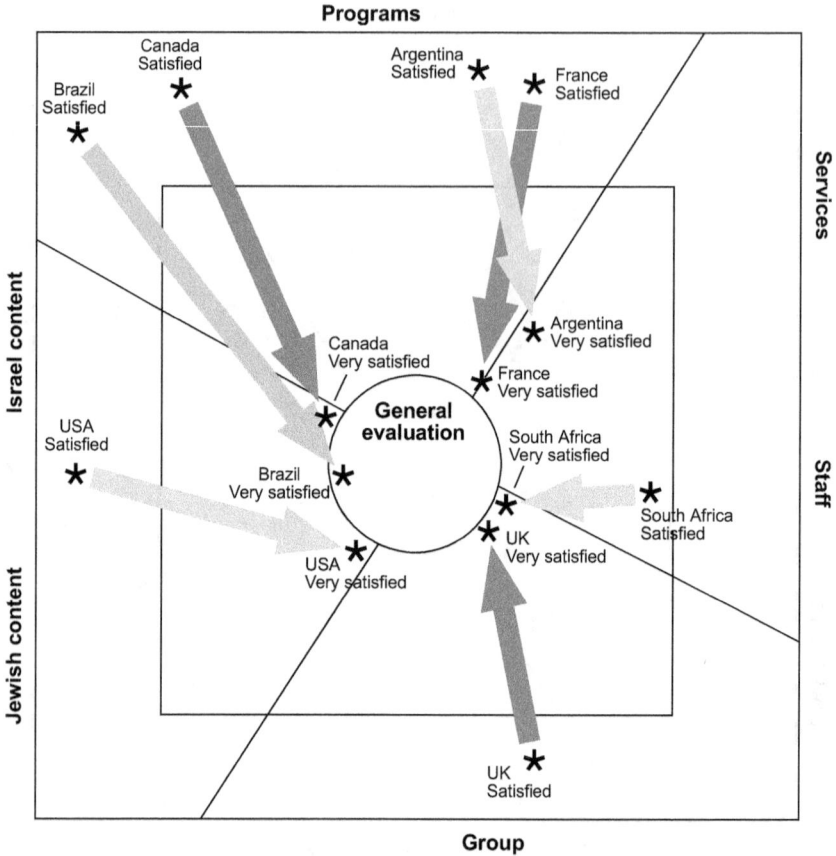

Figure 8 Comparison by level of satisfaction, by nation, 1993–2000

satisfied–very satisfied populations, it is possible to draw strategic conclusions as how to improve the programme – in other words, to bring the merely 'satisfied' closer to the elements from which they were distant and closer to a balanced 'very satisfying' experience. The groups from Canada, Brazil, Argentina and France follow a similar pattern, with the satisfied participants in the Programmes region and the very satisfied closer to the centre. Looking at the case of the USA, we see that the satisfied participants are in the Content region, between the items related to Israel content and those related to Jewish content. They are opposite the Staff region. Content is relatively more important to the American groups. Improving the overall experience for the USA groups seems to be strongly related to the quality of the counsellors and guides. The South African groups follow the opposite trajectory. The satisfied participants are in the Staff region, opposite the Content regions. Therefore, to improve their experience it is necessary to improve the quality of the content of the tour, the educational aspects related to Israel and to Judaism. Finally, the participants from the UK, both the satisfied and the very satisfied, are located in the Group region. The group experience is their point of departure, and remains important to them. A more satisfying, balanced tour, however, would include higher quality programmes throughout Israel.

Satisfaction with the Tour and Previous Educational Background

As discussed earlier, almost all participants in educational tours to Israel have prior Jewish educational background. This provides what may be called 'structural preparation' for the trip (Cohen, E.H., 1999a). Structural preparation differs from specific programme orientations. Structural preparation takes place throughout a child's formative years in a variety of settings: the home, school, synagogue, youth movements, etc.

As noted by Shlomo Gravetz, the late head of the Youth and Hechalutz Department of the World Zionist Organization:

> The Israel Experience cannot be a substitute for a long educational process but should complement such a process. The Israel Experience cannot take the place of central frameworks such as the family, school, Sunday school, youth movements, community centres, and so on. If these frameworks do not exist in the student's life, the Israel Experience cannot provide a basis for a link and connection to Judaism and Israel. (Gravetz, personal communication 1997)

Structural preparation provides the cognitive and affective tools to interpret the experience; the 'vessels' into which the content of the trip to Israel is poured. Like the scaffolding of a building, it enables the participant to stretch their limits emotionally and cognitively and '... permits/encourages travellers to safely go beyond their comfort zones in trying new experiences and articulating new thoughts' (Wall & Klein-Katz, 2007: 6).

Structural preparation deepens the encounter with Israel. Despite the brief duration of the tour (particularly in the case of the Taglit-birthright israel tours), participants are able to recognize and appreciate what is 'authentic'. Even more, their own sense of connection with Jewish and Israeli history and culture prevents the trip from being a superficial glance at exotic sights arranged for tourists (Kelner, 2002; Kelner & Phil, 2001).

Table 15 Impact of participation in local Jewish community on satisfaction with Israel Experience tours

	Never participate	*Rarely participate*	*Frequently participate*	*Very frequently participate*
Not satisfied with tour	8%	5%	5%	4%
Satisfied with tour	43%	46%	44%	38%
Very satisfied with tour	47%	49%	50%	57%

In his book *Informal Jewish Education in North America* Reisman (1990: 21) describes the view of the Judean Hills not just as a beautiful desert, but as the land where his forefathers walked 3000 years ago. Such an interpretation of the landscape requires prior knowledge of the stories of the Bible.

Not only are most Israel Experience participants recruited from the core of the community, those who were most active in their local communities tended to be most satisfied with the tour, as shown in Table 15. Similarly, those who are more frequently involved in local Jewish community activities were more satisfied with the functioning of the group travelling together: 56% of those who participate in community activities at least once a week described the group functioning as 'excellent' compared to 45% of those who participate only once a year.

First Visit Compared with Repeat Visits

One variable that may have a significant impact on the success of the tour is whether or not the Israel Experience tour is a participant's first time in Israel. Half of all Israel Experience participants surveyed between the years 1993 and 2001 had been to Israel previously, as shown in Table 16. Almost a quarter had previously visited more than once, and just over a fifth had been to Israel with a youth group tour prior to the one in which they were surveyed (it is possible that some repeat participants were surveyed more than once).

The rate of previous visits varies widely between the countries of origin. The Western Europeans visit far more frequently than any of the other groups. Programme organizers have to take this into account, because a repeat visit is not like a first visit. Youngsters who have already visited Israel expect a programme appropriate to them and want to deepen their familiarity with Israel and Israelis.

Some organizers emphasize trying to reach those who have not yet been

Table 16 Previous visits to Israel by continent, cumulative data 1993–2001

	North America	Western Europe	South America	Eastern Europe	South Africa	Australia & New Zealand	Together
Previously visited Israel	39%	74%	38%	25%	48%	53%	50%
Previously visited two or more times	16%	45%	6%	13%	20%	20%	24%
Previously visited with a youth group	16%	32%	17%	27%	16%	11%	22%
Participants	27,120	15,889	4286	895	1381	859	50,430

to Israel, those more in the periphery of the Jewish community. In the first years of the Taglit-birthright israel tours, only those who had never been to Israel before were eligible for the free trip. Recently the organization opened registration to those who have been to Israel with family, but not on previous organized educational tours. Other organizers point to the importance of the second visit and even recommend that advertising should be directed towards the parents of youngsters who have already visited Israel. Based on the research carried out by Goldfarb, Professor Steve Cohen (1992) concluded that multiple trips to Israel are necessary to have a significant impact on the attitudes and behaviour of participants. However, this conclusion is liable to be problematic because it is hard to determine with any certainty what is cause and what is outcome. Additionally, family vacations taken as a young child have a different significance than educational tours joined as an adolescent. Therefore the cumulative impact of tours undertaken in various frameworks is hard to assess.

Bubis and Marks (1975) claim that the fact of participation on the part of young Jews visiting Israel in groups manifests self-selection; only those who are already close will come. It is therefore possible to claim, by the same principle, that those who return for a second visit are expressing even greater self-selection.

Influence of Programme Duration

Young Jews wishing to visit Israel on an educational programme may choose from tours of various lengths, from the 10-day Taglit-birthright israel tours to programmes lasting a year or more. The MASA programme, sponsored by the Israeli government and the Jewish Agency, offers a catalogue of more than 150 programmes from five months to several years in length, including Jewish studies, university programmes, yeshiva religious studies, language studies and more. Naturally, the length of time in Israel is a significant factor in the nature and impact of the stay. Potential participants chose programmes based on both logistical considerations and their expectations for the trip. For example, Shapiro (2006: 4) writes that she chose a three-month programme, because it was, '... of long enough duration to be more than simply touristic but short enough that I could return to school in September'.

The classic Israel Experience tour lasts between five and six weeks. By 1998 there was a trend towards shorter programmes, offered in an effort to attract more participants by reducing the cost of the tour. Of the tours from the USA conducted that summer, 21% lasted between three and four weeks, 27% lasted four to five weeks, and 42% lasted between five and six weeks. Only 5% of the groups came for less than three weeks and only 5% came for more than six weeks.

In order to better understand the short-term and long-term impact of tours of various lengths I compared the evaluations of summer tours of various lengths. To focus on only tour length as the variable, I used only data from a single year (summer 1998) and from participants from one country of origin (USA).

I compared programmes of the three durations that were most popular at that time: 22 to 28 days (3–4 weeks); 29 to 35 days (4–5 weeks) and 36 to 42 days (5–6 weeks). The shortest tours were popular both among the youngest (12–15 years olds) and the oldest (18 years and over) cohorts. The four to six week programmes were most popular among 16 and 17 year olds. It is likely that the youngest participants would not yet be emotionally prepared for the longer tours, whereas the oldest participants may have work and study obligations that make it more difficult for them to join the longer trips.

As seen in Table 17, those in the longer tours were somewhat more likely to say they were 'very satisfied'. The longest programmes received the best rating for group functioning and impact of the group on the overall experience. Both satisfaction and group functioning may be, at least in part, a result of the participants' background, as I also found that the longer tours appealed to participants who had greater involvement in their local Jewish communities and were more religious. However, those in the shorter programmes were more likely to have said they thought the programme should be longer and/or more intensive, indicating that the shortest tours may have been too brief to fulfil participants' expectations.

Shye (1986) also found that impact increased with the duration of educa-

Table 17 Comparison of programmes by duration, participants from USA, summer 1998

	22–28 days	29–35 days	36–42 days
Very satisfied	46%	54%	53%
Excellent group functioning	47%	47%	57%
Excellent group impact on experience	54%	57%	65%
Consider self religious	38%	53%	63%
Programme should be longer	45%	38%	40%
Programme should be more intensive	30%	25%	23%

tional programs in Israel on all areas considered, i.e. attitudes related to Israel, to Judaism, to the involvement with the local Jewish community and universal values addressed in the programme.

I also compared evaluations of specific programmes offered within the tours of various lengths. The home hospitality programme (in which participants stay with an Israeli family for several days) and the encounters with Israeli youth (*mifgashim*) programme received more positive evaluations among those in shorter tours. It may be that these activities provided the intimate look at Israeli society necessary to make the short tours meaningful. The Exodus boat tour from Europe to Israel also seemed particularly well suited to the shortest programme. The Gadna programme, which brings participants to an Israeli army base, rates higher as the length of the programme increases, perhaps due to the participants' age and/or Jewish background.

Programmes of different durations appeal to – and thus are most appropriate for – different populations. Longer programmes seem to be better suited to strongly affiliated youngsters, while shorter programmes may be a better tool for outreach to the periphery. Decision-makers, counsellors and other staff members must be aware of the different needs of the participants in tours of varying duration.

Influence of the Size of the Group

Another variable affecting the experience is the size of the group travelling together. As seen above, the functioning of the group has a significant impact on the evaluation of the tours. A group that is too small is liable to create a sense of suffocation and intensify inter-personal conflicts, while a group that is too large is liable to prevent the formation of an intimate atmosphere. From 1993 to 1997 there was a gradual trend towards larger groups,

Table 18 Effects of group size on programme evaluation, USA summer 1998

	<30 participants	30–39 participants	40–49 participants	50+ participants
Would definitely recommend programme to others	52%	57%	59%	68%
Very satisfied	47%	51%	50%	55%
Definitely more aware of community's needs	17%	20%	21%	26%
Definitely enhanced Jewish identity	26%	32%	34%	40%

possibly for economic reasons. In 1998, in response to group feedback in favour of smaller groups, this trend began to reverse.

Nevertheless, as shown in Table 18, the larger the group, the higher the rating of such central general factors as recommendation of programme, satisfaction with programme, enhanced Jewish identity, and enhanced awareness of community needs. (Again, only one national population (USA) is considered, in order to isolate the variable of group size).

In addition, some organizations insist that a number of buses join up for the entire tour, to make logistics and supervision easier, thus increasing exponentially the number of participants at sites. This may have a negative impact on the group experience, as expressed by a participant in one such tour:

> 'I would have liked, at least at the beginning, for the buses to have been separate so that we could have gotten to know the people in our bus better. My brother came back from a tour where there was only one bus, and he had a very powerful experience. He felt a sense of friendship among the people. I feel that I know the people well, but I didn't really have the chance really to get to know 90 kids.'

Hearing about the programme from friends, family or former participants is directly related to group size. The larger the group, the more likely it is that the participants heard about the programme from their friends, family and former participants.

Logistics

While the main emphasis has been on the educational and identity-enhancing aspects of the Israel Experience, as with any tour the mundane logistics must not be ignored. The logistical sphere has been a source of misunderstanding and tension between the programme's marketers abroad and the organizers in Israel. There is a feeling among the organizers abroad that the Israelis do not understand the special needs of their youth, at either the organizational or the material level. The organizers in Israel feel that their colleagues abroad do not have enough understanding of the many technical constraints they have to deal with in Israel. The task of logistic organization is by no means simple; it includes such issues as accommodation, meals, security and timing visits to sites. When large numbers of youngsters come to Israel all at the same time, the staff in Israel is not always able to take into account the special requirements of every group.

The organizational side has a great effect on the participants' feeling of satisfaction, and in this realm there has been considerable amount of criticism, as voiced in the following quotes:

> 'I feel that in general what was lacking was organization. There didn't seem to be a formal chain of authority. The counsellors never knew exactly what was happening and plans were often changed suddenly.'
>
> 'I believe I could have enjoyed the experience more and benefited more if the general organization had been better.'

Food is a particularly problematic component, and complaints about the quality and quantity of food are routine among Israel Experience groups. Some organizers try to respond to the participants' by offering more choices and familiar foods such as hamburgers and pizza. Others feel that Israeli-style food, such as falafel, should be provided as part of the cultural experience, rather than adapting the meals to the home diet of participants.

However, it cannot be ignored that the daily routine of these adolescents has been disrupted, and homesickness often manifests at mealtimes, especially when unfamiliar foods are served. Cohen, E. and Avieli (2004) found that, for international travellers, food may be both an attraction and a source of problems related to health and hygiene, communication, expectations, and authenticity. In some groups, participants spend a considerable amount of money on buying their own food (most often fast food and junk food). Those with special dietary considerations, such as vegetarians, have complained that there are no arrangements to provide for their needs.

Similarly, the accommodation and service staff (i.e. bus drivers) have an impact on the extent to which participants enjoy the trip. The issue of food and accommodation raises a number of questions as to level of 'luxury' that should be provided to participants. This is particularly complex as participants come from backgrounds with different standards of living to which they have become accustomed. Most nights participants stay in hotels, youth hostels or in tourist accommodation provided at a kibbutz. Not all tours patronize the same accommodation. Some (particularly participants from Mexico, who pay more for their tours, and the Taglit-birthright israel tour participants) tend to stay at higher quality hotels (Dani More, general director of Israel Experience programmes, personal communication June 28, 2007). Meals are provided at the hotel or kibbutz (see sample itinerary in appendix). Sometimes box lunches are provided during hikes or other outdoor activities.

Organizers wish to be egalitarian, providing the same standard for participants from all countries. However, some may find the conditions insufficient and uncomfortable, whereas others may be bothered by conditions they feel create a barrier between them and Israeli society.

Preparation and Follow-up

The impact of an educational tour to Israel may be enhanced through orientation programmes and follow-up activities (Rovner, 1976; Strenger & Lichtenberg, 1996).

Orientation programmes, as distinguished from the structural preparation of ongoing involvement with Jewish life at home discussed above, are specific to the upcoming tour. The primary objectives of an orientation programme are to:

- arouse participants' enthusiasm;
- enable participants to form realistic expectations for the trip;
- allow members of the touring group to become acquainted with one another;
- help participants pack properly for the climate and planned activities;
- point out key aspects of Israeli culture that may help participants understand the encounters they are likely to have;
- give background information about sites to be visited.

Trip-specific follow-up activities:

- reunite group members;
- provide a forum for discussing and processing reactions to the trip;
- provide continued learning about Israel and Judaism;
- provide information about upcoming trips to Israel and encourage subsequent visits;
- channel enthusiasm from the trip into other activities.

Significant follow-up activities are practical only if participants all come from the same geographic region. This is often the case for trips organized through synagogues or youth groups, but is less common in national programmes such as Taglit-birthright israel. Participants who live far from one another may stay in touch through mail, email or phone, although this tends to be maintained for only a short time.

'I enjoyed learning about Israeli history and politics in discussions with our counsellors and tour guides. I found that these discussions were also relevant to my Jewish identity. I would like there to be a place at home that would give me the opportunity to continue these discussions.'

There are four basic programme models related to preparation and follow-up. These are:

(1) *the Targeted Model* sees the visit as standing alone and requiring no further activity;
(2) *the Didactic Model* offers preparation before the visit. Preparing the participants for the visit is done to ensure they have the tools to understand what is taking place, to coordinate expectations and to get to know the other participants in the journey;
(3) *the Recruitment Model* emphasizes activity in the home country after the trip. This model requires organization in the countries of origin to await the participants on their return;
(4) *the Ongoing Model* includes all the elements that have been mentioned: preparation, visit and follow-up activity. This model is particularly suitable for youth movements or other frameworks that operate on a regular basis.

In 1994 we asked counsellors accompanying Israel Experience groups how they see the trip to Israel in the context of ongoing involvement with local community activities (Table 19). The counsellors from the US were most likely to see the trip as a one time event, unrelated to previous or subsequent activities. Those from the UK were most likely to see the trip as

Table 19 Counsellors' attitudes regarding the place of the Israel Experience in educational activities over the year

Programme design as:	United States	France	United Kingdom
Climax and summation of the past year	1%	30%	3%
Standing in its own right	65%	39%	46%
A springboard for activities next year	34%	32%	51%
Total	100%	100%	100%

Table 20 Participation in preparatory activities, by continent. Cumulative data for 1993–2001

	North America	Western Europe	South America	Eastern Europe	South Africa	Australia & New Zealand	Together
Never	37%	31%	7%	27%	15%	11%	31%
Once or twice	41%	53%	21%	41%	39%	47%	43%
Three to five times	15%	8%	30%	17%	36%	25%	15%
Six or more	8%	7%	42%	15%	10%	17%	11%

an incentive for future activity. The counsellors from France seem to view the trip as an integral part of ongoing involvement.

Overall, almost a third of participants came on the tour with no specific preparatory activities. Only a quarter participated in three or more orientation sessions. As with other issues, we see there is a significant difference in the prevalence of orientation activities among groups from different countries, as shown in Table 20. South American participants had by far the greatest level of participation in orientation activities; almost three quarters took part in at least three preparatory activities. US participants were the least likely to have not taken part in any orientation activities.

Note

1. The quotes presented are representative of the vast body of personal comments collected over the years of the survey, and therefore attributions to the specific participants are not given.

Chapter 8
Impact of the Israel Experience

In the course of doing the research for this book, we heard or read the reactions of thousands of participants. Most remember their visit as an experience that left an indelible impression on them. There are even those who say that their visit to Israel changed the course of their lives.[1]

> 'The trip was an experience I will never forget ... I finally for once in my life feel some sort of stability and finally feel a part of something ...'
>
> 'I have gained more during my five weeks in Israel than in all my other summers combined ... thank you for giving me an enriching and broadening summer that will affect me for the rest of my life. Israel is forever a part of me now.'
>
> 'I am leaving Israel a different person than when I came ...'

It can be said with confidence that the trip is meaningful for participants: the overwhelming majority says that their programme had an impact on them (52% yes, 37% definitely yes). However, given the significant amount of money and energy invested in these educational tours to Israel, it is important to assess the extent to which they succeed in fulfilling their goals of enhancing participants' Jewish identity, increasing their level of commitment to Israel, and encouraging them to be more involved in their local Jewish communities. While this is a primary reason for the evaluation of the programmes, it is not simple to assess. Even using methods such as control groups, before-and-after surveys and follow-up studies, it is difficult to isolate the impact of the programme from other factors such as the participants' backgrounds and their ongoing involvement in other Jewish educational settings. Bubis and Marks (1975) asserted that participants in Jewish educational programmes are a self-selected population and that in most cases the programme itself could not be credited with instilling beliefs or values, although they may help in strengthening them. Shye (1986) found that initial attitudes and home environment had to be considered, in addition to the conditions of the programme itself, when assessing the impact of an educational trip to Israel. Shye found that attitudes related to Zionism and the Jewish religion were more likely to be enhanced by the programme if they were positive at the outset. Love for and knowledge of Israel, on the other hand, were found to be less dependent on prior attitudes and in this case feelings of detachment could become feelings of commitment.

In evaluating the Taglit-birthright israel programme, Saxe et al. (2004) considered both *conversion* (the programme's ability to instil positive feelings towards Judaism and Israel where they did not previously exist) and *preservation* (maintaining or enhancing such feelings where they did previously exist).

Impact on Jewish Identity

Some parents, organizers and participants expect an automatic and almost mystical positive impact on Jewish identity from the simple fact of visiting Israel. The results of empirical research on this topic, however, have been more ambiguous. In their 1975 study, Bubis and Marks compared different indices of Jewish identity and the changes taking place in these indices as a result of participation in two different programmes: a summer camp in the USA and a visit to Israel. As a result of this study, Bubis and Marks raise two important questions. One is whether the impact of a programme depends on its location in Israel, or if a similar impact on Jewish identity can be achieved through a well-planned programme in the home country. The second question relates to how long the impacts last after the end of the programme. Is there a 'halo effect' immediately after the programme that fades over time?

In his study of participants in year-long programmes at Israeli universities, Herman (1970) found that the Jewish identity of participants in the programme was strengthened during the visit to Israel and that they feel their Jewish identity must include a high level of commitment to the State of Israel. At the same time, studies of Jewish summer camps in the US have also found that participation in the Jewish environment of the camp strengthened Jewish identity (Sales & Saxe, 2004; Zeldin, 2006; Cohen, E.H. & Bar-Shalom, 2006). In the case of summer camps, some young people return to the same camp year after year throughout their childhood and adolescence, thus strengthening the impact of the programme. The return to the same setting is important, regardless of where the camp is located (Zeldin, 2006).

In contrast, the Taglit-birthright israel programme stress the importance of being in Israel, even if only for a very short time. The research study carried out by Goldfarb Consultants (1991) found that respondents who had been in Israel ranked the visit in first place among the events that had sharpened their commitment to their Jewish identity, and many ranked it as the strongest experience of their lives, in terms of Jewish identity.

The specific nature of the impact on Jewish identity may be measured in terms of both behaviour and declared attitudes. The questionnaires distributed to Israel Experience tour participants as part of the ongoing survey included items dealing with issues related to how the visit has changed the behaviour of the participants, such as whether they have kept in communication with Israelis and group members they met on the trip, have increased their involvement in the local Jewish community, take an interest in events in Israel, have returned or plan to return to Israel and whether they are considering becoming Israeli citizens. Changes in the participants' attitudes toward issues related to Jewish identity are examined in comparisons of pre- and post-trip questionnaires and follow-up studies.

In order to study changes in attitude taking place immediately after the visit to Israel, between 1989 and 1994 my research team distributed two questionnaires among participants: the first immediately upon arrival in Israel, and the second soon after their return home. The two questionnaires included identical questions related to Jewish identity. The results are shown in Table 21. Overall, we see that participants entered the programme with a high level of pride and sense of solidarity, and this was strengthened slightly during the course of the programme. At the beginning of the programme the sense of being part of the Jewish people was weaker than the sense of pride in being Jewish, but the impact on the former was somewhat greater. The exceptions to this picture were the Eastern European participants. They not only started the programme with far less sense of Jewish pride and solidarity, but their attitudes were negatively affected. This finding highlights the critical need for programmes tailored to the needs of specific populations. Currently, the Jewish Agency sponsors a number of subsidized programmes for Eastern European Jewish youth, including trips to Israel for 17–25 year old students, and Jewish summer camps, and youth leadership seminars in Eastern Europe and the former Soviet countries.[2] Evaluation of such programmes would be useful in designing more effective educational tours for this population, whose history and current cultural-political climate (i.e. the almost total destruction of the Jewish communities and their institutions during World War II, the Soviet regime, and continued anti-Semitism) have made Jewish identity and connection with Israel particularly difficult.

For all groups, there was an increased sense of the importance of participating in the local Jewish community. As discussed earlier, at least from the perspective of the Diaspora organizers, strengthening Jewish life in the Diaspora has become one of the most important goals of the programme, and it seems that the programme has successfully conveyed this to participants.

In addition, we asked participants at the end of the tour to evaluate for themselves the extent to which they felt their understanding was improved on various issues, and whether the programme positively affected their

Table 21 Attitudes related to Jewish identity at the beginning and end of the tour; percentage answering 'strongly agree', by continent, cumulative data 1989–1994

	North America		Western Europe		South America		Eastern Europe		South Africa		Australia & New Zealand		Together	
	pre	post	pre	post	pre	post	pre	post	pre	post	pre	post	pre	post
I am proud to be Jewish	75%	81%	70%	76%	72%	75%	51%	45%	84%	85%	71%	77%	73%	78%
It is important for me to feel part of the Jewish people	56%	64%	53%	63%	55%	60%	44%	34%	65%	68%	53%	57%	55%	63%
I want to be involved for a few hours each week in my Jewish community	50%	58%	49%	60%	52%	63%	70%	74%	41%	47%	59%	73%	50%	59%

Table 22 Participants' evaluation of program impact on Jewish identity, by continent

	North America	Western Europe	South America	Eastern Europe	South Africa	Australia & New Zealand	Together
Program enhanced Jewish identity (yes/definitely)	83%	77%	83%	71%	88%	81%	81%
Program made me more aware of my community's needs (yes/definitely)	69%	67%	79%	61%	79%	69%	70%
Program improved my understanding of Jewish identity (very/quite)	67%	66%	70%	58%	83%	66%	68%
Program improved my understanding of Judaism (very/quite)	63%	55%	64%	42%	69%	52%	60%

attitudes. Table 22 shows the results for issues related to Jewish identity. The vast majority of participants felt that the programme enhanced and improved their understanding of their Jewish identity and made them more aware of the needs of their local Jewish community. A smaller percentage, although still well over half, felt their understanding of the Jewish religion had been improved. Again we see the program's weaker impact on Eastern European participants.

In 1996 I conducted a survey of students holding positions of responsibility (i.e. secretary, treasurer, activities head, etc.) in Jewish campus organizations, a population from which future leaders of the Jewish community are likely to be drawn (Cohen, E.H., 1997b). The vast majority (77%) had visited Israel, and virtually all (97%) said that visiting Israel has a positive impact on Jewish identity. It is noteworthy that even in countries with relatively low rates of visitation, campus activists still perceive a trip to Israel as having a positive impact on Jewish identity; for example, although only 59% of respondents from Argentina had visited Israel, 95% said they think a trip to Israel has a positive impact on Jewish identity. This reinforces the analysis above regarding the relationship between prior expectations and the impact of the trip.

Impact on Attitudes towards Israel

Particularly from the perspective of the Israeli organizers of the programme, the key goal of the programme is to instil in Diaspora youth a sense of connection and commitment to Israel. However, the impact on attitudes towards Israel was more ambiguous than that on Jewish identity.

The results of the pre- and post-trip questionnaires (Table 23) show that at the end of the trip, a slightly greater percentage of participants said Israel makes them proud and that they consider themselves Zionists. The greatest increase was in the perception that it is important to support Israel. Among participants from South America and Eastern Europe there was a slight decline in the percentage who said Israel makes them proud, and the South Americans were less likely at the end of the programme to call themselves Zionists.

The programme's impact on attitudes regarding a possible future in Israel is even more complicated. Among North Americans, South Americans and Eastern Europeans, the desire to return to Israel for a longer study programme remained the same or was slightly strengthened by the short-term study tour. The other groups expressed *less* of a desire to return for a study programme at the end of the tour. Only among the South Americans do we see an increase at the end of the trip in the percentage who said they

Table 23 Attitudes related to Israel at the beginning and end of the tour, percentage answering 'strongly agree', by continent, cumulative data 1989–1994

	North America		Western Europe		South America		Eastern Europe		South Africa		Australia & New Zealand		Together	
	pre	post	pre	post	pre	post	pre	post	pre	post	pre	post	pre	post
Israel makes me proud	80%	84%	68%	72%	74%	71%	57%	51%	82%	85%	78%	79%	76%	78%
Are you a Zionist? (yes/definitely)	65%	69%	64%	68%	48%	44%	43%	48%	69%	69%	72%	72%	62%	67%
It is important to support Israel (strongly agree/disagree)	66%	77%	57%	65%	61%	72%	68%	52%	60%	67%	70%	74%	63%	72%
Would you like to return to study in Israel? (yes/definitely)	60%	62%	53%	44%	35%	43%	60%	68%	43%	41%	49%	37%	53%	54%
Do you want to live in Israel?	48%	35%	52%	43%	27%	30%	34%	60%	52%	48%	50%	36%	46%	38%
I am thinking about *aliyah* (agree/strongly agree)	25%	32%	27%	33%	21%	27%	66%	36%	28%	39%	26%	35%	25%	32%
I like Israelis (strongly agree/disagree)	55%	49%	41%	36%	26%	26%	70%	55%	36%	32%	45%	37%	48%	41%

want to live in Israel. Among Eastern Europeans, who were most likely to say at the beginning they want to live in Israel, this attitude was unchanged. Negative encounters with Israelis, it seems, may be responsible for some of these unfavourable attitudes, as participants from every country were less likely at the end of the trip to agree with the statement 'I like Israelis'. Preparation for the cross-cultural exchanges and well-mediated encounters may be needed to rectify the trip's apparently negative impact on impressions of Israelis.

Interestingly, every group was more likely, even if only slightly so, to say they were thinking about *aliya* (immigration to Israel). The percentages for this, both before and after the trip, were low. It seems, perhaps, that the trip to Israel succeeded in planting the seed of this idea in the minds of the young visitors, even if few are seriously considering making the move.

In the evaluation of the Taglit-birthright israel programme, which compared participants with non-participants, it was found that those who had gone to Israel were less likely to hold negative images of the country (i.e. torn by internal strife, fundamentalist, militaristic) and more likely to see Israel as a source of pride and as a future home. As with the Israel Experience participants, the Taglit-birthright israel participants were far more likely to think of Israel as a source of pride (62% of surveyed participants) than as a future home (17%) (Saxe *et al.*, 2006).

Impact on Personal Identity

In addition to its impact on Jewish identity, the tour also has an impact on participants' personal development. Inculcating responsibility is no less important a goal of the programmes than the transmission of particular elements of Jewish and Israel content. The leadership of the Jewish community today is aware that from this core of involved and affiliated Jewish youth will come the next generation of leaders. Developing leadership skills was found to be one of the primary goals of informal Jewish education (Cohen, E.H., 1997b, 2001), of which the Israel Experience is an important part.

Most participants say that their Israel Experience programme enhanced their sense of personal independence (45% yes, 36% absolutely yes). Since the participants are adolescents, this aspect of the programme is particularly important. Interestingly, although for many of the issues explored there was almost no difference between male and female participants (in itself a significant finding), we found that the young women benefited particularly in terms of personal independence: 40% of the female participants said the programme 'absolutely' enhanced their sense of personal independence, compared with 31% of the male participants. In an independent study, Levinson and Zoline (1997) concluded that summer trips to Israel have a positive impact on the self-esteem of Jewish adolescents.

Some 59% of participants say the trip to Israel improved their leadership skills. This is particularly significant given that almost half of participants, both male and female, held positions of responsibility in a Jewish youth or community organization prior to their trip to Israel.

Long-term Influence

The Israel Experience clearly has a strong impact on participants. But how lasting is its influence? Are the glowing evaluations at the end of the trip indicative of a real shift in attitude, or a 'halo effect' that quickly fades after return to daily life? In terms of Jewish identity and participation in local community activities, it is hard to isolate the effect of the visit to Israel from other factors influencing the participants' identity over time (i.e. other Jewish educational settings, family and friends). Therefore the question of the long-term influence of the Israel Experience can not be answered unequivocally.

Researchers who have investigated this question found different, sometimes even contradictory answers. Bubis and Marks (1975), for instance, compared the degree of influence on Jewish identity nine months after the end of Jewish informal education programmes in Israel and in a Jewish summer camp in the United States. The visit to Israel was not found to have produced a greater change in behaviour or attitudes of the participants relative to those who stayed in the United States. Bubis and Marks concluded that differences between the groups were due to self-selection: those who went to Israel had stronger prior Jewish affiliation.

On the other hand Kafka *et al.* (1992) found that almost a year after returning home, the influence of the visit to Israel could be seen in programme alumni who internalized the content and attitudes transmitted during the programme into an integral part of their beliefs.

My research team conducted two follow-up studies on the Israel Experience. The first was conducted from June to September 1994, between nine months and a year after the 1993 Summer Israel Experience. The second study, commissioned by the CRB Foundation and the Youth and Hechalutz Department, was conducted among 1996 Israel Experience American alumni 12–16 months after they returned from Israel. Participants from various groups agreed in advance to take part in the follow-up study. Although anonymous, the coded follow-up questionnaires could be compared to the questionnaires that individual participants filled out at the end of their tour of Israel.

Both of these studies confirmed the lasting effects of the programmes. In fact, we found that enthusiasm increased over time. At the end of the visit in 1993, 53% said they were 'very satisfied' with the trip. In the follow-up study, 66% said they had been 'very satisfied.' The sense of a bond with Israel also increased over time. In response to the question 'Has the programme reinforced your relationship with Israel?' 56% percent answered 'yes, absolutely' in the follow-up survey, as compared with 48% at the end of the programme.

On the other hand, a weakening was observed in other indices of Jewish identity. In the follow-up study, 35% of the programme alumni said that the programme had absolutely strengthened their Jewish identity, as compared with 47% who said so at the end of the programme. The weakened influence is even more noticeable with regard to the participants' awareness of the needs of their local community; only 18% said that the programme made them more aware of the needs of the community after nine months, while 31% had said so at the end of the programme. The implications of this are particularly important, as it is in the realm of community involvement that enthusiasm from the trip may be most practically channelled.

Similar results were found in the 1997 follow-up survey of the summer 1996 Israel Experience programme, strengthening the conclusions. As seen in Table 24, a year after the return home, there was an increase in the percentage of respondents who said they were very satisfied with the programme, were definitely influenced by it, and that it enhanced their

Table 24 Long-term impact of Israel Experience, results of 1997 follow-up of summer 1996 participants

	Response at end of tour (summer 1996)	*Response to follow-up survey (1997)*
Very satisfied	63%	77%
Definitely influenced by programme	57%	62%
Programme definitely enhanced my relationship to Israel	62%	77%
Programme definitely enhanced my Jewish identity	50%	42%
Programme definitely improved my awareness of home Jewish community	31%	24%

relationship to Israel. But there was a decrease in the percentage of those who said the programme definitely enhanced their Jewish identity and that it definitely improved their awareness of the needs of their Jewish community at home.

The percentage of programme alumni considering moving to Israel fell drastically after returning home. At the end of the programme, more than half the participants had said they were seriously thinking about coming to live in Israel. In the follow-up a year later, only 8% said they were interested in living and working in Israel. This is the one area in which a halo effect did seem to play a significant role in responses.

Willingness to recommend the programme provides a practical yardstick for measuring the success of a programme. At the end of the summer, 96% of participants said they would encourage friends and peers to join an Israel Experience tour. A year after their return to the United States, an impressive 94% said they had actually done so.

In the follow-up survey, we found that almost all former Israel Experience participants were still in touch with friends they had made on the trip; 97% maintained contact with at least one co-participant, and 80% maintained contact with three or more. Such connections almost certainly help preserve the effects and the memories of the summer experience. However, in the open comment section of the questionnaire, some participants noted that, although they had enjoyed meeting Jewish teenagers from throughout the United States, distance prevented more frequent reunions.

The Taglit-birthright israel programme has included follow-up surveys as a regular part of an ongoing evaluation (Saxe *et al.* 2000; 2001; 2002; 2006). Participants in the programme were surveyed 1 month, 3 months, 12–15 months, 2 years and 3 years after the trip. A control group of those who applied to the programme but did not join a tour was surveyed at each of these intervals also. The long-term evaluation of the control group enables the researchers to isolate effects of the trip itself from other impacts on attitudes.

In comparing participants' responses one, two and three years after their trip, Saxe *et al.* (2006) found that feelings of connection to the Jewish People and to Israel that were still strong a year after the trip had waned somewhat after two or three years. However, some attitudes related to Jewish continuity, such as the importance of raising Jewish children actually increased with the passage of time.[3]

Saxe *et al.* (2004: 7) concluded that, 'The strongest conversion effect was on feelings of ethnic connection – to Israel, to the Jewish people, and to Jewish history,' while there was little conversionary effect on religious practice or community participation. In my follow-up study of the American participants in the summer 1993 Israel Experience tour (Cohen, E.H.,

1995d), I found impact on Jewish identity gradually dissipated, whereas feelings of connection to Israel were even stronger than at the conclusion of the programme. The congruence of the results of these follow-up studies indicate that the continued impact of the trip, with a gradual decline in the influence on Jewish identity, is a structural feature of the long-term impact of educational tours to Israel.

Notes

1. As with the previous chapter, the quotes presented are representative of the vast body of personal comments collected over the years of the survey, and therefore attributions to the specific participants are not given.
2. See http://www.jafi.org.il/iefund/search_results.asp?search4=Eastern+Europe (accessed 11.11.07).
3. It must be noted that this survey is not a comparison of the same individuals, but rather a comparison of the results of a 2006 survey of alumni from various programmes, that is from summer 2005 (1 year post-trip), from 2003–2004 (2 years post-trip) and from 2002–2003 (3 years post-trip).

Chapter 9
Content of the Programme

The Modules

Although Israel Experience tours are organized through public entities,[1] most of the individual activity units, many of the modules that make up the curricular itinerary of the tour are offered through private subcontractors. A module may be defined as:

> A self-contained unit capable of performing a function without outside help. Each module is designed for a specific purpose and is temporary, in the sense that as soon as its purpose has been accomplished, it can be disbanded. As such, modules can be added or subtracted (or shifted) as needed. This introduces flexibility into an organization so that it can keep up with a rapidly changing environment. (Rice & Bishoprick, cited by Kahane, 1997: 29)

In the past 10 years, the number of modules has tripled, indicating that the domain is constantly adapting. Today, some 600 modules are in operation throughout the country (CRB Foundation 1993; Cohen, E.H., 2006b). In 1998–1999, my research team conducted a comprehensive survey of the modules of the Israel Experience programmes. This included an inventory of existing modules, a questionnaire distributed to providers (staff) and an item in the participants' questionnaire asking them to rate selected modules.

These modules offer a huge variety of programmes lasting from a few hours to an entire week. They may be informal activities or seminars and lectures. Some accommodate small groups; others cater for large groups of several hundred participants at a time. The content may include recreational activities, nature, history, religion, political issues, or universal values (such as leadership skills). The following categories and examples give a taste of the variety of the modules:

- recreational activities: emphasis on fun, with little or no explicit educational content (e.g. days at the beach or ice skating at an indoor rink);
- field trips: emphasis on seeing, enjoying and learning about the geography and natural environment (e.g. hikes in nature reserves, kayaking and camel rides);

- guided tours of historic sites, with emphasis on learning about recent and/or ancient history (e.g. tours of the Old City of Jerusalem, battlefields and archaeological sites);
- sites of symbolic religious and/or national importance (e.g. the Western Wall, Masada and Herzl's grave);
- seminars, lectures and discussions on a subject related to Judaism or Israel. Some of these are held in classroom settings, while others take place at a specific, relevant location (e.g. a seminar on the Holocaust at Yad Vashem and archaeological seminars at excavation sites);
- workshops and games to teach skills such as drama, photography or leadership skills;
- visits to museums such as the Bible Lands Museum or the Diaspora Museum;
- experiential activities such as the army training camp at Gadna, kibbutz stays, volunteer programmes with the Israeli ambulance service or in development towns, for example, and visits to Druze or Bedouin villages;
- planned encounters (*mifgashim*) between groups of Israeli and Diaspora youth or home hospitality with Israeli families;
- Some modules combine several elements by visiting sites, integrating recreational activities and hands-on experience, and holding discussions of subjects that come up as a result of the activities, such as a 3–4 day hike from the Mediterranean Sea to the Sea of Galilee (the Sea-to-Sea programme).

An analysis of participants' evaluations of specific modules revealed that the most favourably-rated activities included a range of those considered *important* (concerned with powerful Jewish or Zionist symbols such as the Western Wall and the Holocaust museum), those considered *enjoyable* (kayaking, drama exercises), and those that were *educational* (the Diaspora museum). Some popular modules combined these elements (peace process seminar, encounters with Israeli youth). While content is a factor in a module's popularity, poorly-rated modules often have problems with logistics, planning or guiding. In some cases apparently identical modules led by different guides or held in different places received dramatically different evaluations. In particular, some meetings between young Israelis and visiting youngsters received very high ratings, while others were quite problematic, highlighting the importance of planning and effective guiding.

The location itself is also important to the success of various activities, and the different geographical regions in Israel vary in significance for the participants. Hikes in the Negev are consistently among the most popular activities. The Negev desert offers a beautiful and exotic natural landscape in which participants may experience both physical and spiritual adventure. Jerusalem also offers sites and experiences impossible to find anywhere else, and the time spent in Jerusalem generally affects visitors strongly. The urban environment of modern Tel Aviv, in contrast, received the least favourable ratings among visitors; perhaps it is too similar to cities they have seen in their home countries or in other parts of the world.

As mentioned, the long list of modules from which programme organizers may chose enables tours to be tailored to emphasize specific goals. Not only the choice of sites and activities, but also the way in which the sites are presented may affect the message imparted to participants. The visit to the historical site of Masada provides a clear example. Masada is a plateau overlooking the Dead Sea where Jewish rebels made their last stand against the Roman Empire in the first century of the Common Era. It has become a powerful symbol of Jewish national survival (despite the eventual suicide of the rebels in the face of defeat at the hands of the Romans). The majority of Israel Experience tours visit Masada, most climbing the 'snake path' to the excavated ruins at the top. For most organizers, the visit to Masada provides a setting for helping visiting Diaspora youth understand the history of Israel and its people. But some are uncomfortable with the apparent romanticization of religious and national extremism and martyrdom in the Masada story. David Forman, a Reform rabbi, suggests giving participants more opportunity to learn about current problems in Israeli society, such as absorption of Russian and Ethiopian immigrants and the Israeli–Palestinian conflict, and to discuss these issues among the group and with Israeli peers. He also suggests that visitors to historic sites such as Masada should pick up garbage as they tour, providing an example and a service.

In the questionnaire distributed in 1998, participants were asked to rate selected modules according to seven questions:

(1) Do you think such a programme is *important*?
(2) Were you satisfied with the *guiding* of the programme?
(3) Would you say that your *understanding* of the [relevant issue] has been improved?
(4) Did you *enjoy* your visit to this programme?
(5) When you take in to consideration the various components of the programme, would you say that you are *satisfied*?
(6) Would you *recommend* including this programme in future Israel Experience tours?
(7) How would you rate the *quality* of this programme?

Content of the Programme

The responses to the first six of these questions were analyzed using the Smallest Space Analysis technique, which revealed three regions of related modules, which may be described as cognitive, axiological and experiential (Figure 9). Sub-populations of participants who expressed various levels of satisfaction were introduced into the map as external variables. The least-satisfied participants were located on the border of the Axiological and Cognitive regions and far from the enjoyment variable. The 'satisfied' participants were in the Axiological Region, but closer to the centre of the map. The 'very satisfied' participants were located close to the centre of the map, in the Experiential region, indicating that participants prefer modules offering a balance between symbolic importance, understanding and enjoyment (hence their placement in the centre of the map).

To further explore the evaluations of the modules, the results from all seven of the evaluative questions were analysed using another data analysis technique called the Multi-dimensional Partial Order Scalogram Analysis (MPOSAC) (see description in Chapter 1). Based on this analysis, I found that modules could be effectively evaluated using a Recreational-Cognitive Quality index, which considers the extent to which an activity is enjoyable, the extent to which it increases participants' understanding of the relevant issues, and its overall quality (Cohen, E.H., 2006b). The modules that received the highest evaluation according to this index were:

- *The Kotel:* The Western Wall in Jerusalem (the Kotel) is certainly the most famous site of Judaism, with profound symbolic importance. Visits to the Kotel may be structured or unstructured; an informative, emotional or group-oriented activity. Regardless of the format, the visit to the Kotel leaves a very strong and deep emotional impression on the participants, and also provides an opportunity to learn about Jewish history, and to explore Jewish identity.
- *Kibbutz Misgav Am:* At this kibbutz on Israel's border with Lebanon, various issues such as history, politics and security problems are discussed. One of the aims of the programme is the personal involvement of participants in the ongoing debates, and their personal experience of the reality of the northern border. The participants and *madrichim* reported that the guiding was excellent and the topics were both interesting and pertinent to the current political situation. It should be noted that the participants in the surveyed tour identified with the guide who was originally from North America.
- *Peace process seminar:* This seminar, with no fixed setting, aims to provide participants with an understanding of the Middle East peace process through educational and technical means, such as group

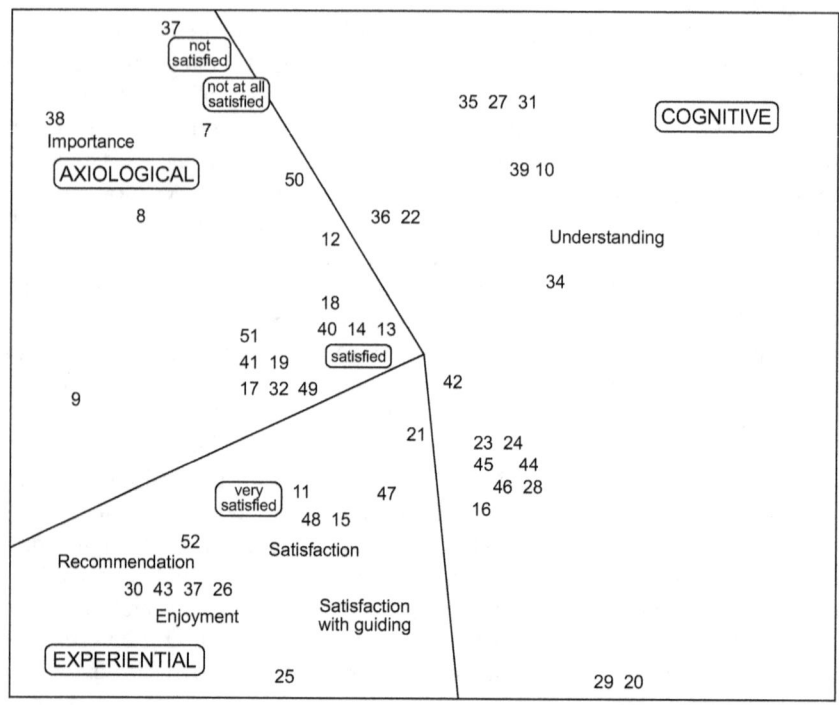

Key:
7 Yad Vashem
8 Kotel (Western Wall)
9 Tree planting
10 Israel Museum
11 Chamat Gader hot springs
12 Peace process seminar
13 Mt Herzl
14 Rabin's grave
15 Nahal David nature reserve
16 Herodian Quarter, Jerusalem
17 Camel ride at Chavat Han
18 Beyond biking
19 Petra jeep tour
20 Beit Guvrin caves
21 Archeological seminar
30 Almog beach
31 Kibbutz Tuval
32 Underwater observatory
33 Shorashim (roots) seminar
34 Misgav Am
35 Kibbutz Marom ha-Golan
36 Kibbutz Malchia
37 Kayaking
38 Masada
39 Ammunition Hill
40 Sde Boker field school
41 Survival activity
42 Melitz meeting with Israeli youth
43 Diaspora museum
44 Machaz meeting with Israeli youth
45 Zofim meeting with Israeli youth
46 NFTY meeting with Israeli youth
47 Yom Tapuz events for South American participants
48 Shabbat programme
49 Gadna army base
50 Canada sport centre

Figure 9 Smallest Space Analysis of participants' evaluation of individual activity units (modules)

discussions and personal experience, group activities, games, creative workshops and audio-visual aids.
- *Yad Vashem:* The programme includes a tour through Yad Vashem museum and its surrounding monuments, led by the group's guides. Often the participants prepare a ceremony held at the 'Hall of Memory.' The tour has a tremendous symbolic meaning for young Diaspora Jews, especially as a part of their visit to Israel. A significant amount of new information is transmitted through pictures, stories and artifacts.
- *Bet Guvrin caves:* Located half an hour southwest of Jerusalem, this is a tour of an ancient city through secret tunnels, caves and archeological findings. Through fun outdoor activity and exploration, the participants learn and experience both history and archeology.
- *Archeological seminars:* guided tours in Jerusalem and its outskirts concerning various historical periods (e.g. the Second Temple) and/or historical figures.

Such activities form the core of the programme. Activities that are high-quality recreational activities but minimally educational, and high-quality learning experiences that are not recreational expand the diversity of the programme, as long as the overall itinerary maintains a balance of each.

Subject-Based Programmes and Specific Content Areas

Within the framework of the general Israel Experience tours, there are a number of central issues that have been addressed repeatedly, although not always in the same way. In this chapter we will mention a few components that have been included in many programmes in recent years, and examine the implications and difficulties they raise. Each of these components expresses in a different way the internal educational conflicts that accompany the entire tour.

In most programmes, these specific content areas form parts of a comprehensive overview of the country. There are, also, programmes (including longer programmes available through the MASA framework) which offer an in-depth exploration of a particular subject such as creative arts, archaeology, kibbutz life, volunteering, Holocaust studies or the environment.

The Holocaust

The Holocaust is one of the central elements in contemporary Jewish identity, touching on sensitive, emotional issues for Jews from a wide variety of backgrounds. The Holocaust directly affected the families of millions of Jews in Israel and throughout the Diaspora. Although the Zionist movement started in the late 19th century, it was only after the Holocaust that the rest of the world accepted the idea of a Jewish state. The Holocaust, therefore, provides part of the justification for the existence of the State of Israel. (And, conversely, it is criticism of the State of Israel that is now providing a justification for Holocaust denial or revisionism.)

It is precisely in relating to the Holocaust that the polarization between classic Zionist ideology and the ideology that justifies continued Jewish existence outside Israel, which characterizes many Diaspora Jews, is most clearly reflected. Many Israelis see the Holocaust as historical proof of the fact that only Israel provides a real solution to the Jewish problem. Israelis frequently make claims such as: 'If Israel had been in existence, the Jews of Europe would not have been wiped out'. Diaspora Jewry relate to the Holocaust as a terrible event that is part of their history and which should be guarded against in the future, but they do not accept the claim that living in Israel is the only option, and in fact some think that concentrating all the Jews in one place would make them more vulnerable. Thus addressing the issue of the Holocaust to Diaspora Jews visiting Israel touches on issues at the very heart of Diaspora tourism.

Regardless of one's political or religious beliefs, learning about the Holocaust may intensify the sense of belonging and shared fate with the Jewish people. At the same time, it addresses universal messages related to prejudice and racism.

Over the years of the ongoing evaluation of the Israel Experience, various questions related to the Shoah were included. Given the stability of the data for other variables, it seems reasonable to use the data collected in given years as representative of the population.

In 1998, participants were asked whether any of their family members personally suffered in the Shoah: 44% answered yes. As may be expected, this varied between home countries, with the highest percentage (67%) among Eastern European participants and the lowest (34%) among South American participants. 45% of North Americans (the largest group numerically) answered that they had family members who had suffered in the Shoah. In 1993 and 1994, participants were asked whether the Holocaust affects their worldview: 90% said it does, 40% choosing the strongest answer, 'yes, definitely'. Interestingly, there was little variation (no more than 5%) between countries, indicating that the Holocaust strongly affected Jews whose families were not directly involved.

Even before coming to Israel, many young Jews, especially those living in the United States, had been exposed to historical and educational material on the Holocaust, such as Holocaust museums or memorial sites, community events and ceremonies, and lessons in Jewish Day Schools or extracurricular Hebrew schools. Holocaust education has become widespread in public schools.[2] Many have seen television programmes or films dealing with the Holocaust, such as Steven Spielberg's *Schindler's List*, or Claude Landsmann's *Shoah*.

In the context of the Israel Experience, the Holocaust is taught in two main ways: visiting Yad Vashem, the Holocaust memorial and museum in Jerusalem, which is virtually a compulsory site, and the pre-Israel tour to Eastern Europe that is included in some tours.

The educational treatment of the Holocaust as part of the Israel Experience touches on three basic themes:

(1) the significance of the State of Israel for the survival of the Jewish people;
(2) the history of anti-Semitism, its ongoing impact on Jewish existence in the Diaspora;
(3) universal lessons regarding human evil and ways of addressing it.

Sometimes the visit to Yad Vashem includes a meeting with a Holocaust survivor, to emphasize the human stories behind the numbers. Also, at the Yad Vashem Children's Memorial, the names of the children who perished in the Holocaust are read aloud, in a moving ceremony.

In the late 1980s, some Israel Experience tours began including visits to Holocaust-related sites in Europe before coming to Israel. These visits enable participants to extend their understanding of Jewish history in Europe and the Holocaust. The first of these tours were connected with the March of the Living, an independent project launched in 1988 in which young Jews from around the world join to walk between the Auschwitz and Birkenau concentration camps in Poland on Holocaust Memorial Day and then fly to Israel for Israel's Independence Day, thus explicitly linking the Holocaust with the creation of the State of Israel. The March of the Living thus became a kind of prelude to the Israel Experience for some participants. Taglit-birthright israel has also begun to offer free tours joining the March of the Living.

Beginning in the late 1990s, Israel Experience tours offered programmes that started with a few days in Prague. Participants see the remains of the Jewish community in Czechoslovakia, which flourished for over 400 years, and then visit the Theresienstadt concentration camp, only some 30 miles northwest of Prague, an extreme and visual illustration of the annihilation of a once-lively community.

The visit to Prague was very important in terms of my personal experience in learning about the Holocaust. It was a 'living experience'. It was there that I gained a wider understanding of the Holocaust, of Israel and of Yad Vashem. (participant quoted in Cohen, E.H., 1997c)

Young Israelis also participate in some of the programmes in Europe, particularly the March of the Living. Meetings between Israeli and Diaspora youth in this context are particularly emotional, and the participants find common ground in the shared history of the destruction of European Jewry. In this way, the Holocaust sites in Europe function as 'contact zones', defined by Pratt (1992: 6) as '... the space in which peoples geographically and historically separated come into contact with each other and establish ongoing relations, usually involving conditions of coercion, radical inequality, and intractable conflict.' Such contact zones also play a role in tours for African-Americans to Africa (Bruner, 1996; Richards, 2005).[3]

Despite the emotional common ground of the Holocaust sites, tensions still arise between the perceptions of different groups. For example, during a tour of Theresienstadt, the Israeli organizers wanted to end the ceremony by singing the Israeli national anthem, Hatikva ('The Hope'). This initiative prompted objections from the Reform movement counsellors, who said that Hatikva is not the anthem of all the Jewish people, and that singing the Israeli anthem gives the message that the response to the Holocaust should be *aliya* to Israel. They saw this as expropriating the memory of the Holocaust for ideological and political purposes. Many leaders of the American Reform movement, in contrast, prefer to link the memory of the Holocaust with the Jewish continuity in the Diaspora as well as in Israel. They emphasize the transition from a state of victimhood to one of power and strength, but without presenting Israel as the only solution. Yet another approach is stressed among members of *Habonim* (literally, 'the builders'), a socialist-Zionist youth movement linked to the Kibbutz movement. They stress the universal, humanist and social message of the fight against social injustice wherever it exists.

Some counsellors attempted to bridge the differences in perception. At the end of the visit to the Children's Memorial at Yad Vashem, one of the Israeli counsellors said:[4]

> My lesson from the Holocaust is that now the Jews have a country and I want you to feel at home here. It is my country, and it is also your country. Every Jew can come here. ... But this message is very personal. Try to think for yourselves what personal lesson you take with you from everything we have seen, learned and felt here. There is no right and wrong here, just a clarification of the lesson that I, as a Jew and as a human being, can learn from the story of the Holocaust.

Content of the Programme

The counsellor invited the participants to consider this complex and confusing subject and to search for a personal position, but did not hesitate to also express her own position. It may be advisable for counsellors to be given specific training in order to deal effectively and sensitively with the many questions and painful issues raised in the aspects of the tour that address the Holocaust. Israeli and visiting counsellors may not have the same perspective. Their differences may be confusing and counter-productive if they lead to arguments between counsellors, or they may be informative to participants if handled well, with honesty and openness. In this way, counsellors may act as role models, allowing participants to see their own human reactions, rather than giving standardized speeches.

In many groups, the counsellors carry out special preparations prior to the visit to Yad Vashem, including holding a discussion, watching a film, and holding a memorial ceremony. Some less conventional preparatory activities were tried, with unclear results. For example, some counsellors led activities that participants did not know were related to the upcoming visit to Yad Vashem. The group was taken on a bus journey of several hours without knowing their destination. The aim was to illustrate the uncertainty experienced by victims of the Holocaust. In another group, participants were asked to write everything that was important to them on a piece of paper, and then the counsellors collected the notes and burned them in a very impressive ceremony, explaining that: 'This is the way people felt in the Holocaust.' It is doubtful whether these attempts did in fact promote an understanding of the Holocaust or identification with its victims, or if they were only confusing and humiliating to the participants. As these programmes develop, it will be important to document the relative success of various educational activities.

Another potentially confusing, yet important, aspect to Holocaust education is that two messages are bound together: the particular message, distinguishing between the Jewish people and all other nations; and the universal message, relating to the Holocaust as an event of importance to all humanity. Counsellors may ask participants to consider other acts of genocide that have occurred or are occurring in the world and to discuss whether the Holocaust was a special case, or if it is only special to Jews because of their personal connection to it. They may challenge participants to think about how they will answer people who deny the Holocaust, or who equate Israel's treatment of Palestinians to the Nazi's treatment of the Jews. These are real issues that Diaspora Jews may face, and the Israel Experience visit to Yad Vashem gives young Jews a chance to explore the issues candidly in an all-Jewish environment.

The survey of participants included a number of questions designed to assess the impact of the trip to Israel on attitudes towards the Holocaust. Between 1993 and 2001, at the end of their trip participants were asked to what extent they felt the tour improved their understanding of various issues, one of which was the Holocaust. Overall, 82% said their understanding of the issue improved: 30% chose the strongest category ('very' improved), 27% responded 'quite' improved, and 25% said it was 'somewhat' improved. Eastern European and South African participants were most positively affected in this area, perhaps because they were exposed to less information about the Holocaust prior to the trip and therefore learned more that was new to them.

However, while answers to most issues were stable over the years of the survey, in this case we saw a steady decline in the degree to which participants felt they learned about the Holocaust. Whereas in 1993, 41% chose 'very improved', by 2001 this has dropped to only 26%. This may not necessarily represent a decline in the quality of the programme offered at Yad Vashem. Whereas Yad Vashem was once almost the only museum dedicated to the memory of the Holocaust, over the past few decades, numerous museums commemorating the Holocaust have opened. The US alone has over 20 Holocaust-related museums, the largest of which in Washington, DC opened in 1993. The first official Holocaust museum in the UK opened in 1995. Additionally, *Schindler's List* was released in 1993. The apparent decline in positive evaluation may reflect participants' increased prior knowledge about the Holocaust. As more Holocaust museums open (for example, Paris dedicated a Holocaust memorial museum in 2005) the guides at Yad Vashem may need to offer more advanced or in-depth programmes.

The Exodus programme

The Exodus programme is another special pre-Israel segment of the tour offered as part of the Israel Experience. Rather than flying into the airport outside Tel Aviv, participants are brought from Greece, Italy or France to the port in Haifa by ship (participants from non-European countries arrive in Europe by plane). The shipboard voyage may be a continuation of a pre-Israel programme visiting Jewish sites in Europe.

The programme was founded in 1994. It quickly grew from one ship the first year to six ships (more than 2500 participants) in summer 1996. The programme has continued every summer and, particularly in combination with the increased number of programmes beginning in Europe, has proved to be a popular and powerful part of the Israel Experience.

The 3–4 day voyage is essentially a re-enactment of the illegal immigration to British Palestine in the years before the establishment of the state. [A full exploration of this programme may be seen in my own chapter in *Tourism, Diasporas and Space*, Cohen, E.H., 2004c.]

The ship-board programme includes various simulation activities. This can be illustrated by a description taken from the on-board observational research of an American participant in an Exodus programme from Athens.

On embarking, the participants were checked in by counsellors disguised as British soldiers. On the ship there were signs in Hebrew and different areas named after towns in Israel. The ship's captain announced, 'This journey links past, present and future.' All day the loudspeakers played Hebrew songs, and the participants learned Hebrew and folk dances. The participants were divided up into committees and worked on performances that made a connection between the Holocaust and immigration to Israel. The activities carried out on board the ship included hearing the testimony of an illegal immigrant, watching a drama group attempting to illustrate the image of illegal immigration, and listening to a local radio called 'The Voice of Israel'. Participants were also asked to discuss in groups the dilemmas of concern to the illegal immigrants at the time: should they stay in Europe, or emigrate to Israel or to the United States? Questions were raised relating to anti-Semitism, the status of minorities, questions of physical, emotional, psychological and economic security, and so forth. Participants also spent one Shabbat on board ship, when an attempt was made to create a special atmosphere and to emphasize traditional Jewish elements. Discussions were also held on major issues of our times, such as Jewish identity, racism, Zionism and Israel.

On the last day on board the participants staged a play in which four figures appeared, dressed as illegal immigrants, representing four possible responses to the expected attack by the British: passive resistance, active resistance, surrender and a diplomatic solution. An argument developed among these figures, and groups of participants were asked to decide the best strategy to adopt. During the show, a plane appeared over the ship and distributed leaflets in the name of the British Mandate, demanding that the illegal immigrants surrender.

When the shores of Israel came in sight, the participants divided up into small groups and read the Proclamation of Independence. At this stage, issues of concern in modern Israel relating to the Proclamation of Independence were raised: military service for Arabs, the Law of Return which grants all Jews automatic citizenship on arrival, problems of immigrant absorption, and so on. The participants were brought together to watch a film on the United Nations vote and the Proclamation of Independence, and there was considerable excitement expressed in an outburst of singing and dancing. One participant said this about the arrival in Israel:

It gave me a feeling of having overcome something, I worked hard to get here and I have a feeling of satisfaction at having made it.

The Exodus programme raises a number of important issues related to informal education and simulation activities in tourism.

The use of symbols as an educational device

The Exodus programme and its simulation activities are laden with symbols. Use of symbols is a common educational tactic, particularly in informal education, allowing complex messages to be conveyed in emotionally powerful ways. Indeed, symbols are commonly used throughout the Israel Experience programme, as well as in Jewish summer camps and other programmes whose goals include identity enhancement and transmission of values. One of the group organizers from a youth movement in the United States cautioned that symbols without sufficient content are empty, and over-use may lead to rejection and ridicule. The use of symbols representing values, figures or historical events takes on the desired meaning for the educators if those values, figures or events are familiar and relevant to the students. Any gap between the aspiration to provide a strong, meaningful experience and the way the participants perceive these symbols is liable to lead to them missing the point. This question becomes particularly significant in the case of the Exodus programme: the activity itself represents a symbolic re-enactment and simulation of a historical event, and so its success depends on the relevance of the symbol for the participants. Different models of the ship programme have been adapted to the needs of the different organizations, and thus these symbols have achieved their full formative force.

As in the case of Holocaust education, there are different attitudes towards the message to be presented. Some organizers expressed the feeling that the programme over-emphasizes the transition from victimhood to revival (the Holocaust to the founding of the State of Israel) through symbols of strength and power.

Balance between cognitive and emotional elements

The closed environment of the ship makes careful planning even more crucial in order to balance fun, learning and meaningful emotional experiences. The educational messages of the Exodus programme may be given in various ways: hearing testimony of survivors of the original voyage; role-playing games in which participants must consider and grapple with dilemmas inherent in the historical events, singing and dancing, re-enactments of events, films, readings, lectures and more. Organizers must balance the educational, social and emotional elements of the trip, within the logistical restrictions presented by the ship environment, in order to create a meaningful, enjoyable experience.

Also related to this issue is the question of how realistic to make the re-enactments. Clearly, participants will not be asked to endure anything resembling the actual hardships withstood by the passengers on the original Exodus ship, and yet the programme is not meant to be a luxury cruise either. Somehow a taste of the refugees' experience must be portrayed within the limits of what paying tourists will accept. The issue of portraying harsh conditions to vacationing tourists in a realistic way is also relevant to heritage tours related to the African slave trade (Dann & Seaton, 2001).

Co-ordination with the subsequent tour of Israel

Essentially, the Exodus programme is a preliminary to the tour of Israel. It is meant to set the emotional stage for the experience in Israel. Thus, the educational message and the tone of the trip must be compatible with that of the subsequent programme. At the same time, it is not simply an orientation activity, but rather a full and powerful programme in its own right. The counsellors in Israel must take into account the experience that the participants had on the ship. The Exodus programme is a historical re-enactment, but participants disembark in modern Israel. The simulated environment of the ship and the real environment of Israel must be brought into congruence for the participants.

The kibbutz visit

The kibbutz stay was a significant element in the programme for groups who came during the 1950s and 1960s. At that time, the kibbutz was presented as a living example of the utopian social dream. Zionism is no longer inherently linked to socialist ideals and the kibbutz itself no longer represents a pioneering lifestyle for Israelis. There has been a trend towards privatization among most kibbutz communities (Ben Rafael, 1997; Mittelberg, 1988). At the same time, the kibbutz is a unique form of Jewish community life and an important part of Israeli history and society.

There are different formats for Israel Experience groups visiting the kibbutz, usually staying for a few days. In many of these visits, participants work in different branches of the kibbutz economy. Sometimes the kibbutz stay is utilized for a meeting with young Israelis.

Based on the evaluations of the Israel Experience overall, and particularly the follow-up surveys, it seems that the kibbutz stay is often difficult and ineffective for the participants. 20% of the participants were dissatisfied with the kibbutz programme. A quarter said they were 'very satisfied' with the kibbutz programme, whereas more than half were very satisfied with the tour overall. In 1994 and 1995, I conducted a specific study of the kibbutz stay as part of the Israel Experience (Cohen, E.H., 1995e). The results showed that a third of the participants were not satisfied with the work component of the kibbutz stay. Well over half (58%) felt their work did not make a real contribution to the kibbutz. Work with children was the most preferred of the work options, followed by agriculture. Work in industrial or service aspects of the kibbutz was particularly unpopular.

Between 1994 and 1997, questionnaires included items related to the personnel involved with the kibbutz stay. The results show clearly that this was an area that could use improvement. Half rated the kibbutz liaison, the house mother and the kibbutz educator as only fair, poor or unsatisfactory. Almost a quarter felt the time on the kibbutz was too long. They were disappointed that they did not have more interaction with kibbutz members, and were kept at a distance. We found that in many cases, no member of the kibbutz has been assigned to act as a liaison between the group and the kibbutz.

Despite all this, when asked to which places in Israel they would like to return to spend *more* time, the second most frequently chosen option was the kibbutz: 84% said they would recommend a kibbutz stay to others. It is possible that the kibbutz is still attractive because of its position in Israeli history and mythos. However, careful planning is needed to provide a meaningful kibbutz stay. It is not possible to assume that visiting a kibbutz will be automatically and naturally exciting and fulfilling for visitors, even if this once was the case. Detailed, precise organization is required to realize the untapped potential of the kibbutz stay as part of the overall Israel Experience. Organizers must examine whether the visit enables the participants to gain a real understanding of what the kibbutz means and in what way the time on the kibbutz ties in with the broader aims of the visit to Israel. Additionally, there needs to be more intentional co-ordination between the visiting group and the kibbutz.

There have been efforts to improve and reframe the kibbutz visit as part of the Israel Experience (Mittelberg, 1997). Joel Magid of the United Kibbutz Movement describes (personal communication, 1997) attempts to use the kibbutz as a place for meeting young Israelis. Yossi Amir, kibbutz representative for the youth movement *Hashomer Hatzair* (literally The Young Guard) worked to change the format of the kibbutz stay by adding activities more directly related to the content of the tour, reducing work hours and allocating skilled people to deal with the youngsters during their kibbutz stay. A study on possibilities for kibbutzim to expand the activities they offer to Diaspora youth (Kerem *et al.*, 1989) identified traits of successful programmes and common problems. Good kibbutz programmes include a clearly defined educational aim coordinated with the larger tour programme, staffed by dedicated, interested kibbutz members who understand the needs of the visiting Diaspora youth. One common problem was an incompatibility between the expectations of the hosts (volunteer labour) and the visitors (an educational and meaningful part of the larger quest for Jewish identity). Related to this was fatigue on the part of the kibbutz members, who did not see the visitors as significantly contributing to the kibbutz, and therefore were reluctant to dedicate time and energy to overseeing their activities. It was recommended that the kibbutz develop educational programmes drawing on their unique features (i.e. nature, history, arts) which would be profitable enough for the kibbutz to dedicate the staff and infrastructure necessary to offer a quality programme that would better meet the needs of the visitors. Indeed, a number of kibbutz throughout Israel have done this, offering specialized educational programmes to young people and adults in areas such as the environment, health, archaeology, Jewish-Arab dialogue and 'life on the northern border', which provide ways to combine the kibbutz stay with an exploration of issues of interest to the visiting groups.

The kibbutz stay represents an interesting phenomenon within a tour programme that has existed for many decades. The programme must constantly adapt to changes in Israeli society, as well as to the changing needs and expectations of the participants, and the goals of the organizers. It exemplifies a paradox within heritage tourism, which must strive to fulfil the desire of visitors to experience something that existed in the past while operating within contemporary reality. The socialist-collective striving for a utopian ideal, which formed such a basic part of early Zionist and Israeli history, can hardly be found today. Attempting to portray this myth may only lead to disappointment and disillusionment. Nevertheless, the kibbutz does still exist as a major facet of the Israeli landscape. The kibbutz movement is in a state of flux, and this may be in itself interesting to visitors. The kibbutz may offer a platform for discussing the evolution of Israeli society.

Memorial sites

During their stay in Israel, groups visit memorial sites representing part of the Israeli national ethos. Visiting memorial sites is a common feature of heritage tourism, as these are places where there is a concentration of symbols that are intended to arouse certain feelings towards key historical events or personalities and to create a sense of commitment to the values and the culture they represent (Schwartz, 1997). In order to really understand a memorial site and its system of cultural and ethical connotations, it is necessary to have some prior orientation. It is not enough to know the historical facts commemorated by the site, it is also necessary to internalize the culture underlying its establishment. For the Israel Experience participants, who for the most part do not have the necessary background to appreciate the sites to which they are brought, the Israeli counsellors must act as cultural mediators, explaining the sites and their significance. For example, during a group visit to the military cemetery on Mount Herzl, an anthropological researcher observed the following:

> The campers [participants] wander among the graves for two or three minutes and then sit down in small groups and talk quietly. The atmosphere is serious, but it appears that most of them are not studying the graves, whose meaning for the most part they are unable to understand. The counsellor gathers them together and says that everyone can find his own way to connect to something common to the entire Jewish people. She notes that almost every Israeli wandering among the graves will find a few names that he knows or his parents know personally. Some of the names will at least sound familiar. They will remember when and where they fell. She talks about Israel as a country in which the army plays an important role and says she doesn't want Israel to appear to be a militaristic country but it is impossible to ignore the special significance of the army: Everyone serves in the army and there is a consensus as to its necessity.

This description highlights the importance of the counsellor-guide in making Israeli symbols relevant to Diaspora youth. The participants feel the serious and sad atmosphere, but the content does not speak to them directly; it does not awaken a feeling of identification and belonging. Many are not able to read what is written on the graves. Even if they can read Hebrew letters, the names hold no meaning for them. The counsellor explains in personal terms what the site means for her and for other Israelis, thus making it real and relevant.

The grave of Yitzhak Rabin has become a focus of pilgrimage for many groups since the summer following his assassination in 1995. Among the groups who visited in the first years following his death, most Israel Experience participants were familiar with Yitzhak Rabin. Close to half of the participants surveyed in 2000 indicated that Rabin was one of the symbols representing their identity as Jews. In contrast with other memorial sites that document events with which the young visitors are unfamiliar, they wanted to see Rabin's grave and tended to become emotionally involved. They felt that the national trauma that followed Rabin's assassination was something that happened to them as well. The televised reporting on the assassination brought Diaspora youth face to face with something very contemporary and relevant in Israeli reality.

Furthermore, the site embodies a dichotomy: on the one hand it symbolizes an event that created widespread empathy in Israel and throughout the world, while on the other hand his assassination by a radical Israeli Jew opposed to Rabin's efforts to make an agreement with the Palestinians clearly symbolizes the deep schism in Israeli society. Regardless of their own political views, almost all the visitors felt that the place symbolized something very important (AJC, 1996, 1997). They felt they could directly take part in the culture of mourning for Rabin that emerged among Israeli youth, and which many participants had seen on television prior to their own visit. In this case, it is possible to say that the media acted as a mediator, linking Diaspora youth to Israeli youth. As time passes, naturally, the groups will increasingly consist of participants who are too young to remember this event from 1995, and the level of personal connection will be likely to fade.

The following observation illustrates the difference between the experience at Rabin's grave and that at Mount Herzl:

> The counsellor asks the campers what they remember of the assassination. One of the campers says, 'In England we felt as if we were in Israel, so many people came to visit each other and talk about what happened.' Another says 'I felt proud to be Jewish and that he [Rabin] had done such a lot, and angry that he wasn't allowed to finish the task'; 'It was very moving to see the ceremony on television, with all the leaders from all over the world,' notes another camper.

At Rabin's grave the counsellors were able to bond emotionally with the participants. Counsellors talked about their personal experiences and feelings at the time of the event and about the importance of the event in contemporary Israeli society. According to the observer's report, the participants genuinely listened to the counsellors and empathized with their feelings. The group and counsellors discussed the painful issues and questions raised by the assassination of the prime minister by an Israeli Jew. As groups visit who were too young to remember Rabin, the counsellors need to provide more of their own personal memories in order to make the visit meaningful. It will be interesting to monitor how this memorial site will be understood by the next generation, when even the counsellors do not personally remember Rabin or his assassination.

Rabin's grave provides the opportunity to observe the process of formation of a memorial site. Because of its relative newness, this site does not yet have a defined form of presentation. Some groups held ceremonies at

Rabin's grave, directed by the counsellors. Some read excerpts from Rabin's own words or speeches given at his funeral. Some sing 'Let the sun rise', the song sung by Rabin at the peace rally just before he was killed. A moment of silence is often part of the ceremony. Many lay stones on the grave, a common tradition at Jewish cemeteries.

The impact of visits to memorial sites is strongly dependent on the prior knowledge of participants and on the ability of the counsellors to make the memorial meaningful to visitors. The timing of the visit may also be important; what activities precede and follow the visit to the site will affect how visitors remember it.

Mifgashim (encounters with Israeli youth)

For much of the time in Israel, the young Diaspora Jews travel in an isolated environment, having few in-depth interactions with Israelis aside from the counsellors. The *mifgashim* and home hospitality units of the tour offer opportunities for the visiting Diaspora youngsters to meet and talk with their Israeli peers. These mediated encounters have come to be included in virtually all Israel Experience tours. The *mifgashim* programme touches on the issue of authenticity in tourist encounters. They are not spontaneous, but are planned and mediated. Nevertheless, the discussions are not scripted, the young Israelis are not actors, and the meetings allow for spontaneous expression of feelings and emotions. It may be described as 'staged authenticity' (MacCannell, 1973). In practice, the meetings may provide an environment more conducive to candid discussion than a chance meeting in the street.

The meetings generally last several days, during which time the two groups live together. They take part in a variety of recreational and social activities, and discussion groups. The aims of the *mifgashim* programmes are to create personal, social contacts between visiting youth and Israeli youth, thus helping the two groups to better understand one another; and to make Israeli society more personal and relevant for the visitors (Avivi, 2000; Bar-Shalom, 1998; Ezrachi & Sutnick 1997).

The sociology of tourism points to the cross-cultural encounters made possible through international travel. 'Tourism matters', write Jack and Phipps (2005: 1) because, 'it invites us to engage in exchanges of life with others', and it '... has the potential to teach us some radical lessons about the possibility of living a different, everyday life when we are not tourists' (Jack & Phipps, 2005: 157). The *mifgashim* give Diaspora Jews a chance to explore the possibility of a different life, if they lived in Israel. The meetings give both the Diaspora and the Israeli youth a chance to be exposed to styles of Judaism with which they may not be familiar. For example, Israelis tend to emphasize national aspects of identity, while Americans emphasize religious aspects (Cohen, S., 1995). Thus, the meetings may be mutually beneficial in terms of creating a feeling of Jewish Peoplehood, in expanding the participants' understanding of what it means to be Jewish, and in personal, emotional and social development (Bar-Shalom, 1998).

Avraham Infeld, one of the programme initiators, observed (personal communication, 1998) a meeting between young members of the Reform movement in the United States and young Israelis from middle or upper-middle class backgrounds. He said that while the two groups were identical in terms of dress, the difference in their relationship to Jewish tradition became apparent after the first meal, when the rabbi announced they would recite the traditional Grace after Meals. While many of the members of the American youth group knew the prayer by heart, they did not understand the Hebrew words. At the same time, the secular Israelis were unfamiliar with the prayer, but understood the words. This sort of paradox, according to Infeld may be used as a starting point for dialogue on different faces and experiences of Judaism – a meaningful educational experience for both groups.

However, the encounters are not always easy, as they are hampered by language, cultural, and even religious differences. Although all the participants are Jewish, the Israelis may be secular, whereas the visiting youngsters (particularly from some home countries) are often more religious. The Israelis may shy away from spiritual discussions, emphasizing daily life in Israel, whereas the participants from abroad are often more religious and expect a spiritual experience. There may also be cultural differences in styles of expression, such as physical contact, openly discussing personal feelings, etc.

The discussions and activities are generally conducted in English. Although English is part of the Israeli school curriculum, the participating Israeli youth were not necessarily recruited from English-speaking families, and their level of speaking and understanding of English varied. In the case of groups from non-English-speaking countries, the language of the meeting was not the native tongue for any of the participants.

In addition to their common Jewish heritage, the participants are linked through the universal youth culture of sports, music, the Internet and fashion. It is interesting to note that while adults are often disturbed by the 'Americanization' of Israel (Goldberg, 2002; Heilman, 2002), for the young visitors it is precisely this global youth culture that makes the meeting between the two groups easier.

Since 1993, my survey of the Israel Experience programme included questions regarding the encounters with Israeli youth. Overall, the encounter programme received favorable ratings, although this varied from year to year, and between different individual programmes. The survey of modules revealed that virtually all participants in some *mifgashim* were satisfied, whereas in others almost a quarter were not, indicating that the encounter is not automatically positive, but is strongly affected by the organization and facilitation of the programme.

In 1995, my research team conducted an in-depth study of the *mifgashim* programme, in which both the visiting Americans and the Israeli participants were surveyed (Cohen, E.H., 1996c, 2000). A fundamental problem in the organization of the *mifgashim* was uncovered during this research, from an unexpected direction. My research team prepared a questionnaire to distribute to the Israel Experience tour participants and a parallel questionnaire in Hebrew to distribute to the Israeli youth. Many of the organizers were surprised at the inclusion of a questionnaire for the Israelis and expressed the opinion that there was no need to distribute them at all. They assumed, it became clear, that the *mifgashim* were for the benefit of the visiting youth and the role of the Israeli was to provide this inter-cultural experience. They did not see the programme as a mutually beneficial encounter. The idea that the Israelis might learn something about Judaism or might expand their perception of what it means to be Jewish through meeting their peers from other countries quite literally had never occurred to many of the organizers of the 'encounter' programme! Eventually we convinced them of the importance of distributing questionnaires to the Israeli participants as well, and the results, quite naturally, greatly enriched the study. This experience provided an insight into the programme that proved valuable in assessing its strengths and weaknesses. It also reminded me as a researcher of the link between qualitative and quantitative research, and that a key observation may be made even during the distribution of the questionnaires.

Although virtually no participants from either group said they were dissatisfied, the Americans were more likely to say they were 'very satisfied' (46%, compared with 24% of the Israelis).

For most participants, this represented their first in-depth meeting with their peers from the other group, although it was somewhat more common for the Americans to have met Israelis prior to this programme than vice versa. Approximately 60% of the participants said that the programme gave them a better understanding of their peers from the 'other country' and that they established personal connections with them. The vast majority (86% of the Israeli participants and 80% of the Americans) said that the meetings helped them better understand people their age from the other group. This shows how a planned, mediated meeting may counter the phenomenon found in mass tourism, in which both hosts and guests form and maintain stereotypes of one another based on superficial contact (Reisinger & Turner, 2003).

Observations of the meetings showed that the Israelis were keener than the Americans to make contact with the other side, but came up against more obstacles. One common difficulty encountered by the Israelis was making inroads into the cohesive group that the Americans travelling together had already formed. At the same time, the Israeli participants attached greater value to the meetings. Many more Israeli participants said that they were prepared to recommend the programmeme to their friends and would like to see the *mifgashim* programme extended to all youth groups visiting Israel. As seen in Table 25, the young Israelis attributed far more importance to the meetings as an essential aspect of understanding Israel than did the Americans. This highlights an important difference in the attitudes towards the visit as a whole as well as towards the *mifgashim* in specific. It should be remembered that the Israelis did not participate in the rest of the tour, and therefore may not have had a clear idea of the various ways the group 'got to know Israel'. Nevertheless, it seems that for the Israelis, it is virtually unthinkable that visitors can understand their country without meeting them personally. The Americans consider meeting Israelis an important part of getting to know the country, but perhaps not necessarily the most essential.

There are several different types of *mifgashim*. One model includes creative workshops and discussions of issues related to Israel, Judaism and general subjects of interest to adolescents. Another model includes mainly leisure activities, the primary aim being to simply create an encounter between the youngsters.

There was no difference in the level of knowledge that the participants acquired about the other country in the two types of programmes among

Table 25 Responses of the Israeli and overseas youngsters to the question: What things do you think are important for American youth in order to get to know Israel better?

	Unimportant		Important		Very important	
	Israelis	Americans	Israelis	Americans	Israelis	Americans
To spend a week with Israeli youth	1%	15%	29%	54%	69%	27%
To acquire Israeli friends	1%	14%	28%	45%	70%	39%

either the Israelis or the Americans. The most serious difference between the models is in the mutual perception of the other groups. In the leisure activities, there was greater emphasis on the differences between Israelis and Americans, while in the workshops they tended to emphasize what was common to the two groups. Nevertheless, the participants in both models recommended increasing the number of excursions and recreational activities; in other words, they wanted to have more fun together.

In addition to the encounters with Israeli youth, some Israel Experience groups place participants with an Israeli family for a weekend. These home hospitality weekends may be a highlight of the programme, or a source of disappointment and stress. Only half the participants rated the home hospitality as good or excellent. For a quarter, it was unsatisfactory or poor. Although the counsellors invest considerable energy in matching hosts and guests, they are not always successful. However, we also heard and read numerous positive comments by the participants regarding the home hospitality. These comments sometimes reveal as much about the visitors' home community as they do about the hospitality programme: for example, the American participants were frequently impressed by the very fact that their Israeli hosts eat family meals together and particularly with the festive Shabbat meal Friday night, common even among non-religious Israeli families.

There are a number of ways for improving the encounter and home hospitality programmes. Although the vast majority of tour participants said that they wanted personal encounters with Israelis and thought that the *mifgashim* should be included in future tours, there were many disappointments with the meetings expressed by the participants and observed by my research team.

There is a need for better preparation for the meetings, particularly among the visiting youth. Whereas in many cases, the Israelis were chosen after a careful selection process and were specially prepared for the meetings, the overseas participants were not always made aware of the difficult aspects of such encounters and had not undergone a prior selection process.

Very sensitive issues may be raised in these meetings between young Israelis and young Diaspora Jews – issues at the core of contemporary Jewish life and Israel–Diaspora relations such as the import and implications of the mandatory army service the young Israelis will soon be serving, the difference between living as a minority or part of the majority, what it means to be a Jew and part of the Jewish nation, and more. These meetings are central to the goals of the Israel Experience as a whole, but are also among the most difficult to carry out.

Some of the institutions involved in the Israel Experience and Taglit-birthright israel tours have begun producing materials to help prepare participants for the encounter and to train counsellors in leading them. *Mifgashim* facilitated by specially trained counsellors result in a more positive – and more predictable – experience. The facilitators are trained to anticipate difficulties that often arise, to spot and mediate problems before they escalate, and to lead activities proven to be effective and enjoyable (Bar-Shalom, 1998).

Volunteering

Participants in some Israel Experience tours have the opportunity to volunteer with various organizations. Generally in the framework of the short tour, the volunteer experience lasts only a few hours or at most a few days. For participants particularly interested in volunteering, specific volunteer programmes are available, such as with Magen David Adom, the ambulance service or Livnot U'lehibanot, a programme lasting several months that dedicates a significant portion of time to community service.

Doing volunteer work has become an increasingly popular way to spend at least part of the time during a tourist vacation. In response to widespread information about the negative impacts that some forms of mass tourism have on destinations, 'volunteer tourism' has emerged as a subset of the larger 'sustainable tourism' movement. Tourists who dedicate part or all of their vacation to helping with social, environmental or health-related organizations '... are seeking a tourist experience that is mutually beneficial, that will contribute not only to their personal development but also positively and directly to the social, natural and/or economic environments in which they participate' (Wearing, 2001: 1).

There is a long and well-established history of Diaspora Jews volunteering in Israel, beginning with the establishment of the State. In 1948, during Israel's War of Independence, approximately 3500 overseas volunteers came from 43 different countries to help with the war effort.[5] The Hebrew acronym Mahal is used to describe volunteers with the Israeli Defense Forces. Volunteers have come to Israel during all of its wars. Generally, they do not join the combat directly, but work in place of soldiers on reserve duty, especially on kibbutzim, or in other non-combat roles. In 1982 Brigadier General (Res.) Davidi established a body called Sarel which brings volunteers aged 17 to 70 to Israel to work in the army for short periods of time. Today some 500 volunteers come to Israel each year in the framework of Sarel. Volunteers work in the army itself, releasing people from reserve duty. Recently, for example, these volunteers packed gas mask kits for the civilian population.

Though the Israel Experience is not, itself, a volunteer programme, participants in some groups volunteer time with various social programmes such as in development towns, senior citizens' homes or health care programmes. Participants in Israel Experience tours may be considered a self-selected group of young people who have a prior interest in both personal development and in the welfare of the destination country. Therefore, the opportunity to volunteer with various Israeli organizations may be integrated into the tour itinerary. Volunteering, even for very short periods of time, allows Diaspora youth to feel a greater connection to Israel and to feel a sense of contribution. Of the participants surveyed between 1993 and 2001, approximately a third took part in a volunteer programme. Those who took part were likely to rate the programme as good or excellent.

Many groups spend time on an army base, through *Gadna*, the Israel Defense Force's pre-military training youth corps. This is not strictly a volunteer programme, but rather is offered to give visiting youth a taste of the military service required of Israelis. Most participants rated the experience favourably. Girls were just as likely to find the programme positive as the boys were.

Jonathan Cohen, of the Melton Centre for Jewish Education in the Diaspora recommends (personal communication, 1998) that tour participants at the very least visit social and community help programmes. He sees this as a way to offset the superficial nature of the 'consumer spirituality' that leaves tourists with a spiritual and religious buzz with no lasting, meaningful impact. Instead of being given only pseudo-events, visitors may be shown and even participate in the real-life drama taking place in places where people have created something special and carried out meaningful social acts. For example, a visit to Yad Sarah (a network of health care volunteers throughout Israel) or to a development town, may become a spiritual experience, particularly when experienced in combination with the other activities throughout the tour.

Bar/Bat Mitzvah programme

Some programmes offer an opportunity for participants to celebrate their bar/bat mitzvah in Israel. In some cases, a tour is specially organized for a group of participants all of bar/bat mitzvah age (12–13 years old).[6] In other tours, post-bar mitzvah participants (14–17 years old, or even older) take part in a special ceremony, often at the Western Wall or another holy site, to mark their passage into young adulthood. There is generally a prayer ceremony and reading from a Torah scroll, followed by singing and dancing. As with the Israel Experience as a whole, the bar/bat mitzvah ceremony is planned according to the needs of the group. In some cases this may be a group of Orthodox youth coming for a traditional bar/bat mitzvah ceremony in Israel. In other cases, participants well past the age of bar/bat mitzvah (as in the case of many Taglit-birthright israel groups), who are less familiar with the traditional ceremony, may hold a communal ceremony at the Kotel or at another site such as in an ancient synagogue or at one of Israel's Conservative synagogues (where the restrictions on females' participation common in Orthodox settings will not be imposed) (Gilad Levian, tour organizer for Israel Experience, personal communication, 2007).

The bar/bat mitzvah programme is particularly popular among groups from the USA, as well as among some South American groups. Although the vast majority of participants (83%) had already celebrated their bar/bat mitzvah, for many the programme in Israel holds special significance due to the location and the fact that it is done by choice, rather than at the insistence of their family. Particularly for American youth, we found that the bar/bat mitzvah in Israel was perceived as a 'fixing' (*tikkun*, in Hebrew) for the first ceremony, which may not have been a meaningful experience for them. This is particularly significant as, for many American Jewish youth, Jewish education ends with the bar/bat mitzvah ceremony.

Visiting students

The bulk of this study has dealt with participants in short-term tours. However, longer study programmes may be considered another example of educational tourism. In addition to the 4–8 week programmes offered during school vacations, there are also longer programmes, sometimes organized through Jewish Day Schools. For example, Jewish Day Schools in South Africa have offered various opportunities for students to spend several months during the school year in Israel (Rafi Barnett, Jewish Agency for Israel, personal communication, 2007).

While they may all be considered examples of educational youth tourism to Israel, there are a number of differences between visiting student programmes at universities and the Israel Experience programmes, beyond the simple issue of duration. While universities in various countries may coordinate their exchange programmes, there is not the same relationship of parallel Diaspora and Israeli public institutions working to organize the programme as is found in the case of the Israel Experience. University programmes, in general, do not have the explicit goal of influencing Jewish identity or instilling an emotional connection to Israel. In fact, although the majority of visiting students to Israel are Jewish, not all are, whereas the Israel Experience and Taglit-birthright israel programmes are designed specifically for Jewish participants. Some long-term programmes, such as yeshivas or seminaries have a stronger focus on religious studies.

Between 1994 and 1996 I directed a study of visiting foreign students in Israeli universities and colleges (Cohen, E.H., 1998). In 2004-2005 I conducted a study of year-long programmes in Israel for French-speaking students (Cohen, E.H., in press-b). The French-speaking students were in various educational settings, including high schools, local colleges, universities and religious schools (*yeshiva*). They provide a valuable comparison to the other studies, which focused primarily on students from the United States. Although non-Jewish students were included in the study, in the following discussion only the Jewish students are considered, as the non-Jewish students, a small minority of visiting students in Israel, constitute a distinct population with different goals and expectations.

Diaspora Jews who study in Israel for longer periods of time are motivated by similar goals and have similar experiences to those who come on short tours. In fact, it was found that 72% of the students participating in the one-year programme had already visited Israel in the framework of the Israel Experience. Of the French-speaking students, 90% had previously been in Israel, and two thirds had visited Israel four times or more.

Despite the differences in the short- and long-term programmes, many characteristics of the short programmes seem to be even more strongly emphasized in the visiting student programmes. For example, the educational background of visiting students is even stronger than that of participants in summer tours. In other words, the self-selection of those with prior Jewish background is even more intensive for those making the commitment to be in Israel for a longer period of time. Also, although the students have chosen to enrol in formal educational institutions, the informal learning and emotional aspects of the time in Israel are equally important to the overall experience, as expressed by this student:

> I had an amazing time in Israel and learned an amazing amount of things. I learned how much you can learn outside of books – and how great it is to see history and be involved in another part of the world so intimately. I learned a lot about myself ... I haven't even had a chance to reflect ... because I have been too busy bombarding myself with new experiences. (female, age 21, semester student from Maine, 1995–1996)

My own studies of visiting students in Israel and those of my colleagues (Herman, 1962, 1970; Friedlander *et al.*, 1991; Kerem, 1988; Mittelberg & Lev-Ari, 1994) found differences in terms of Jewish identity and educational background among the populations of students attracted by the various long-term programmes available. For example, half of the visiting students in Israeli universities came from a background in Conservative Judaism which was the case for only a quarter of those in the Hebrew language study programme offered through the Oren kibbutz *ulpan* programme, the remainder coming from less religious, secular or unaffiliated homes. My analysis of French students in Israel found that the different types of institutions tended to attract students with different value orientations. For example, those in universities valued self-actualization more than those enrolled in career-oriented colleges, who held more traditional and family-oriented values (Cohen, E.H., in press-b).

In their study of participants in the one-year visiting student programme at Hebrew University, Friedlander *et al.* (1991) looked at the social background, the motivation for the journey and the elements of Jewish identity reinforced by the visit. Participants were asked about their attitudes at five different stages of the programme. As reasons motivating them to come, the students gave the following factors: the desire to travel to foreign countries, taking time out before starting a career and family, and having an enriching experience. In Israel, they expected to achieve the following goals (in order of importance): to learn about Israel (especially social issues), to learn Hebrew and to promote their academic achievements. Being part of a predominantly Jewish student body, as well as the location in Israel, reinforced the Jewish identity of the students surveyed. Studying in Israel strengthened the students' motivation to be active in the Jewish community upon returning home. As with the short-term programmes, many alumni returned to their home countries with a greater interest in participating in local Jewish activities.

In my study of visiting students (Cohen, E.H., 2003c), I examined the factors involved in joining a year-long study programme. The students were asked to what degree the following elements were important in their decision to study in Israel: academic studies, religiosity, ideology, the social aspect, tourism and learning a language. On comparing the degree to which each of these factors is important to students, it appears that the lowest ranking was given to academic studies. The tourism motivation is strikingly important, taking first place. In other words, Jewish students join a study programme in Israel as a means to see Israel.

In a multi-year analysis that compared different respondent profiles, I developed a typology of students according to their motives for joining the programme. The findings indicate that the most significant motives for joining the programme, on which all the other factors are also based, are religion and tourism. That is, the religious bond and the search for the tourist experience provide the best explanation for the differences among the different types of student:

(1) 25% of the population declared that they were strongly motivated by both religion and tourism;
(2) 29% selected religion but not tourism to describe their motivation;
(3) 31% indicated tourism but not religion as their motivation;
(4) 15% did not mention either of the two factors as important motives for joining the programme.

When we compare the populations of the different groups with regard to different issues such as world outlook and evaluation of the programme, considerable differences are revealed: those who chose religion as an important factor in their motivation were found to have come from the heart of the Jewish community. They are much more interested in focusing on Jewish studies during their time in Israel than are those who came for more tourist or academic reasons. They also were more likely to be studying in Israel along with friends from their schools and communities back home.

The Oren Kibbutz programme

While the other visiting students' programmes were similar to, if more intensive than, the short-term tours, studies of the Oren kibbutz *ulpan* (language study) programme found that it represents a significantly different approach. Participants live, work part-time and study on a kibbutz. The emphasis is on Hebrew language, although there are also field trips and seminars and workshops on Jewish and Israeli history and current events, archaeology, arts and drama.

Mittelberg and Lev-Ari's (1994) research on the Oren kibbutz ulpan programme focused on two spheres. One was a comparison of students without a previous background in Judaism (22% of participants) with those who had already participated in Jewish educational frameworks in the past. The other was a comparison of the religious kibbutz experience and the experience on a non-religious kibbutz.

In direct contrast to the findings of the Israel Experience and the general visiting students, in this case it was found that the *lower* the level of Jewish education the student brought to the programme, the *greater* his or her satisfaction with the educational activities. Furthermore, for the group of students with no Jewish background, the educational activities had no relevance for predicting whether they would enjoy the stay. This is the opposite of the findings of the survey on Israel Experience programmes, in which participants with a relatively strong educational background have the context to understand and thus enjoy the programme better than those with no background. The explanation the researchers gave for this finding among the Oren kibbutz participants is that the more idealistic the motivation for joining the programme, the harder it is to fulfil the expectations. Thus, the more remote the student's background, the lower his expectations and the more he will be satisfied. On the other hand, students with a Jewish educational background have high expectations and it is easier for them to feel frustrated or disappointed with the programme. Nevertheless, Mittelberg and Lev-Ari found that, among the participants in the Kibbutz Oren programme, there was an increased sense of Jewish identity and with it an increased willingness to participate in community activities.

Overall, we may conclude that the success of an educational, heritage tourism programme for Diaspora Jews in Israel depends on two converse parameters: one is related to previous Jewish background and the other to the degree of idealization and level of expectations of the visit. The degree of preparation and Jewish background has a positive effect: the deeper the background the more meaningful the visit. The degree of idealization has a negative effect: the greater the idealization and the higher the level of expectations, the greater the disappointment is liable to be.

Class visits

Some Jewish Day Schools organize class trips to Israel. If the trip takes place during the summer or winter vacation, it is similar to other Israel Experience tours organized through youth groups or synagogues. One significant difference is that the teachers may use class time to give background on the sites they will visit, Israeli history and culture and geography, basic Hebrew phrases, and more. They also can provide an opportunity for students to discuss their expectations and worries, providing ideal conditions for in-depth preparation for the journey.

Some Jewish Day Schools offer programmes in Israel of several months in duration during the school year. In this case, the visit will represent part of the formal study and will sometimes even end with exams and grades. In particular, the trip to Israel may be expected to improve students' Hebrew, as language skills are an aspect of international study not easily replicated in the home classroom (Ritchie et al., 2003). Nevertheless, the fact of choosing to come to learn in Israel demonstrates that the organizations are interested in giving their students an educational experience whose dimensions are not solely cognitive.

There are a number of accredited high school academic programmes for visiting students in Israel. These may be non-denominational or associated with a branch of Judaism (Orthodox or Reform). In this case, students will not be with their classmates from home, but will study for a semester or a year with students from other geographic areas.[7]

Notes

1. Following the expansion of the Israel Experience at the end of the 1970s, there was an expectation that commercial bodies would play a larger part in this tourism market, but in a survey carried out in 1992 it emerged that public entities were still responsible for the majority of the programmes (Cohen, E.H. & Keisar, 1993).
2. According to the Task Force for International Cooperation on Holocaust Education, Remembrance and Research, Holocaust education is an official part of the school curriculum at some level in Austria, Croatia, France, Germany, Greece, Luxembourg, Switzerland, the UK and the US. See individual country reports available at: http://www.holocausttaskforce.org/teachers/index.php?content=educational_reports/ (accessed 11.11.07).
3. Another interesting link between tourism related to the slave trade and tourism related to the Holocaust is the role of the hosts. Richards (2005) notes, 'To attract tourists, Ghanaians must remember a history they learned to forget,' referring in part to the role Africans played in the slave trade. Similarly, European hosts must face a chapter in their history many would prefer to forget. In some tours interactions with non-Jewish local youth have become part of the programme, adding yet another emotional encounter, which raises difficult questions and issues for the adolescent participants.
4. All unattributed quotes from participants and counsellors in this chapter are taken from the open comments section of the questionnaires (which are anonymous) or from observations conducted by my research team.
5. See http://www.mahal2000.com/about/history.htm (accessed 11.11.07).
6. For a sample itinerary of such a programme see www.jewishadventures.com/bar_mitzva_bnei_iti.asp (accessed 11.11.07).
7. See http://www.israelexperience.com/JewishAgency/English/Jewish+Education/experiences+in+Israel/Short+term+Programs/High-School+Academic+Programs/ (accessed 11.11.07).

Chapter 10
Informal Education and the Israel Experience

Education encompasses both the formal acquisition of knowledge and the informal learning of values, beliefs, modes of thinking and types of behaviour (Cohen, E.H., 1997d). In his longitudinal study of youth movements, Kahane (1997) concludes that informal education has increased in importance in the postmodern age, providing youth with the tools they need to navigate the rapidly changing world in which they must live and work.

Informal (or 'non-formal')[1] educational activities are diverse. Some are unplanned, such as learning from friends or family in the course of daily life. Some use educational materials provided by others, but outside a group structure, such as independent learning from books, trips to museums, computer programmes and the Internet. Others are planned educational activities, but outside a classroom environment, such as voluntary or community-based educational activities for young people or adults.

The educational aspects of the tour programme are experiential and interactive. The journey is the curriculum, the people, places and events encountered are the texts and the guides and counsellors are the teachers. The social context of the educational journey is paramount. The programme is theme-based, as opposed to subject-based (Chazan, 2002).

A number of characteristics of an informal educational framework are relevant to understanding the Israel Experience tours.

Balance between Cognitive and Emotional Dimension

Educational theory differentiates between *cognitive* (intellectual), *affective* (emotional) and *instrumental* (behavioural) aspects of learning. All of these are contained, in varying degrees, in the Israel Experience programme. The three types of learning may be addressed in different activity modules, but are often linked within the same activity. Even informal, recreational activities may contain a cognitive element. For example, during hikes tour guides teach about history, geology and ecology. Singing songs along the hike may add an emotional element to the activity. Participants may also learn practical skills, such as how to understand Israeli road signs, or the

Hebrew phrases necessary for using the bus system. Some counsellors teach participants Israeli slang expressions. Knowledge of this kind creates a sense of intimacy and makes visiting youngsters feel closer to Israeli society.

Similarly, although the seminars included in the tour are similar in style to formal education, they often touch on emotional issues such as the Holocaust or the Israeli–Palestinian conflict. The group may discuss how they may best respond to real situations they may encounter at home, such as acts of anti-Semitism against their community or synagogue, rallies against Israel on their school campus, or people who deny the Holocaust. Thus we may see how informal education links the cognitive, the emotional and the instrumental.

The types of learning must be balanced. Most organizers agree that one of the keys to the success of the Israel Experience is that informal elements play a more important role than do formal elements in the programme. Even sponsors and organizers who themselves are involved with formal education agree that the informal aspects of the tour to Israel are essential. In fact, even teachers from overseas Jewish schools who take part in the training seminars in Israel have requested a more informal, hands-on type of learning programme in Israel. As summed up by Professor Walter Ackerman (1986), the late scholar, teacher and administrator involved for decades in Jewish education in Israel and abroad: 'The organizers plan a study programme in Israel and the teachers want an Israel Experience'.

Over-emphasizing cognitive elements may become boring for visitors on their summer vacation. Additionally, their educational background must be taken into account, so that the lessons are neither patronizing and redundant, nor confusing and frustrating:

> The guides expected us to know more than we did about Judaism and Israel. They kept asking questions that we could not answer and that made it feel like a test.[2]

Generally speaking, the affective aspect of the tour is dominant. In their comments on the tour, the emotional impact is consistently emphasized:

> Going to the Western Wall touched me deeply and those feelings will stay with me forever. For the first time in my life, I feel some kind of stability and finally I feel part of something. Coming to Israel makes you feel wanted and important.

On the other hand, an excessive desire to put across an emotional message is likely to come across as spurious, and sometimes provokes feelings of guilt:

They [the guides] made me feel guilty that I was an American citizen. We went to Yad Vashem today and one of the Israeli guides said to us: 'You didn't behave properly, you didn't cry'.

Importance of the Group

Emphasis on interpersonal relations is another key element of informal education. As discussed previously, the functioning of the group is critical to participants' satisfaction with the tour. To facilitate positive group functioning, the counsellors must teach and model interpersonal communication skills. The *mifgashim*, kibbutz stay, volunteer work and home hospitality elements of the tour provide particularly challenging opportunities to learn about cross-cultural communication and social skills.

Comments written by Israel Experience participants in the open question at the end of the survey illustrate the link between the group and the educational impact of the tour:

I think this trip strengthened my ties to Israel. The group was amazing. There was such a strong feeling of closeness.

I just wanted to say that this was the most amazing summer. It's not the programme but the friends I made that turned it into such an experience.

The connection made in the first quote between the participant's ties with Israel and the feeling of group closeness is instructive. Indeed, as a framework that makes use of informal tools the group also directly transmits part of the educational message and fulfils the educational aims of the visit: through the group experience, the participant also experiences a sense of belonging to the wider Jewish public.

Positive inter-personal relations are essential because the participants have virtually no time away from the group. The participant sees Israel as part of a group. Almost all time is spent in structured group activity, even if the activities are 'informal' in nature. This type of informal education, therefore, is quite different from the 'backpacker' type of travel, which is unstructured and allows for significant time alone.

Kahane's Elements of Informality

According to sociologist Reuven Kahane, the unique contribution of informal education lies in its ability to adapt itself to changes taking place in the surroundings and to make innovations, while maintaining social continuity and a commitment to values. In this way, students explore possibilities for contributing to society and its values. Characteristics of informal education such as autonomy and spontaneity have been widely adopted in post-modern youth culture, and are adapted to ambiguous situations. Therefore, informal education is an important tool for socialization in a rapidly-changing society.

In his analysis of informal education, Kahane (1974, 1975, 1988, 1997; Kahane & Rapoport, 1988) proposed a set of indicators designed to compare the level of 'informality' of a given educational activity (from 'very informal' to 'not at all informal'). This approach, based in part on a long-term study of Israeli youth movements, is particularly suitable for a study of Jewish educational tourism to Israel. Kahane's indicators are: autonomy, dualism, expressive instrumentalism, modularity, moratorium, multiplicity, symbolic pragmatism, symmetry and voluntarism

- *Autonomy:* participants in informal educational frameworks may express themselves and make decisions freely, with minimal consideration for the opinions of outgroups (i.e. adults, established societal institutions). In the case of the Israel Experience, this may refer to the all-Jewish environment, enabling participants to candidly discuss issues such as Israeli politics, the Holocaust or Jewish religious tradition without worry about what non-Jews might think (that is, feeling no need to be either apologetic or defensive). Additionally, the all-youth environment allows participants to discuss issues among their peers, without worry about the opinions of parents or teachers.

- *Dualism* refers to the co-existence of two or more orientations that may parallel, overlap or even contradict one another (for example, co-operation and competition) within a single social or educational framework. In the Israel Experience, the concept of duality may be displayed through the ideals of commitment to Israel and involvement in the home Jewish community. The two orientations may be emphasized during different activities, or by different counsellors, enabling participants to explore both.

- *Expressive instrumentalism* refers to the manner in which rewards are achieved in informal education. In formal frameworks the reward for the effort invested in the educational activity is expressed in grades or diplomas. This reward is generally delayed. First work and effort must be invested, and only at the end of the process (months or even years later) is the reward received. In informal frameworks the reward is immediate: the fact of participating in the group and the activity gives pleasure and satisfaction. Participants may acquire rewards such as self-confidence, a positive self-image and friendships. This type of reward is very appropriate to the Israel Experience. Pride in being Jewish and the pleasure of being part of a Jewish community are reinforced. Specific activities may improve participants' physical abilities, self-confidence, leadership and communication skills.

- *Modularity* in Kahane's terminology is an 'eclectic construction of activity sets according to changing interest and circumstances' (Kahane, 1997: 26; see also a systematic presentation of the issue in Cohen, E.H., 2001). This is reflected in the menu of modules, from which the itineraries of the Israel Experience tours are developed, providing a variety of recreational, educational, social and spiritual activities. The wide variety of activities undertaken during the visit to Israel enables the tour to appeal to a wide variety of youth. For some the physical effort of a hike in the Negev may be the highlight of the tour, filling participants with self-confidence and leaving them with memories of the natural beauty of the land. For others the ideological, religious, or spiritual fervour brought out in a visit to the Western Wall or a Shabbat celebration may be more meaningful. Working on a kibbutz, digging in an archaeological site, singing and dancing, talking with Israelis and of course the interaction within the touring group itself – each has its own appeal, the combination of which is more powerful than any single type of activity could be.

- *Moratorium* refers to the temporary suspension of social repercussions, providing opportunities for young people to play a variety of adult social roles without fear of failure. It is one of the major advantages of an environment in which the group of peers replaces the family. Thus, for example, in youth movements or camps young people may take temporary leadership roles and may try out different identities (for example, becoming more religious than they are at home). When the youngsters return home, these temporary identities may be dropped. Moratorium also characterizes the role of the young counsellors.

Moratorium is commonly expressed in several areas during the Israel Experience tours. One involves couples experimenting with relationships; since the length of the tour is limited, there are few complications if the relationship doesn't work out. The other involves experimenting with taking a stand on various issues related to Judaism and Zionism. The youngsters have the opportunity to work out problems of identity and to express various opinions, which may be changed during the course of the programme.

- *Multiplicity (also sometimes called multiplexity)* refers to a wide spectrum of activities, roughly equivalent in their value and importance, which may be used as means of achieving the educational goal. The goal may not appear to be directly linked to the activities; for example, the goal of increasing self-esteem may be achieved through sports and art.

    The goals of the Israel Experience, as discussed, primarily related to increasing participants' sense of Jewish identity and connection to Israel. Organizers hope to achieve these goals through activities such as hikes, days at the beach, visits to holy sites, meetings with Israeli youth and seminars on Israeli politics, each of which touch on a facet of the relationship of the participants to Israel, to each other (and by extension to the Jewish people) and to Jewish history and tradition.

- *Symbolic pragmatism* involves giving significance to otherwise mundane actions or objects and at the same time, expressing symbols in a concrete, functional way. Summer camps and youth organizations use symbols such as logos, songs and rituals to create a sense of belonging and a sort of local culture among participants (Cohen, E.H., 2004b; Sales & Saxe, 2004; World Association of the Scout Movement, 1998). The symbols may be specific to the camp or movement, or they may be related to a broader religious or national identity.

    In the case of the Israel Experience, symbols related to Judaism and to Israeli national identity are frequently invoked. Symbols related to the sponsoring youth movement may also be used, and in some cases a group touring together will create their own symbols – mascots, for example, or ceremonies, songs that become anthems or t-shirts to express group solidarity.

    The use of such symbols is likely to reinforce the participants' identification with the values that are being taught, or to serve as a reminder of impressive events experienced by the group during the trip, and thus help strengthen group solidarity. Among other things, the counsellors can take advantage of the long journeys as an opportunity to reinforce certain effects. If the participants stay in touch and continue joint activities on their return home, these symbols will have an important effect in preserving the group feeling and recreating experiences relating to the values that have been internalized.

- *Symmetry* according to Kahane refers to 'a balanced, reciprocal relationship based on equivalence of resources and mutual coordination of principles and expectations in which no party can impose his or her rules on another' (Kahane, 1997: 26). In an informal education framework there is a reciprocal relationship among individuals in the group. Although there are instructors, the hierarchy of authority is de-emphasized.

During the tour of Israel, there is a high degree of symmetry even between the youngsters and those responsible for them (primarily the counsellors). For example, participants may explore and offer answers to ethical or philosophical questions raised during the trip, rather than being told the 'correct' answer by an authority figure. The opinions of the counsellors and guides are valued based on their own knowledge and personality, not on their position. Naturally, there are many issues over which the participants do not have equal say, particularly those related to logistics and security. Therefore we could say that for the indicator of symmetry, the Israel Experience and Taglit-birthright israel tours are 'less informal' than a group of independent friends travelling together, but 'more informal' than a classroom setting. The age of the participants is an important factor. Programmes organized for adults offer more symmetry in relations, allowing for free days and even in some cases allowing for changes in the itinerary based on the group's decision (Klein-Katz, 1990, 1991; Reisman, 1993).

- *Voluntarism* refers to 'a relatively constraint-free pattern of choice (of goals, means, affiliations) in which the cost of changing one's mind is minimal' (Kahane, 1997: 26). Informal frameworks are characterized by a high level of voluntary action in joining, participating and leaving. Although the Israel Experience is voluntary with regard to joining the programme, the great distance from home and the heavy burden of responsibility of those who have undertaken to look after the participants does not (other than in very exceptional cases) allow any degree of voluntary action in terms of participating in specific activities or leaving the group. The complex logistics do not leave much room for manoeuvering.

One of the tasks facing the organizers of the Israel Experience is to find ways to give participants a feeling of greater choice and strengthening the voluntary dimension in their participation. A few Israel Experience programmes have given participants the option of choosing among a number of activities, usually on given days of the tour. Participants were very satisfied with this experimental programme. The counsellors may provide opportunities for participants to have some degree of choice, although this sometimes puts them in conflict with the organizational headquarters.

Overall, although external factors place limits on the informal nature of the Israel Experience tour, many of the essential factors that characterize informal education are fundamental to the nature of the tours. The distinctive features of the tour enable the programme to provide a type of Jewish educational experience not possible in a classroom setting. Since the Israel Experience is limited to a few weeks, it may be most effective in the context of other informal settings such as Jewish summer camps and youth organizations, in which young people may take part over the course of many years.

Some educators have questioned the possibility of transmitting values and feelings such as a sense of 'peoplehood' through formal – or at least through exclusively formal – settings (Cohen, S. & Wertheimer, 2006; Henze, 1992; Jeffs & Smith 1990, 1996). In the world of Jewish education, there has been an emphasis on the importance of informal settings (Ackerman, 1986; Reisman, 1990; Chazan, 1991; Cohen, B. & Schmida, 1997). These settings provide an environment in which young Jews, most of whom are a minority in a non-Jewish dominant society, may explore and develop a sense of being Jewish.

Notes

1. Coombs and his colleagues distinguished between informal and non-formal education, defining *informal* education as learning in daily life situations, and *non-formal* education as planned educational activities taking place outside the classroom (Coombs *et al.*, 1973; Coombs & Ahmed; 1974). Nevertheless, the two terms are still used interchangeably throughout the literature. Here the term 'informal education' is used in the broader, more inclusive sense.
2. All unattributed quotes from participants and counsellors in this chapter are taken from the open comments section of the questionnaires (which are anonymous) or are observations conducted by my research team.

Chapter 11
Staff of the Israel Experience

The Israel Experience tours are the result of the coordinated work of many institutions and individuals in Israel and in the participants' home countries. The personnel from abroad include heads of the organizations (youth movements, synagogues, schools, etc.) who do the planning and determine general policy, the organization's coordinators and group leaders sent to Israel to co-ordinate and oversee the programme on the ground (these people are usually somewhat older than the counsellors), and the counsellors from the home community who accompany the groups. Sometimes groups are also accompanied by people who specialize in a certain field, such as, for example, a rabbi or a professor specializing in Holocaust studies.

The personnel from Israel include heads of the Israeli sponsoring organizations and departments, people appointed to liaise with the different organizers of groups from abroad, coordinators, tour guides, leaders of specific module activities, medics, security guards, bus drivers and the Israeli counsellors who accompany the groups.

The personnel dealing with the Israel Experience in Israel can be divided into two groups: temporary staff, whose services are hired just for the period when the groups are visiting (an estimated 1500–2000 people, not including lecturers and experts) and permanent staff (50–100 people), who coordinate the programme throughout the year.

Importance of the Counsellors

I will focus mainly on the temporary staff, because they are in direct contact with the participants during the tour. The counsellors have a particularly crucial role in the programme. I have collected data on the counsellors from the participants, from other staff and from the counsellors themselves. The anthropological observations of programmes conducted by my research staff also include information about the counsellors. The counsellors are almost universally referred to by the Hebrew term *madrichim*.

My own research and that of others have all consistently pointed to the decisive, positive role of the *madrichim*. Their ability to act as positive and well-received role models for the participants has been found to be one of the key differences between a mediocre programme and an excellent one

(Cohen, E.H. *et al.*, 2002). Similarly, charismatic leaders and counsellors in Jewish summer camps were identified as one of the main elements in creating the 'magic' of a successful camp experience (Zeldin, 2006).

The counsellors are like the conductor of an orchestra who can never forget the score. They are involved with logistics (accommodation, meals, transportation, etc.) and with organizing the programme's educational aspects. They set the tone and pace of the programme. They help the participants work through the moods and emotions of the intense experiences that are integral to the tour. They are the most important factor in motivating participants. The counsellor is an essential mediating link in the chain of factors that can determine the degree of success of the Israel Experience. Emotional support, ideological guidance and educational backing are roles that only the counsellor can fill.

The participants formed deep and warm relations with the counsellors. Year after year, both the Israeli and home country *madrichim* were rated as good or excellent by more than 80% of the participants. In their own words:

> I love the way the staff related to us. They were our staff, but they were also friends.[1]

> The staff was excellent and they were always there to help.

> We had a great staff: you could talk to them any time. They respected us. It was like a friendship and not like a student–teacher relationship.

The counsellors had a similarly warm and personal interest in the participants, beyond that of a simple summer job. One American counsellor described the nature of her position and motives for becoming an Israel Experience counsellor in this way:

> I want to give campers [participants] the opportunity that I was given, a framework in which they can come and create personal ties with Israel. I wanted the campers to understand it here, I wanted them to understand what they saw and to create a bond. In general our role was to make sure that the campers were safe, that the programme was carried out properly, that they kept on schedule, that the campers' needs were met. Our group was an experienced group from an American youth movement and we wanted to keep with the style of American informal education: to see all sides of the subject, and to make the campers aware of Israel and all the things that are going on here, such as the peace process. I wanted the campers to understand what they were seeing.

The staff of the Israel Experience tours is not transparent; that is, they do not simply provide technical guidance. They act as role models and interpreters. They mediate the encounter between the visitors and what they see in Israel. Denar Dahan, coordinator of summer programmes for French-speakers for the Jewish Agency, stresses that guiding which brings out the significance of sites visited will influence the participants' personal identity (personal communication, 1999).

During our years of observations of Israel Experience tours, we found that counsellors are sometimes expected to lead educational activities in the absence of a professional tour guide or activity leader, and they did not always have the necessary knowledge or skills to do so well. Additionally, sometimes counsellors have to take time out during an activity to solve logistical problems. We found that, in cases where the counsellors operated the programme themselves, the result was confused and of a not particularly good quality. In particular, the counsellors did not adequately prepare or orient the participants for the upcoming activity. Only in certain cases, such as at the visit to Rabin's grave described earlier, was the personal rapport of the counsellors with the participants sufficient to carry out a meaningful activity.

Many of the counsellors are students: 60% of the Israelis and 86% of the overseas counsellors. Among the Israeli counsellors there are more women than men (61%), whereas among the counsellors from abroad only 45% are women. This, in part, has to do with the army requirements of young Israeli men. We also found that a far lower percentage of the Israeli counsellors define themselves as religious.

In 1995 and 1996, as part of the on-going survey of the Israel Experience programme, my research team conducted a special study of the counsellors (Cohen, E.H., 1999b). In addition to the questions pertaining to the counsellors that were included in the questionnaires distributed to the participants, a separate questionnaire was distributed to the counsellors. They were asked about their professional background and their experience in working as counsellors, as well as their general educational and Jewish background. The counsellors were asked how they view their role and how they feel such a programme should be planned.

Just over half of the counsellors (52%) are doing this job for the first time, but there is a stark difference in experience between the Israeli and the home-community counsellors. Among the counsellors from abroad, most are working as Israel Experience *madrichim* for the first time (two-thirds of those from the US and France and 85% of those from the UK). In contrast, only a third of the Israelis are first-time *madrichim*. However, when we take into account work in other educational frameworks, we see that the difference is far less. Only 15% of the counsellors from abroad and 12% of the Israeli counsellors are working with young people for the first time; all the others have already served as youth instructors in other settings such as camps or youth movements.

Although the Israelis had more experience, they were less likely to feel adequately prepared for the job. Some 58% of the Israeli counsellors said they received appropriate training, compared with 71% of their colleagues from abroad. One Israeli counsellor noted that the visiting *madrichim* were

> ... better prepared and more cohesive as a group before the programme. Even before the summer started they already had clear expectations of themselves and defined roles, while we didn't!

On the other hand, Israeli counsellors had a stronger rapport with the Israeli institutions that sponsor the trips. The Israeli counsellors were more likely to say that they felt that their work was being effectively followed up by the organizers: 71% of them said that they received frequent follow-up, compared to only 51% of the overseas counsellors. The Israeli counsellors also had the obvious advantage of sharing a language with the other Israeli staff and organizers, thus in some cases receiving better information prior to or during the trip. Some Israeli counsellors suggested that overseas counsellors should be recruited who have been in Israel before and who speak at least some Hebrew.

Thus we see that a significant percentage of the *madrichim* feel they could use better preparation and/or more follow-up from the organizers in order to deal with the many complex situations with which they were faced during the tour, leading to some degree of uncertainty during the programme.

The division of authority and labour between the Israeli and visiting staff members can reflect different educational emphases. If the educational emphasis is on Jewish life in the home community, then the staff members accompanying the group from abroad and representing the home organization should set the tone and determine policy. Israelis in this case serve both as experts representing the Israeli dimension and as technical and logistical assistants.

Another approach sees the Israel Experience as first and foremost presenting Israel to Diaspora youth. In this case, responsibility for organization, education and content should lie primarily with the Israeli personnel. The Israeli counsellors can either position themselves as authorities representing Israel, or they can try to minimize the differences between themselves and the participants and foreign counsellors.

The *madrichim* help the participants interact with Israel and bring them out of their tourist bubble in order to see how Israel is simultaneously familiar (as the centre of Jewish culture) and foreign. Israelis just out of the army may be most successful in connecting the visitors to the State of Israel.

Israelis who are immigrants (or children of immigrants) from the participants' home country may have a better understanding of and empathy with the participants, and may soften the culture shock of the group. These counsellors can also be figures with whom to identify, and they serve as examples of people who lived the life that participants lead, but chose to come and live in Israel.

> I found that there was a difference between the American tour guide and the Israeli tour guide. It was much harder for me to understand the Israeli. It created a different experience when we had a guide who had lived part of her life in the United States.

Some of the home country counsellors felt they had to represent the interests or concerns of the participants when problems with the Israeli counsellors arose because of a lack of understanding and familiarity with the lifestyle from which the participants had come. For example, some participants felt the Israeli counsellors made them feel guilty. A young Canadian said that he had two Israeli counsellors: one wanted to persuade him to immigrate to Israel, while the other was looking for contacts abroad in order to leave the country. Naturally the youngster ended up confused.

At the same time, when foreign counsellors are in control of the group, they may mainly stress the home community's values and ensure that the community's style dominates the visit, which can create a sense of missed opportunity.

The framework of the programme requires intensive teamwork, and this is sometimes difficult to maintain under the pressure of the tour and given the differences between the foreign and Israeli staff. Nevertheless, the difficulties were more apparent to the counsellors than to the participants: 63% of the participants said they thought their counsellors worked very well together as a team, while only 47% of the counsellors felt this way.

In addition, there is a need for smooth communication between the staff who accompany the groups and the office staff of the sponsoring institutions. The pre-planned schedule and tight logistics seldom allowed the counsellors to make changes that they may have felt were necessary to provide the participants with the best possible experience. For example, if the counsellors felt that more time was needed at a given site in order to answer questions, hold a discussion or provide time to sit and reflect, they rarely had the opportunity to change the schedule to allow this. Some 26% of the counsellors felt there was no way to change the programme without prior approval; 36% felt that they could only occasionally do so, and 45% of the counsellors answered that they had sometimes been told about certain parts of the programme only at the last minute. At the same time, 16% said that last-minute briefings were the norm, suggesting that changes could be made from the administrative side.

It should be noted that each year there are technological innovations that make communication between the counsellors and coordinators and the centre easier: The increasing number of cellular/mobile telephones given out to the counsellors in many groups in the past few years is the best indication of the considerable importance that the system attributes to effective communication. At the same time, the dependence on these phones is liable to create a situation in which the office coordinators solve problems arising in the field over the telephone and the counsellors who accompany the group are less inclined to take responsibility.

Attitudes and Worldview of the Counsellors

While the *madrichim* share some of the characteristics of tour guides and also of teachers, they are more than pathfinders and mentors. They are role models, and as such, their personal beliefs, attitudes, behaviour and personalities are as important as their knowledge. The educational message of the trip to Israel includes various aspects of Jewish identity, such as attitudes towards intermarriage, religion, involvement in the Jewish community and, of course, Israel. The beliefs of the counsellors affect the way each of these is presented to the participants. Therefore, to understand how these messages are passed to participants in the course of the tour, it seems crucial to understand to what extent the counsellors personally hold the views that the programme is meant to transmit.

The complex nature of the educational message invites many difficulties and internal struggles. Putting across an educational message effectively depends on the content and resources that the organizers present and the training that the counsellors receive; it also depends on the personal character and experiences of each counsellor. A counsellor from abroad described one aspect of this difficulty:

> One thing that troubled me was that lots of counsellors were not able to answer a variety of 'Jewish' questions that they were asked in the summer. We take the best of our 'young adults' to lead these muddled and confused youngsters towards a slightly clearer Jewish identity, but who are the leaders? What is their Jewish identity? It's not clear.

A surprising picture emerges from a comparison of the attitudes of the participants, the counsellors from Israel and the counsellors from abroad on questions relating to Israel and Judaism. The foreign counsellors espouse more explicitly Zionist views and are more religious than the

Israeli counsellors. The attitudes of the participants are apparently more similar to those of the Israeli counsellors.

However, the similarity in the responses of participants and Israeli *madrichim* to questions regarding Israel and Judaism may be misleading. While one of the central messages of the tour is that the Israeli and Diaspora Jews belong to the same people, the Israeli counsellors and tour guides come from a material and spiritual world that is largely foreign to the youngsters they are leading. The Israelis' attitudes to Judaism may not be in line with those of the organizations that sponsor the trips. The disparity between the attitudes of the Israeli and the foreign counsellors raises the question of what messages are conveyed to the participants. Particularly in the area of religious content, there seemed to be a lack of coordination between the Israeli and home-country counsellors.

As discussed earlier, Jews in various countries and contexts relate to Judaism differently. Israelis tend to focus on the national aspect of Jewish identity, while for Americans in particular, Judaism is first and foremost a religion (Cohen, S., 1996b; Cohen, S. & Horenczyk, 1999). The educational derivative of this difference is particularly striking in the framework of the Israel Experience. While the Diaspora community is looking for a spiritual encounter and personal experience, the Israelis are offering a nationalist experience with historical emphases.

It is instructive to look at the types of young adults recruited as counsellors from Israel and from each of the home communities. The counsellors from the United States, for example, tend to come from the core of the community. They are relatively religious and concerned with passing on Jewish tradition. While there are, of course, populations of very religious Israelis, the counsellors for the Israel Experience tours tend to come from more secular communities. There may be an assumption that Israelis will have an innate understanding of Judaism, as expressed in the following statement by Mordechai Bar-On, who served as head of the Youth and Hechalutz Department of WZO during the 1970s:

> The Israeli teenager has far more Jewish perceptions and associations, more Jewish spiritual symbols ... than the Jewish teenager in the Diaspora. This is not because he is better, but because he speaks Hebrew and the Jewish sources are easily accessible to him, [because] every expression he uses is steeped in the Jewish sources [and because] he lives in a country where the culture and religion are Jewish. (Central Zionist Archives, June 17, 1982)

Whether or not this is still true, the Israeli counsellors may not necessarily be able to transmit a sense of Jewish religious identity to participants from Diaspora countries. One Israeli counsellor commented, 'What I felt was missing was a bit of preliminary preparation and background on the subject of religion'.

An American counsellor noted, 'It seemed as if the Israelis were trying to minimize the Jewish aspects of the programme. For example, no time was allocated for prayer'. Another American counsellor said: 'We had to provide the Jewish side of the programme, because the Israeli counsellors were secular'.

Not surprisingly, the Israeli counsellors expressed the strongest feelings of affinity with the State of Israel. But the visiting counsellors, too, felt closer to Israel than did the participants they were leading: 96% of the counsellors from the United States said they felt close to Israel, compared with only 75% of the American participants.

To take one example, there was a particularly striking gap between the Israeli, French and American counsellors and the American and French participants with regard to a very central issue in Jewish education in the Diaspora, the question of intermarriage, as seen in Table 26. In order to give the most accurate comparison with the data collected in the survey of counsellors, only the participant data from 1996 is in the table.

The counsellors from the USA expressed by far the strongest opposition. The Israeli counsellors were largely ambivalent. The level of objection expressed by the French counsellors was between that of the Israelis and the Americans. Given that the rate of intermarriage among Jews in the USA has surpassed 50%, among French Jews is between 30% and 40%, and in Israel is only 5% (Della Pergola et al., 2005; Cohen, E.H., 2002a), it seems that these figures more accurately portray the degree to which the various groups of counsellors are concerned with this issue, rather than actual acceptance of intermarriage within the various home communities. Nevertheless, the ambivalent attitude of the Israeli counsellors may influence or confuse the participants.

Table 26 'If a member of your family was willing to marry a non-Jewish partner, how would you react?'

	Counsellors from:			Participants from:	
	Israel	USA	France	USA	France
There's nothing wrong with it	9%	4%	1%	19%	12%
I'm ambivalent	43%	8%	25%	16%	15%
I am somewhat opposed	21%	21%	32%	31%	26%
I strongly object	26%	68%	42%	33%	47%

The difference in the attitudes expressed by the participants from the USA and their home-country counsellors was graphic. It is likely that a significant percentage of the participants have close relatives, even parents, who are married to non-Jews. As mentioned, the American counsellors tend to be recruited from a relatively religious segment of the American Jewish population. These figures indicate that the American counsellors hold quite different views on core issues from those of the members of the groups they are leading. The counsellors and participants from France have more similar views to one another. In fact, in this case the participants are somewhat less tolerant of intermarriage.

Qualities of an Excellent Counsellor

Both the surveyed counsellors and the participants were asked what qualities they felt were most important in an 'outstanding' counsellors. Table 27 shows the responses of the participants and those of the counsellors from Israel, the US and France. The participants' evaluations of traits necessary for an excellent counsellor are lower on almost every item than the evaluations of the counsellors themselves. There is no consensus among the participants as to the qualities required to make an outstanding counsellor. In general the qualities rated most important by the participants are in the field of interpersonal relations: taking care of individual's needs, listening to participants, creating a good atmosphere, respecting participants and their religious choices, being a good friend, and being able to put the programme across.

The counsellors clearly place more emphasis on taking responsibility and on the ability to solve problems. The participants preferred counsellors who give them a lot of freedom. The Israeli counsellors emphasized skills such as listening, motivation, the ability to transmit the goals of the programme, and taking care of individual participants. The American counsellors put more emphasis on knowledge about Judaism and about Israel. Compared to their American counterparts, the counsellors from France put more emphasis on taking care of the group as a whole as well as taking care of the individual participants and put far less emphasis on knowledge about Israel or Judaism.

As we have seen in relation to other issues, the characterization of an ideal *madrich* differed among participants from different home communities. Participants from North America placed far greater emphasis on knowledge about Judaism, particularly in comparison with those from South America and Eastern Europe. Those from South Africa were most concerned that the counsellors know a lot about Israel. As mentioned

Table 27 An outstanding counsellor is one who has these qualities (percentage responding 'very important')

	Counsellors from			Participants 1995
	Israel	United States	France	
Takes responsibility	89%	89%	78%	65%
Is respectful towards the participants	85%	77%	75%	72%
Knows how to listen	81%	67%	74%	65%
Is highly motivated	78%	51%	67%	59%
Knows how to create a good atmosphere in the group	78%	74%	71%	67%
Knows how to solve problems	68%	72%	54%	49%
Knows a lot about Israel	68%	82%	46%	59%
Is a role model for the participants	66%	65%	44%	32%
Respects each person's religious choices	62%	73%	72%	67%
Has the ability to put the programme across	62%	39%	52%	66%
Takes care of the group as a whole	60%	57%	71%	62%
Takes care of each individual	54%	32%	50%	58%
Is a good friend	53%	68%	26%	56%
Understands the Jewish community where the participants live	52%	33%	24%	22%
Has Zionist views	37%	32%	14%	17%
Helps each participant in his/her own personal search	28%	36%	28%	35%
Knows a lot about Judaism	26%	44%	19%	32%
Encourages the participants to take responsibility towards the community	24%	49%	26%	19%
Encourages the participants to make *aliya*	13%	6%	13%	13%
Gives the group a lot of freedom	6%	8%	9%	31%

earlier, a very high percentage of South African Jews attend private Jewish schools, so may see their trip as an opportunity to learn specifically about Israel, rather than about Judaism (which they can learn about at home). The Eastern European participants were the most likely to say that an excellent *madrich* is one who understands the participants' home country (66% say it is 'quite' or 'very' important, compared to 46% of those from North

America). In the context of the relatively lower satisfaction across the board expressed by Eastern European participants, and their small numbers, this may be an indication that they feel their particular situation is not well understood by the programme organizers, and their appreciation of counsellors who do understand their specific needs.

There were some differences in emphasis between male and female participants, noteworthy in part because overall so few differences along gender lines were found. The girls expressed more strongly the importance of counsellors treating participants with respect, knowing how to listen, having a sense of responsibility, creating a good group climate and taking care of the group.

It seems that the model of the teams of Israeli and home country counsellors, is a valuable one, if each is trained and understands the role they may best play. The home-country counsellors may translate the experience for participants, particularly if they have been in Israel several times themselves. The Israeli counsellors provide the link to Israeli society necessary to distinguish the trip to Israel from a summer camp in the home country. While it did not always work perfectly, the model of the two teams of counsellors may be valuable for other heritage and Diaspora tourism programmes. The key seems to be prior training of both teams and clarity of the expectations for each.

To some extent, the dynamic between the teams of Israeli and home country counsellors may be seen as a microcosm of Israeli–Diaspora relations, reflecting many of the tensions and challenges as well as the mutually beneficial results in terms of education and exploration of the plurality of contemporary Jewish identity.

Notes

1. All unattributed quotes from participants and counsellors in this chapter are taken from the open comments section of the questionnaires (which are anonymous) or are observations conducted by my research team.

Chapter 12
Marketing

Expansion Plans

From time to time the organizers of the Israel Experience declare that they want to double the number of participants, to make the visit to Israel a rite/right of passage for every young Jewish girl and boy, and to reach out to the population that has distanced itself from community organizations. After a wide-scale research on the Israel Experience, Annette Hochstein (1986) came to the conclusion that doubling the number of participants was a realistic goal. Yet participation in 2000 was not much higher than it had been in 1987, and year after year the people who come in the end are very close to the core of the Jewish community. The Taglit-birthright israel tours have succeeded in attracting large numbers of participants by eliminating the question of cost, and yet even this programme seems to be primarily attracting participants with some prior ties to the Jewish community.

Schematically, four segments of the target population can be distinguished:

- *Segment 1* comprises those involved in a Diaspora Jewish community who feel affiliated with Israel to some degree.
- *Segment 2* represents disaffected individuals who are distant from the local Jewish community but attracted to Israel.
- *Segment 3* characterizes Jews who are active in their local community but are alienated from activities connected with Israel.
- *Segment 4* characterizes Jews who are distant from both the local Jewish community and from Israel.

Each segment of the population requires a different marketing approach. Currently, the vast majority of participants come from the first segment of the population. Shifts within this population, such as the increased number of participants who attend Jewish Day Schools, or the decreased emphasis on political youth organizations, may require the specifics of marketing to be adapted. However, they remain within the network through which the tours have traditionally been advertised.

Those in the other segments are either outside the communication network through which most advertising for the tours takes place, or have little interest in coming to Israel. Reaching them would require great effort, and convincing them to join a tour to Israel would require even more. As we see, marketing of Israel Experience programmes is intimately intertwined with issues of Israel–Diaspora relations and Jewish identity.

Obstacles to Participation

The questionnaire distributed to Israel Experience participants asked if they had friends who had applied to the programme but did not come. Those who said they did could then indicate why they thought their friends did not join the tour, even though they had expressed interest in it. Additionally, in July and August 1998 we conducted individual informal interviews with 60 youngsters from English-speaking countries participating in Israel Experience summer programmes. We asked them if they had friends or acquaintances who had wanted and/or planned to come to Israel this summer but did not and, if so, why not. This combination of quantitative and qualitative methods is particularly useful. The questionnaire reached far more respondents (tens of thousands), but offered only five multiple choice options for why friends did not come (cost, other commitments, parents' objections, inconvenient dates or summer school). The interviews provided an opportunity for participants to elaborate and to offer other explanations that we may not have considered when designing the questionnaire.

Over one-third of the teenagers interviewed in 1994 noted that they had at least one friend who would have liked to have participated in the Israel Experience but in the end did not come. We estimate that this population represents some 5000 youngsters each year. This group is the most reachable pool of future participants, and therefore the first population to target in order to expand participation.

Cost

Over half said it was because the trip was too expensive, although this reason declined in importance during the course of the survey, falling from 62% in 1994 to 48% in 2001. The expense of the trip was a particularly large hurdle for youngsters from South Africa and Australia/New Zealand (airfare from these distant countries significantly increases the cost of the trip.) Although the Taglit-birthright israel programme has largely eliminated the obstacle of cost, at least for a first trip, 79% of their alumni said finances were an obstacle for a subsequent trip (Saxe et al., 2006).

The participants we interviewed indicated that programme choice often depended on cost and the availability of scholarships. Some said that their friends and acquaintances who did not join an Israel Experience programme had not known about scholarship options. Some interviewees added that people can be embarrassed by taking charity and that even those who know that money is available may not apply for it, or may not qualify for it.

Participants who define themselves as 'definitely religious' are most likely to say they have friends who did not come to Israel because of the cost of the programme.[1] If we assume that participants tend to have friends of a similar background and level of religious identification, we can conclude that programme cost is a bigger obstacle among the religious population. This may be because Orthodox Jewish families generally invest a large proportion of their budget in education (private Jewish Day Schools), and they tend to have many children. Thus setting up scholarship funds or subsidized trips may help increase participation from this segment of the population.

Security, safety and other parental concerns

The least-mentioned reason for non-participation was safety and security. In the questionnaire, this could be expressed as 'parental objection': 30% of the respondents indicated this as a reason their friends did not join the tour. South Africans were the most likely to select this as a reason for non-participation (46%) and Eastern Europeans the least (17%). Also in the personal interviews, security issues were generally discussed in the context of parental concerns (i.e. their parents were worried about safety).

It can be assumed that parental objections are a more important factor than appears in the data, as adolescents tend to minimize the importance of parental influence. Girls were slightly more likely to acknowledge parental concern as a reason that their friends did not participate (31% as opposed to 25% of the boys).

Parental objections extended beyond the expected concerns about terrorism in Israel. They also included parents' concern that their children were too young or not mature enough to leave home for the summer, and parents who discourage Jewish involvement in general.

Some aspects of the issue of safety concerns, of course, are dependent on the volatile political situation, and are largely out of the hands of Israel Experience organizers. The best they can do is reassure parents that all possible security measures are taken. As mentioned, different Diaspora populations react differently to the security situation in Israel; some actively send 'solidarity missions' specifically during the most difficult times, whereas others cancel tours.

Alternative summer plans and conflicting obligations

These were commonly given as reasons for friends' non-participation: 46% of respondents indicated that interested friends had other obligations, and 22% said the dates of the tour were not convenient. Some potential participants chose alternative summer activities, including driver education classes, camps in the home country, summer jobs, summer school or college programmes, as well as travel to other destinations.

Offering a greater variety in available dates may be possible, although the tours are already arranged around school vacation schedules. Summer school, much to the dismay of those enrolled, is largely unavoidable. However, this seemed to affect only a small percentage of the potential participants: only 10% of respondents indicated this was why their friends did not join the tour. Scholarships, subsidized programmes and free programmes may allow some to participate who would otherwise take summer jobs.

Major 'competitors' are summer camps, especially Jewish summer camps. Some friends and acquaintances of Israel Experience participants work as counsellors at summer camps. Others simply do not want to miss a summer at the camp that they have attended for years. Given the shared objective of enhancing Jewish identity, the organizers of the Israel Experience programme do not want to discourage participation in Jewish summer camps. Instead, collaborate efforts may be possible.

Greater publicity about the enjoyment of a trip to Israel (for example through schools and community centres), may help encourage Jewish youth to visit Israel rather than other tourist destinations.

Initiative and awareness

Although this was not included as an option in the questionnaire, in the course of the interviews some participants mentioned friends who had not come on the tour because they learned about the programmes too late to register, were too slow in signing up, did not actively follow the process through or did not know about the variety of programmes offered. Others were uncertain or unenthusiastic about the tour. Some interviewees referred to friends who talked about joining an Israel Experience programme but never actually took the initiative as 'lazy' or 'sell-outs'.

Some interested youngsters were not accepted to specific programmes of their choice (e.g. the Poland trip) or were aware of only certain programmes that did not appeal to them (e.g. programmes arranged through Orthodox organizations), and were not aware of alternative options that might have been attractive to them.

While teachers and staff at community centres have not been found to be very successful at recruiting participants, they may be able to give guidance to those who express interest in trips, helping through the registration process. Additionally, given the high level of computer literacy of young people today, websites providing information and on-line registration for tours may help alleviate this mainly logistical obstacle to participation.

Sources of Information about the Programme

Another marketing-related question asked how participants learned about the Israel Experience programme. It has consistently been found that most participants learn of the tours by word of mouth. A 1992 study carried out in Canada (Goldfarb Consultants, 1992) who found that, among the youngsters who came to Israel, 57% encouraged others to follow in their footsteps. Among their sample, of those who had participated in an Israel Experience tour, most heard of it by word of mouth through Jewish friends or organizations. Only 22% learned about it from advertising.

I, too, found that, for the most part, participants found out about the existence of the programme through informal advertising, that is, through friends, former participants, members of youth groups and family members ('horizontal marketing') and not through media or official institutional channels ('vertical marketing') (Cohen, E.H., 1999c).

Over 70% of participants said they learned of the trip from friends: 41% said specifically that they learned about it from a former participant and 36% through a youth organization (more than one option could be cited). In addition, more than one- third heard about the programme from family members and youth organizations. In contrast, fewer than 10% said they learned about the programme from posters, newspaper, radio or TV. The only non-personal form of advertising that seemed to have any impact was mail brochures: 28% said they learned of the programme in this way. Mail brochures are a more targeted type of advertising, and were probably sent to addresses of families with some connection to a synagogue or other Jewish organization. Furthermore, most participants noted that the first to influence their decision to come to Israel were friends and family members (Cohen, E.H., 1995b). Similarly, almost three-quarters of Taglit-birthright israel tour participants learned about the trip through favourable word of mouth from friends and family (Saxe *et al.*, 2004: 33). Follow-up studies of both the Israel Experience and the Taglit-birthright israel programmes have confirmed that former participants often recommend the programme, thus serving as effective agents for transmitting information about the programme and marketing it. All this attests to the importance of the informal social network in marketing the tours.

Within the United States, the largest pool of participants numerically, if not per capita, it has been found that some states are over-represented in relation to their Jewish population, and others are under-represented. The most dramatic example of over-representation is Michigan: 6% of Israel Experience participants come from Michigan, a state in which less than 2% of the country's Jews live. Significantly, there was a surge in participation from Michigan in 1996 and 1998, years in which the Michigan Jewish community organized special Israel Experience programmes. The results of this effort are clearly seen, and may serve as a marketing guide for states (such as New York) whose participation rates are lower than their portion of the US Jewish population.

In general we can say that marketing for the Israel Experience is less dependent on advertising than it is on the level of education and activity within the Jewish community. Diaspora communities whose members, as a whole, feel close to Israel and consider Israel to be an important part of their identity are more likely to encourage their children to visit Israel, whether with their families or in the context of group tours. The effect is cumulative: the more likely a youngster is to have a friend who has gone on a tour, the more likely that youngster is to go on a tour him/herself.

According to the results of Levenberg and Isaacs' 1991 marketing study of the Israel Experience, the marketing strategy must address the parents of youngsters in the target population. Although 42% of the parents who said they were not considering the possibility of sending their children to visit Israel gave cost as their main reason, Levenberg and Isaacs claim that the issue of cost is, in fact, an issue of prioritization. If parents were made to feel the cost of the programme was justified in terms of the long-term educational impact, they might be more willing to pay for it.

Levenberg and Isaacs recommend using creative means for convincing young people and their parents of the value of the trip, including stories, music and artwork of alumni and Israelis to illustrate the meaning of the visit and the educational advantages it offers. Young people slightly further out in the periphery of the community, who may be reached through such events, can then pass the word to their less involved friends, thus gradually expanding the informal marketing network.

Programme alumni are a particularly important source of information about the tour, for two main reasons. First, their advice, as people with first-hand experience, is reliable. Second, they share a common language with other potential participants, whereas adults in the community may not. Currently, most of the recruitment carried out by alumni is informal and unorganized, based on personal conversations. Alumni of the programme could be encouraged to participate in the marketing activity directly and in a structured way, for example by presenting slide shows of photographs from their trips to local schools and youth groups. The websites for many programmes (Israel Experience, Taglit-birthright israel and specific youth movements) now provide a place to post and view videos and photographs from tours – a new form of advertising and recruitment by alumni. It has even become possible for participants to communicate with family and friends via the Internet during certain activities, for example from the top of Masada. This enables those at home to have a 'virtual Israel Experience', as well as providing a new dimension to the experience of the participants, although it raises questions of whether or not the online communication may distract from the actual experience. While this is still rare, it may be included in greater number of tours in the future.

Reaching Unaffiliated Jewish Youth

Thus far we have discussed young Jews who are already involved in the Jewish community, even if only marginally. They include thousands of individuals who are aware of the group tours to Israel and may be reached through a focused marketing policy through the traditional channels. It is reasonable to assume that by making an intensive appeal to these youngsters it will be possible to achieve a real increase in the number of participants. These potential participants are accessible because they or their families are already connected to the network of the Jewish community.

We know less about how to reach Jewish youth on the fringes of the community – those who are not affiliated with Jewish community institutions. The fact that they are on the periphery is the main obstacle to their participation in the Israel Experience. The regular channels do not reach these youngsters because they and their families are not connected to them and may even stay away from them deliberately.

However, some Jews who are not attracted by and do not participate in local Jewish community life *are* nonetheless interested in Israel. They may be reluctant to contact the organized community for this purpose, or may not even be aware of whom to contact. In such cases, it should be possible to use alternative routes, such as the Internet and other places where information about general summer camps or tours is available.

Marketing that targets parents (or even grandparents) might be particularly effective with the non-core population. For those already active in the Jewish community, Jewish friends are common and influential. Those far from the core have fewer Jewish friends who may recommend a tour to Israel. Family members, even if they are not particularly involved in the Jewish community, may still have some feelings about the importance of

Jewish continuity or solidarity with Israel and therefore be open to the idea of sending their children on a tour to Israel.

These are logistical questions. More complicated are questions of content and programming when marketing to unaffiliated Jewish youth. What types of messages and what types of programmes are specifically appropriate for young Jews who have little or no Jewish background and involvement? They lack the structural preparation to understand and appreciate the programme in its classic form.

With regard to recruiting non-organized youth, another problem also arises. As described above, there is a direct relationship between the degree to which the participant is involved in the life of the Jewish community and the degree of satisfaction with the programme in Israel. It can therefore be assumed that Israel Experience programmes as they are currently conducted will not answer the needs and aspirations of Jewish youth from the more remote periphery. The programmes are liable to disappoint them and perhaps even lead them to have negative attitudes towards Israel.

There are three basic models for integrating participants who are remote from the core of their local Jewish community into existing Israel Experience groups: the integration, heterogeneous and exclusive models.

(1) *Integration model*: Small numbers of youngsters who are not involved with a youth organization may take part in tours organized by youth groups. This model has been used by groups that originate in the UK. The summer groups coming from England are usually very homogeneous, consisting mainly of members of youth movements who participate in activities throughout the year. In order to preserve the distinctive style of their groups, the youth movement organizers are prepared to include only a few non-member participants in each group. This model has had considerable success since it enables the distanced youngsters to experience the visit through the eyes of their more involved peers and does not require a major revision of the existing programme curriculum. This may be considered analogous to integration models in schools that encourage students who have less background in a given subject (for example, immigrant students learning a new language) to study with those who are more proficient.

However, care must be taken in order to avoid discouraging interested youth who are not members of youth groups from participating. Some years ago, the Jewish Agency in France adopted a policy directing all youth who expressed interest in an Israel Experience tour to various local youth movements. The intention was to improve the long-term educational impact of the tour by providing a framework to absorb the youngsters on their return. The actual result was that many of these young people did not join the groups organized by the youth movements, and most of them simply did not come on a group tour to Israel. They were interested in a direct connection with Israel, but not in an ongoing connection with the Jewish community in their country.

(20 *Heterogeneous model:* A group may consist of approximately equal numbers of youngsters who are close to the core of the community and those who do not participate regularly in Jewish activity. This model runs the risk of causing tension and spoiling the visit for all. This dynamic has been found to be problematic and disruptive in other areas of educational tourism, in which some members emphasize learning or particular values (such as ecological awareness), whereas others are more interested in sight-seeing and recreation (Ritchie et al., 2003).

(3) *Exclusive model:* Special trips may be organized for young people who are not involved in the local Jewish community. This was done by the Youth and Hechalutz Department of the WZO in France in the early 1990s (prior to the policy shift of directing inquiries to youth movements, as described above,). Approximately 250 youngsters took part in these tours each year. This solution provides an avenue for attracting young people who have deliberately kept apart from their Diaspora Jewish community, but would like to see Israel, to better understand its issues, to feel a sense of solidarity and closeness with Israel. These programmes should emphasize touring and interactions with Israelis, rather than issues of Jewish identity. It may be that these participants would experience deeper and more far-reaching changes as a result of the tour than their previously-involved peers.

In any event, consideration must be given to the special needs of disaffected youth. If they are to be included on any significant scale, it will be necessary to formulate not only marketing strategies, but in fact a new programme. Staff will have to be trained in order to ensure that these youngsters understand the sites they see and the activities in which they participate, given that they have little or no Jewish educational background. The Israel Experience programmes are generally designed for a population that is familiar with the language, symbols and codes of Jewish communal life. Participants from the periphery are less familiar with these Jewish communal concepts. Their sense of belonging and affiliation cannot be assumed, but must be nurtured and created almost from scratch.

Young Jews in the community periphery have a different conception of what the Israel Experience should be. We know that these marginally-affiliated youth are most interested in programmes which stress emotional experience, touring and recreational activities, and that shorter and/or lower-cost programmes most appeal to them, and therefore these should be emphasized in marketing to this population. As shown in Table 28, they want a less ideological (less religious and less Zionist) programme. This contrasts with the responses obtained from participants from the community core who recommend a longer programme that is more Jewish- and group-oriented.

Deliberations on questions of recruitment raise the question whether the goal is quantity versus quality, that is, an investment in the Jewish people or training an elite to be future leaders of the Jewish community. Using the criteria of making the tour a rite/right of passage for all Jewish youth, as is repeatedly suggested by Jewish educators in the Diaspora, the success of the Israel Experience programme is measured by the number of participants.

However, we have seen that the Israel Experience is particularly enriching for those who have already absorbed a degree of Judaism before coming to Israel and have been prepared for the experience. The question arises, therefore, whether it may be more worthwhile to focus on quality programmes for interested young people. This idea also ties in with Steve Cohen's (1992) approach, which sees the second visit to Israel as being of greater significance.

The resources allocated to the Israel Experience are limited, and so it is necessary to choose between the attempt to include a large number of youngsters and the desire to train leading elites who in the future are likely to influence their students and others who come in contact with them after their return home.

Table 28 Programme recommendations according to frequency of involvement in local Jewish community (participants from USA, summer 1998)

	Seldom (once a year or less)	*Regularly (once a month or more)*	*Frequently (once a week or more)*
Programme should be:			
less religious	24%	17%	12%
less Zionist	19%	12%	11%
less academic	32%	25%	20%
more sports-oriented	37%	32%	27%
more Jewish-oriented	16%	24%	30%
more group-oriented	35%	37%	41%
longer	32%	38%	47%

If training educators is the goal, it may be even more effective to expand the Israel Experience tours to those who are already working in the field of Jewish education. According to my study of staff in Jewish informal educational settings (Cohen, E.H., 1992b), although the vast majority has visited Israel, only about 7% have received any training in Israel. In recent years, the Department of Education of the Jewish Agency[2] has significantly enlarged its training department. A study of teacher training programmes in Israel found that:

> Without question individuals are personally enriched. They strengthen and/or renew their bond with the land and the people of Israel. Beyond that, they bring home resources, approaches, ideas, and questions that shape their teaching, regardless of the subject matter. At the deepest level they rethink not only the content of their teaching, but also actually *how* they teach. (Grant & Pomson, 2003: 14)

Given the importance of informal education in teaching young people values and identity, and the impact of a visit to Israel on the way in which those working in informal Jewish education carry out their work and put their experience across to their students, Jewish educators in the Diaspora may be seen as a target group of primary importance.

Notes

1. Youngsters in this group are also most likely to say that their friends did not participate because the dates were not convenient, their parents objected, or there were security concerns, but these differences are relatively small.
2. Formerly the Youth and Hechalutz Department of the World Zionist Organization.

Chapter 13
Conclusions and Reflections

The Role of Youth Tours to Israel in Contemporary Jewish Identity

Tourism provides a lens through which numerous sociological phenomena may be examined. Group tours bringing Diaspora Jewish adolescents to Israel are a specific case of tourism with a narrowly targeted population and explicitly articulated goals. Nevertheless, such tours may be seen as a microcosm in which many of the fundamental questions related to travel, identity and education are played out. The Israel Experience tours are the longest-running, most consciously designed and most thoroughly documented example of educational heritage tourism. They have proven to be an excellent vehicle for looking at issues of identity, pedagogy, evolving relations between a Diaspora population and their 'home country', youth travel and more.

In this book, we have given a broad, overall view of the many facets included in the Israel Experience: Jewish identity, Israel–Diaspora relations, informal education, adolescent identity formation, tourism etc. As well as looking at each aspect in its own right, we aimed to offer a mapping of the field as a whole using a combination of qualitative and quantitative research techniques. There has been increased recognition that these two types of research may be considered in conjunction rather than in opposition, with fruitful results. The vast database collected from tens of thousands of participants allowed us to identify large trends, confident that they do not reflect flukes or idiosyncrasies. The interviews, observations and participant comments to open questions put individual voices and faces to the numbers. In some cases observations and discussions produced unexpected insights that proved to be turning points in our understanding of an issue.

The analysis of the Israel Experience contributed to our understanding of contemporary Jewish life. With the creation of the State, Israel, which for centuries had been a religious symbol and messianic dream for most Jews, became a destination of migration and tourism. Israel is a central component of Jewish identity, even for those who have never visited it. For those who have, the visit may be an expression of pride and solidarity, an opportunity to explore their heritage and a religious pilgrimage, as well as a recreational vacation. Many participants in the educational tours describe the visit (particularly if it is a first visit to Israel) as a turning point in their lives – a peak experience.

The tour to Israel, as we have seen, is one aspect of an ongoing process of Jewish education and socialization. We had to look at the tours in the larger educational and community context in order to find out what participants expect and need, what assumptions about Judaism and Israel they bring with them, what activities will interest and move them, and what type of personnel will most effectively transmit the programme to them. There is no 'one-size-fits-all' Israel Experience, and a flexible menu of possible itineraries, linked through common underlying objectives, has been developed in order to provide a satisfying tour for participants from different home communities. The subsequent development of the short Taglit-birthright israel tours and the long MASA study programme further highlight the need and demand for diverse options in educational tourism to Israel.

The synergy between the informal educational model and the wide appeal of Israel make the educational tours popular among a range of religious and political streams in the Jewish world. Formal Jewish education, at least in the United States and France, has become predominantly the domain of Orthodox, or at least strongly religious, Jewish families.[1] Informal settings such as camps are much more popular among the non-Orthodox. Israel is an issue that attracts and concerns Jews from across the spectrum of religious practice. The choice of what types of Jewish education parents provide for their children is an indicator of their hopes and expectations for the next generation and has a real impact on the direction that Jewish community life and culture will take. Sending one's children to Israel on an educational tour represents a distinctive type of Jewish education within the larger framework.

While the distinctive features of the subpopulations of the tour participants must be considered, there are many commonalities between them. Almost all come from strongly-affiliated Jewish backgrounds, and their previous education set a context for understanding and appreciating the tour. Additionally, virtually all participants are adolescents or young adults who have not yet begun a career or begun to raise a family, and thus the tours may be considered part of the field of youth travel and youth leisure. The group and the counsellors were found to be particularly crucial to the tour, both in terms of the enjoyable social experience that the teenage travellers expect, and in the quest for identity that is common to many cases of youth travel and, indeed, contemporary travel in general. Thus, some of what was learned about Jewish identity, Jewish education and Jewish travel to Israel may be applied to the larger fields of ethnicity, education and the sociology of tourism.

Diaspora Tourism to Israel: A Search for an Authentic and Holistic Jewish Experience

MacCannell, who helped pioneer the field of sociological tourism studies, contends that modern travellers are seeking authenticity and the wholeness missing in their fractured lives (MacCannell, 1976, 1992). This perspective has been enriched, contested and expanded by other researchers, who have differentiated between various types of tourists, streams of tourism and outcomes of the tourist experience. Determining what is authentic and what is not in terms of tourism has proved to be difficult, and in an era of virtual reality and the spread of a global consumer culture, the concept of authenticity may be of decreasing importance to post-modern travellers (Cohen, E., 2007). In the case of the Israel Experience tours, it may be asked whether the visitors wish to see (and whether organizers wish to show them) the 'real' Israel or a reflection of their own idealized image of it.

MacCannell's (1976, 1992) second concept of seeking holism through travel may prove to be of more lasting relevance. For the Israel Experience participants, it is particularly germane. The trip to Israel is indeed related to a search for holistic identity among Diaspora Jews. In Israel, it is hoped that they will integrate the diverse aspects of their identities as Jews and find an authentic face for Judaism at the turn of the millennium. The tours enable participants to examine issues of identity in an effectively all-Jewish environment, something rarely available to most young Jews at home. The group travelling together, the staff and the Israelis they meet (with the rare exceptions of activities in Bedouin villages and the like) are all Jewish, and they represent multiple aspects of Judaism and multiple possibilities for Jewish identity.

Although the members of the group are essentially homogeneous in terms of age, nationality and background, the trip exposes participants to aspects of the Jewish world that they may never have encountered before: Israeli teens from Tel Aviv, soldiers in the Israeli army, Holocaust survivors, kibbutz members, immigrants from Ethiopia, ultra-Orthodox Jews praying at holy sites, nature guides, beggars, bus drivers, medics, etc. The assimilation of these diverse aspects of the Jewish people into a consolidated image allows each visitor to form a consolidated image of him/herself. This may be analogous to Lacan's 'mirror stage' of intellectual development (Lacan, 1949/1977; Homer, 2005), in which the image in a mirror provides a perception of the whole self, uniting the fragmented experiences of an infant. The infant instinctively smiles at this image, and is pleased when it smiles back. The almost universal satisfaction with the overall programme in Israel is this smile: the nascent Jewish identity seeing for the first time the unification of what had been fragments.

The Limitations of a Successful Programme

The tour should not be unduly idealized. The impact, while significant, is limited by numerous factors. The tour is short. Confronted suddenly with myriad images and sometimes conflicting messages, participants may not have sufficient time to work through the complex emotions and ideas presented in the programme. Follow-up, subsequent trips and continued or increased involvement in the Jewish community at home help alumni to process the questions and new ideas raised by the trip.

The trip tends to reinforce existing views rather than radically overturn them. Within weeks or months the vast majority of programme alumni return to their pre-trip routines. Those who were already active in their local Jewish communities may intensify their involvement. Some return for subsequent trips, either as part of another group tour or in a different format such as longer study programmes or unstructured visits with family or friends. And, although the percentages are low, there are those who eventually decide to move to Israel. This major decision is often reached after a number of repeated visits, in which case it may be said that the first visit as a teenager with a youth group initiated the subsequent process that eventually led to the decision to make *aliya*. Little empirical data has been collected that tracks the life trajectories of tour alumni over the years and decades following their trip. However, not a few of those currently in positions of leadership in Jewish institutions cite a trip to Israel in their youth as one of the inspirations for their later life decisions.

While encouraging immigration to Israel was once an objective, it has all but been abandoned in favour of goals related to the concerns in the Diaspora, such as preventing assimilation and inspiring youth to be future leaders of their home communities. In the early years, the Israel Experience was intimately tied to the concerns of the Zionist movement. The participants, many of whom were members of Zionist youth organizations, were expected to be concerned primarily with the needs of the new State. Today, it may be said that the Israel Experience and subsequent programmes such as Taglit-birthright israel and MASA are at least equally concerned with the needs of the Diaspora community, which appears to be in more of an existential crisis than does the State of Israel. Travel to Israel has become a tool for maintaining and strengthening Jewish life in the Diaspora. Participants are encouraged to feel a sense of connection to Israel and to consider it their spiritual homeland, but not necessarily (and in some cases, decisively *not*) to think of it as a possible home. This is particularly true of the American participants, who represent the largest population numerically.

The tour programme raises both ideological and practical issues regarding the mutual responsibilities of Diaspora Jews towards Israel, and of Israel towards Diaspora Jews. Perceptions about who supports the programme and who benefits influence the message and logistics of the tour and its component parts (particularly noticeable in activities such as the encounters with Israeli youth).

The impact of the tour may be limited by the extent of the preparation and follow-up. Preparation, as discussed, includes both the long-term structural preparation provided by years of Jewish education and community involvement and specific preparation for the tour or for individual activities. A visit to the Western Wall, for example, is likely to be more meaningful to a group of young travellers who have known about and seen pictures of this holy site since their childhood, who are given historical background about it by their guides before arriving, who discuss together the meaning the Wall has for them and prepare written prayers to put in the cracks (a common tradition) before actually going, than it will be for a group who shows up with little familiarity with the history and significance of the stone wall. Guides need to know how much structural preparation the members of their group have so that they can make specific preparation interesting, meaningful and understandable. Follow-up, too, may be structural (continued or increased education and community involvement) or specific (reunions) and both of these help prevent diminishment of the enthusiasm generated by the trip.

The importance of structural preparation raises the paradox of the inability of the programme to reach unaffiliated Jewish youth, despite repeated attempts to do so. It is now clear that a programme for Jews at the further periphery of the community would require new recruiting methods and a new educational approach to the curriculum of activities. Alternatively, organizers may focus energies and resources on encouraging return trips, which have been found to have cumulative impact, and on training those already at the core of the community to be future leaders, rather than on attempting to bring 'all Jewish youth' to Israel.

However impressive and moving a visit to the Holy Land may be, it should not be assumed that the simple fact of coming to Israel is sufficient to achieve the goals of the programme. The realities of modern Israel raise many difficult issues and present a cacophony of images and experiences that may be confusing or disturbing to participants. The educational message must be carefully planned and executed, and the staff must be trained to address the questions that arise. This does not mean that the message must be didactic or overly explicit. It may be transmitted indirectly, through symbolism or via seemingly unrelated activities (such as social activities intended to create emotional bonds with co-travellers or with Israeli peers). While some have criticized such message-driven interpretation by guides as interfering with 'authentic' tourism (Reisinger & Steiner, 2006), part of the role of the counsellors is to facilitate discussions about what participants are seeing, allowing them to express their opinions, raise questions and draw their own conclusions. At the same time, there *are* educational and ideological goals to the Israel Experience trips. For such a programme to fully realize its potential impact, there needs to be agreement and understanding among the staff and organizers as to the educational message to be transmitted to participants, and it must be appropriate to the group. If not, the programme may inadvertently give participants confusing, contradictory or even negative impressions.[2]

Coordinating a programme with a cohesive educational message is not simple, as the goals of the programme are not understood in the same way by all the various parties involved. The organizers from Israeli institutions and Diaspora community institutions, the Israeli and home-country counsellors, the participants from various home countries, their parents and their teachers each have their own objectives, emphases, underlying assumptions and value structures that colour their perspective on the trip.

Unlike many other examples of tourism, the Israel Experience tours have goals that are not primarily economically driven (although indisputably economic questions do arise). The attitudes towards the trip to Israel are rooted in larger issues related to Israel–Diaspora relations, contemporary Jewish identity and education. The Israeli governmental institutions that sponsor the trips are still guided by a Zionist ethic in which Israel is the centre that Diaspora Jews should support and, ideally, make their home. Recognizing the reality that few will in fact immigrate, in this view the Diaspora Jews come to Israel to experience 'real' Jewish life, and to express their commitment to support the State. The Diaspora community institutions and the parents of participants, on the other hand, are increasingly concerned with Jewish continuity in their own countries, and are likely to see Israel primarily as a means to inspire youngsters to consider the importance of their Jewish heritage. They may be more interested in a dialogue about the pluralistic faces of contemporary Jewish identity, of which being Israeli is only one manifestation (and not necessarily the most authentic one). In this case the Jewish People, rather than Israel, are the centre. In the context of ongoing participation in summer camps in the home country, day school or extra-curricular Hebrew school and youth movements, the tour to Israel is a special field trip, at the end of which return to life in the home country is assumed.

The adolescent participants have their own set of goals and expectations for the trip. Expectations, as we saw, have an impact on the experience; indeed in order to understand the outcome of the tour it is essential to know the attitudes, knowledge and expectations that participants bring with them. First and foremost, participants want to have a good time with their friends. Nevertheless, they are a self-selected group, more strongly connected to Israel and their Jewish heritage than their peers who chose other ways to spend their school vacations. They expect spiritual and personally-enriching experiences during their travel. In this way, the trip to Israel is similar to other examples of youth travel. To some extent, the tourists meet themselves through their interactions with the Other, even when those others are members of the same religious-ethnic group. Although the purpose of the trip is to intensify Jewish identity and participants are encouraged to think of Israel as their homeland, interaction with the foreign environment has the impact of reinforcing their identity as *American* Jews, *Argentinean* Jews, *French* Jews, etc. Indeed, the finding that the attitudes expressed on virtually every issue presented in the survey differed most significantly along national lines (whereas attitudes between girls and boys were virtually indistinguishable) highlights the impact of the dominant society in which the participants live. The images of Israel and the role that Israel plays in the identity of participants from various backgrounds reflect the emphases of the Jewish educational systems, which in turn reflect the values of the surrounding society. Young people from France may be seeking community while those from the US seek spirituality; members of Orthodox and Reform youth movements may react differently to the same sites. For Israel Experience tours to effectively speak to participants, organizers and staff must have a sensitive awareness of these differences, and must be able to adapt the programme to fit the needs of participants from different backgrounds.

The tour has an integrative format, simultaneously incorporating aspects of all types of travel: recreational, existential, spiritual, educational, heritage, volunteer tourism, and even 'dark' (*thana-*) tourism (i.e. sites related to the Holocaust in Europe or at Yad Vashem, and battlefields).[3] The use of independently-run educational units (modules), the flexible model of informal education, and the pre-disposition to appreciate the experience based on educational and cultural background, have enabled the programme to meet the needs of a variety of travellers over the course of decades with an impressively high degree of satisfaction. In this way, it may serve as a model for other programmes in the rapidly-expanding field of heritage-diaspora tourism. The virtually universal satisfaction has shifted the focus of programme evaluation to identifying factors that differentiate the most thoroughly satisfied from those who are 'merely' satisfied, thus providing an evaluative model for fine-tuning already successful education and tour programmes.

Rite/Right/Write of Passage

Rite of passage

Part of the significance of the Israel Experience is its timing in the life of the individual. Most, if not all, traditional cultures have some sort of initiation rite of passage to mark the passage from childhood to adulthood. In Jewish culture this is the bar or bat mitzvah ceremony held at age 12 (for girls) or 13 (for boys).[4] In traditional Jewish society, after reaching the age of bar/bat mitzvah, the individual achieves a new level of personal responsibility. This includes taking on the observance of the religious commandments from which children may be exempt or held to lenient standards (for example fasting on Yom Kippur). Additionally, at this age, children reach a level of moral development that allows them to be held accountable for their actions (for example, according to Jewish law, if a child is caught stealing the parents are held accountable, whereas after the age of bar/bat mitzvah the young adult may be held accountable).

The bar/bat mitzvah ceremony is still widely practised even among Jews highly assimilated and minimally observant of Jewish tradition: 83% of Israel Experience participants said they personally celebrated this rite of passage. However, as a rite of passage, the timing of the bar/bat mitzvah ceremony is not fully in sync with the realities of adolescents today. In Western societies 12 or 13 year olds do not achieve any real level of independence from their parents or accountability in the eyes of the law. They are far from thinking about marriage or leaving home. Adolescence has become a much longer stage of life, and the independence and responsibilities of adulthood are achieved much later than they were in the days when Jewish tradition emerged.

The Israel Experience tour takes place as the teenagers are nearing the end of high school and beginning to think about leaving their parents' home, whether to continue their studies at college and university, or to begin to work. The timing of the rite of passage is relevant to their lives. The popularity of the Taglit-birthright israel tours among even older adolescents further illustrates this point. Young Americans between the ages of 18 and 26 are still likely to be single, without children, and not yet involved in a career-track job. They are still discovering themselves and taking the first steps towards independence. The trip to Israel is meaningful at this juncture in their lives. We repeatedly heard participants compare spiritually-moving experiences during the tour such as praying at the Western Wall or seeing the sun rise on Masada with the bar/bat mitzvah rituals they went through with little enthusiasm or understanding several years previously. Not only the organized bar/bat mitzvah programme offered in some Israel Experience programmes, but the tour as a whole serves as a contemporary rite of passage, in sync with the realities of their lives.

Right of passage

In the choice of their name, the Taglit-birthright israel tours made explicit the concept of the trip to Israel as a right received by virtue of birth into the Jewish People.[5] The Israeli government, Jewish community institutions and private philanthropists have been partners in forwarding this idea since the inception of the tours at the founding of the State. The Right of Return was passed in 1950, granting all Jews essentially unrestricted entry into the country and virtually automatic citizenship, should they choose to apply for it.

It cannot be ignored that today the promotion of the idea that a trip to Israel is the birthright of Jews worldwide is taking place in a political context in which attitudes towards Israel are polarized. Anti-Israel sentiments are being expressed through street protests and boycotts (such as by Britain's union of college and university professors in 2007), and by academic and popular media channels. Despite treaties signed between Israel and its neighbours Jordan and Egypt, the Muslim world (including the growing Muslim population in Europe) continues not only to criticize Israel's policy towards the Palestinians, but also to question the right of Israel to exist at all and to advocate the Right of Return for Palestinian refugees. Meanwhile, at the other end of the political spectrum, the neo-conservatives and American Christian Right have apparently adopted Israel as a symbol of the fight between the Christian West and the Muslim East, thus supporting Israel because of their own political agendas and/or religious ideologies.

It is beyond the scope of this book to delve into the historical, political and sociological reasons that have given rise to these attitudes towards Israel. Nevertheless, we may say that against the background of this complex context, the group tours for Jewish youth may be seen as a public affirmation of the connection between Diaspora Jews and Israel. Tours allow young Jews to express pride in their sense of peoplehood. Thus, the tour is more than a personal rite of passage; it is a communal assertion of a right of passage to Israel. It has become, admittedly, a right with few obligations attached; as already discussed, the pressure to actually immigrate, join the army and build the country physically, has essentially been dropped from the itinerary. Participants are expressing their right of *passage*, not of return. They are passing through, coming to Israel and going back home. Nevertheless, it is an expression of solidarity and group pride.

It also must be taken into account that the trip to Israel is a journey to the Middle East, where travel for Jews in other countries in the region may be dangerous (if not outright prohibited, as in the case of Saudi Arabia). Even travel to the West Bank, Gaza and some of the Arab population centres throughout Israel have become dangerous and have been dropped from many tour itineraries. Particularly during the worst years of the Al-Aqsa *intifada*, the threat of terrorist attacks hung over all of Israel. In this context, tourism to Israel becomes an expression of a political right to travel.

In general, the right to be tourists, to travel unimpeded by political barriers, was expected to be part of the new global village in which travel was among the goods and services available to all (with the money to buy), particularly after the fall of the Soviet Union and the lifting of the Iron Curtain (Munar, 2007). The reality, of course, has been quite different. Tourist destinations, airlines and railways have been targeted in terrorist attacks such as those in Bali, Egypt, India, Madrid, Turkey and New York City.

Additionally, being in Israel gives Jews the freedom to be openly Jewish. While there are essentially no legal prohibitions against practicing Jewish tradition in the home countries of the Israel Experience participants, there are some cultural and practical barriers to looking 'too Jewish'. These stem both from the threat of anti-Semitism and from a political culture that relegates religious and ethnic affiliation to a strictly private sphere (as, for example, in France). Even in countries where there is little threat of violent anti-Semitism, peer pressure may cause young Jews to be embarrassed or uncomfortable wearing outward symbols of their religion. In many Diaspora communities men are seen wearing a kipa (skullcap) only in Orthodox neighbourhoods or inside a synagogue or Jewish community centre. In Israel, the visitors will see many men and boys wearing a kipa, as well as other public signs of Judaism such as large Star of David emblems or tee-shirts with Jewish symbols or Hebrew writing. In Israel, the Diaspora youth may openly display their Judaism with comfort.

Write of passage

As the sharing of memories of the trip to Israel with others is also an important part of the adventure, a third homonym may be suggested: the Israel Experience as a write of passage. Writing about personal experiences in order to make them real and understandable to oneself, as well as to share them with others, has long been a tradition in journals, diaries, memoirs and autobiographies. This has now become even more widespread through Internet technology such as blogs, through which individuals (particularly young people), routinely post their daily thoughts. Numerous writings, photographs, and videos from Israel Experience and Taglit-birthright israel alumni have been posted online.

The importance of narrative to the meaning of travel has been explored by researchers such as Jack and Phipps (2005), Kelner and Phil (2001) and Noy (2002a, 2002b, 2003a, 2003b, 2004a, 2004b; Noy & Cohen, E., 2006). Jack and Phipps (2005: 114) write that 'The act of story-telling had important social, formative and temporal functions for tourists ...'. This includes both personal memories of the trip and 'official' stories, including the myths about places visited presented to tourists by guides and locals. Stories are exchanged among fellow travellers, and are presented at home as a sort of oral souvenir. Through narrative, scattered memories may become coherent stories with themes, analysis, and conclusions drawn about the experience. This process is sometimes encouraged by the tour counsellors, for example in holding discussion groups in which participants are asked to write or talk about and then share their feelings about their Jewish identity or perceptions of Israel. Kelner and Phil (2001: 9–10) recount that in such sessions, 'Isolated fragments from life were retrieved, like a bag of mosaic tiles. Sometimes these memories were arranged to give them some sense of coherence ... What was not germane to this narrative was filtered out'. As a participant-observer of Israel Experience tours, Habib (2004) documented the wide diversity of opinions and viewpoints about Israel and Judaism expressed by youngsters on the tours, despite the relatively homogeneous message presented by the organizers. Based on his in-depth study of the place of Israeli backpackers (young Israelis who travel to other countries for their journey of personal and social identity discovery), Noy (2003b) concludes that the stories of a rite of passage such as a first international travel experience provide the traveller with cultural capital (status) and symbolic meaning. Noy's comment on Israeli youth travelling abroad may be applied to Jewish Diaspora youth traveling to Israel:

> ... I soon realized that it could be said that they travel *for the stories*. They travel after they have heard numerous stories, which pre-shape the itinerary of the travel and the experiences it bestows. And they progress and 'mature' during the trip – they all declare they do – in correlation with the achievements that such (predominantly romantic) journey and adventure narratives entail. (Noy, 2003b, emphasis in original)

In looking at the trip to Israel as a contemporary rite of passage, participants' perception of it as their right as Jews and the stories they tell to others (co-alumni and non-participants), we may discuss the educational process behind the way Israel is remembered, in other words, the pedagogy of memory. Activities such as dramatic re-enactments, visits to historic sites and memorials, and hearing or reading testimonials from witnesses to historic events link personal memory to history (Müller, 2002; Sturken, 1997; Shackel, 2001). The participant 'remembers' the original event through the activity, which has a planned, intentional message. The political and cultural implications of this are myriad. As an historic event is presented through the lenses of various ideologies and re-interpreted in light of subsequent events, it may become, '..a collective and mobile script in which we continue to scrawl, erase, rewrite our conflicting and changing view of ourselves' (Adams, 1988: 49).[6] For example, in the Israel Experience the 'memory' of the Holocaust is inextricably tied to the creation of the State of Israel. Visitors to Yad Vashem walk out of the museum into modern-day Israel, and the destruction of Eastern European Jewry will be remembered in this context. The sequence of activities during the course of the trip will have an impact on the way they are remembered and their long-term educational impact.

Towards a Model of Heritage Tourism and Directions for Future Research in the Field

The preparation of this book has been a fruitful and rewarding project. As the tour to Israel provides a holistic picture, an image of the traveller's self with all parts united, so the preparation of this book has enabled me as a researcher to see a holistic picture of this phenomenon whose component parts I have been studying for more than two decades. Indeed, it is part of a personal journey that began with my own participation, at the age of 15, in an Israel Experience tour organized through the community youth group in France of which I was a member. Following this tour which for me, as for so many other participants, was a pivotal experience, I went on to become a counsellor, and a community camp director. Eventually I moved to Israel and became the educational director for the Youth and Hechalutz Department's tours from French-speaking countries. Finally, I embarked on a career of studying the Jewish educational phenomena that helped to influence the direction of my own life.

I hope that this holistic picture will enable those working in or doing research on the Jewish community and educational system to see in a wider context the particular aspects with which they are involved.

The educational tour to Israel, clearly, has become a widespread and important part of Jewish education and Jewish identity formation among adolescents living in countries around the world. In the modern/postmodern era, ethnic and religious education is more likely to take place outside the home, and group identification has increasingly become a matter of choice. Travel, particularly heritage tourism, may play an important role in both the education and the identity of many diaspora, minority and immigrant populations other than the Jewish people. I hope that the insights offered in this book provide useful guidelines for researchers investigating parallel phenomenon among other populations. Of particular importance in research on educational heritage tourism are the role of the guide, the political culture of the home community and its surrounding society, the structural preparation (educational background) of the tour participants, the relationship between the 'diaspora' and the 'homeland' populations, and the explicit and implicit goals of all involved parties (sponsoring institutions, organizers, participants and parents). I look forward to seeing the results of such research, thus enabling me to see my own work on this case study in an emerging mega-model of heritage tourism in the 21st century.

Notes

1. For example, in the USA, 91% of children aged 6 to 17 from Orthodox families attend Jewish Day Schools, compared to only 4% of those from Reform families. In other Diaspora communities such as those in South America, the dynamics of the Jewish Day School is different. As seen in Table 5, the vast majority of Jewish students in South America attend Jewish Day School, although this is not a strongly Orthodox population.
2. For an interesting account of training guides to transmit a predetermined message and to discourage 'inappropriate' interpretations at sites related to the Nazi era in Germany see Macdonald (2006).
3. Thana-tourism is a recognized, if relatively new, term in tourism studies referring to tourism to sites of tragedies, a technical term for 'dark' or 'grief' tourism. See for example Dann & Seaton (2001). See also http://www.grief-tourism.com/category/types-of-grief-tourism/thanatourism/ (accessed 11.1.07).
4. For an in-depth analysis of Jewish rites of passage see Goldberg (2003).
5. The root of this concept of the birthright is Biblical, invoking the story of Jacob receiving the birthright (primogeniture) instead of his brother Esau, and thus passing it on to his children, the Children of Israel.
6. This quote from a Vietnam War veteran refers to the Vietnam War and its place in contemporary American identity, but the insight may be applied to events in Jewish or Israeli history such as the Holocaust, the Israeli War of Independence or the Six Day War. (Adams, 1988, quoted in Sturken, 1997: 86).

Glossary of Hebrew Terms

Aliya Immigration to Israel. From the Hebrew root 'to go up', this word has much stronger ideological and religious connotations than the word 'immigration'.

Ashkenazi Jews of European descent; from an old Hebrew term for Germany; one of two main branches of Jewish tradition (see also *Sephardi*).

Hasidic A movement within Orthodox Judaism originating in 18th century Eastern Europe; from the Hebrew roots meaning 'piety' and 'kindness'; the Hasidic movement emphasized song, prayer and attachment to a particular rabbi, in addition to religious study; many members of Hasidic sects wear distinctive clothing from the Eastern European tradition.

Havdala Ceremony performed at the end of the Jewish Sabbath (Shabbat); literally 'differentiation'.

Hechalutz pioneer.

Intifada Uprising of Palestinians against Israel involving strikes, riots and attacks against Israeli soldiers and civilians; from an Arabic term meaning 'shaking off'; the 'first intifada' refers to a Palestinian uprising beginning in 1987, the 'second intifada' or 'Al-Aqsa intifada' began in September 2000.

Kibbutz Communal settlement in Israel, usually agricultural, based on socialist and Zionist ideologies. From the Hebrew root 'to gather'.

Kipa Skullcap worn by Jewish men and boys; also commonly known by the Yiddish term *yarmulke*.

Masa Journey; name of project offering long-term (semester or year) educational programmes in Israel.

Ma'abara Transit camp for new immigrants to Israel in the early days of the State.

Madrich (feminine, *madricha*; plural, *madrichim*) Counsellor or guide.

Mifgashim Structured meetings or encounters, in this context between Israeli and Diaspora youth.

Glossary of Hebrew Terms

Olim Immigrants to Israel. From the Hebrew root 'to go up'.

Sephardi Jews descended from the Jewish communities of Spain and Portugal who spread throughout the Middle East and North Africa; from the Hebrew word for Spain; one of two main branches of Jewish tradition (see also *Ashkenazi*).

Shabbat Jewish day of rest; Sabbath; lasts from sundown Friday until just after dark Saturday night.

Shoah The Holocaust, the destruction of European Jewry by the Nazis; literally, 'calamity' or 'destruction'. The Hebrew word Shoah has come to be preferred by many Jews and Jewish or Israeli organizations to the term 'Holocaust', which is derived from a Greek word referring to a completely (*holos*) burnt (*kaustos*) sacrificial offering to a god.

Taglit Discovery; part of the name of the free 10-day tour programme to Israel, 'Taglit-birthright israel'.

Tzitzit Garment with fringes at each of its four corners, worn by religiously observant Jewish men.

Ulpan Intensive Hebrew study.

Yeshiva traditional school or study hall for learning Jewish religious texts; from the Hebrew root 'to sit' or 'to meet'.

Zionism nationalist movement for a Jewish state in the Land of Israel.

Zionist One who supports the existence of a Jewish state in the Land of Israel.

Appendix
Examples of Itineraries

Sample programme, Summer 2007

[Details taken from the Israel Experience website.[1] Comments in italics were not in the original website, but were added for clarification for the purposes of this book.]

'All programmes are "tailor made" to meet the needs and interests of each client. This is done through an ongoing and open dialogue to ensure that the programme meets the educational agendas and needs of the client. With this said, this is a sample youth programme that was built for one of our clients. This can give you a general idea about the educational elements, the logistics taken into consideration and of course a general idea about what there is to do and see in beautiful and wonderful Israel."

Day 1 – Welcome to Israel

Afternoon:	Arrival in Israel.
	Opening ceremony.
	Check into hotel.
Evening:	Hamat Gader – natural hot springs.
	Dinner.
Overnight:	Kibbutz Nof Ginosar *[by the Sea of Galilee]*.

Day 2 – Galilee

Morning:	Breakfast.
	Zippori – home of the Mishna *[Jewish canon law]* and Israelites under Roman rule.
	Kfar kedem – including donkey ride *[a recreated village showing life in a Jewish community in the Galilee at the time of the Mishnaha 2000 years ago]*
	Chov Achziv *[beach on the Mediterranean coast]*
	Rosh Hnikra – cavernous sea grottoes *[ancient passage hewn in the cliff between Lebanon & Syria to the North and Israel & Egypt to the South. Now there is a cable car ride]*.
	Lunch.
Overnight:	Kibbutz Nof Ginosar *[by the Sea of Galilee –Kinneret]*.

Appendix: Examples of Itineraries 203

Day 3 – The Golan Heights

Morning:	Breakfast.
	Hike in the Golan Heights – Jilabun *[waterfall]*.
	Mt Bental – Observation point *[view into Syria – also an old Syrian bunker from before the Six Day War with machine gun emplacements looking down into Israel]*.
	Kibbutz Neot Mordechai – Sandals factory.
Afternoon:	Visit the Talmudic Village at Katzrin.
	Check into hotel – Rimonim, Tzfat.
	Kabbalat Shabbat & Service.
Evening:	Shabbat Dinner.
Overnight:	Rimonim Hotel, Tzfat.

Day 4 – Shabbat in Tzfat

Morning:	Breakfast.
	Tfila *[Synagogue prayers]*.
	Walking tour of Tzfat.
Afternoon:	Shabbat Lunch.
	Menucha *[rest]*.
	Text Study/Discussion about the Parshat Hashavua *[Torah portion of the week]*.
	Havdala *[close of Shabbat ceremony]*.
Evening:	Disco boat on the Sea of Galilee.
Overnight	Rimonim hotel, Tzfat.

Day 5 – Carmel

Morning:	Breakfast.
	Kayaks on the Jordan River.
	Hike in the Arbel *[cliffs overlooking the Kinneret]*.
Afternoon:	Swimming in the Kinneret.
	Lunch.
	Check in to the Shfaim Hotel.
Evening:	Eve of IDF Memorial Day – participate in a ceremony in Hertzeliya.
Overnight:	Shfaim Hotel.

Day 6 – IDF Memorial Day and Mifgashim

Morning:	Breakfast.
	Mifgashim *[planned encounters]* at Netivot-Sedot Negev *[development town in the Negev]*.

Afternoon: Eve of Independence Day – celebrations in Netivot.
Evening: Dinner at Hotel.
Overnight: Netivot-Sedot, Negev.

Day 7 – Independence Day
Morning: Breakfast.
Army Base – Hatzerim/ Machane Natan [*army base and airforce museum*].
Rappelling at the Ramon Crater.
Afternoon: B.B.Q at Park Timna [*the world's most ancient copper mines*].
Camel rides.
Overnight: Mirage Hotel, Eilat [*resort town on the Red Sea*].

Day 8 – The Beauty of Eilat & The Bedouin
Morning: Breakfast.
Hike at Mt Tzfaot/other.
Snorkelling at the Red Sea.
Underwater Observation [*looking at the Coral Reefs from a glass bottomed boat*].
Afternoon: Lunch – on own.
Bedouin hospitality and camel ride.
Evening: Lecture: The Desert Wildlife & Kumtzitz [*camp fire & songs*].
Overnight: Roded-Kfar Hanokdim [*desert lodge*].

Day 9 – Masada & The Dead Sea
Morning: Breakfast.
Drive to Masada [*Herodian Mountain Fortress*].
Masada for sunrise [*climb up Snake Path or take cable car*].
Leisurely hike in the Ein Gedi oasis.
Afternoon: Float and relax at the Dead Sea.
Transfer to Jerusalem.
Haas Promenade – observation point [*overlooking Jerusalem*].
Evening: Madrich Activity – Preparation for visit to Yad Vashem [*counsellor activity for visit to Holocaust Museum*].
Overnight: Kings Hotel, Jerusalem.

Appendix: Examples of Itineraries 205

Day 10 – Memory and Continuity

Morning:	Breakfast.
	Early wake up for T'fila at the Kotel [*Prayers at the Western, or Wailing Wall – Holiest Jewish site – remains of the Second Temple*].
	Kotel Tunnel [*tunnels that lead underground beneath the streets of the Old City and running along the length of the Western Wall*].
	Yad Vashem [*Museum of the Shoah, or Holocaust*].
	Mount Herzl [*Israel's military cemetery & burial place of many great leaders and Prime Ministers, including Yitzhak Rabin*].
Afternoon:	Givat Ha-Tachmoshet [*Ammunition Hill, site of one of the deciding battles for Jerusalem of the Six Day War, cemetery & museum*].
	Shabbat Preparation.
	Kabbalat Shabbat & Service.
Evening:	Shabbat Dinner.
	Oneg Shabbat [*Joy of Shabbat –singing etc.*].
Overnight:	Kings Hotel, Jerusalem.

Day 11 – Shabbat in Jerusalem

Morning:	Breakfast.
	Shabbat Service.
Afternoon:	Kiddush and Lunch.
	Yemin Moshe and Mishkenot Shaananim [*first new Jewish settlement areas built outside the Old City by Moses Montefiore and other philanthropists and dominated by a large windmill*].
	Havdala.
Evening:	Harel Mall [*shopping centre*].
Overnight:	Kings Hotel, Jerusalem.

Day 12 – Jerusalem in Antiquity

Morning:	Breakfast.
	The Jewish Quarter [*of the Old City*].
	The Southern Wall excavations [*excavations of the Southern Wall of the Temple Mount*].
	Graduation at the Kotel.
Afternoon:	Machon Ha-Mikdash [*Temple Mount Institute-museum*].

	Museum on the Seam – a unique installation dedicated to the notion of Coexistence [art museum].
Evening:	Festive Dinner.
	Depart to Ben Gurion Airport.

Itinerary for a Youth and Hechalutz Department Group, Summer 1997

June 27	Arrival, opening ceremony, preparation for Shabbat.
June 28	Western Wall, Havdalah, free evening.
June 29	David's Citadel Museum, the Herodian quarter, Western Wall, southern wall excavations.
June 30	Beit Guvrin caves, Beit Guvrin pool, drama activity.
July 1	David's Tomb, Mt Zion, Mahane Yehuda, special game.
July 2	Nachal Mashash, short abseiling, 'Attrakzia' water park.
July 3	Nachal Arugot, Flour Caves.
July 4	Masada, the Fin, Ein Ovdat, Ben Gurion's grave, preparation for Shabbat.
July 5	Shabbat at Sde Boker field school: Ben Gurion's grave, Nachal Havarim.
July 6	Alpaca farm, Mt Tzefachot, free evening in Eilat.
July 7	Kibbutz Ketura – seminar, swimming in the sea, Nachal Kasui.
July 8	Coral Beach, underwater observatory, camels, Bedouin hospitality.
July 9	Tour of Jaffa, propaganda seminar.
July 10	'Discover Tel Aviv' (game), cable water skiing, flea market, free evening.
July 11	Special Shabbat programme – family hospitality in Nachlat Binyamin.
July 12	Family hospitality in Nachlat Binyamin.
July 13	Special programme.[2]
July 14	Special programme.
July 15	Special programme.
July 16	Special programme.
July 17	Special programme.
July 18	Nachsholim seaside fun.
July 19	Free Shabbat (possibility of staying at Nachsholim).
July 20	Tree planting in Jerusalem Forest, Yad Vashem – preparation.

Appendix: Examples of Itineraries 207

July 21	Yad Vashem, Mt Herzl.
July 22	Sachne, Mt Arbel, Kinneret cemetery.
July 23	The Good Fence, Mt Hermon, Tel Faher – hike, Hamat Gader.
July 24	Water activity, Kibbutz Neot Mordechai, Katzrin – park and museum.
July 25	Nachal Jilbon, Safed, preparation for Shabbat.
July 26	Group Shabbat in Tiberias, sailing on the Kinneret.
July 27	Roots seminar, Acre – Knights' Halls.
July 28	Special programme.
July 29	Nachal Kaziv, Har Halutz, hospitality at Ein el Asad.
July 30	Maccabiah, Lebanon Beach.
July 31	Maccabiah, Rosh Hanikra.
August 1	Keshet Cave, special programme, preparation for Shabbat.
August 2	Group Shabbat in Jerusalem.
August 3	Israel Museum, Chagall Windows, special programme, farewell party.
August 4	Departure.

Sample Daily Programmes

Programme 1 (Group's first day in Israel)

7:30 am	Breakfast at Jerusalem Forest youth hostel.
8:15	Travel to ceremony at Armon Hanatziv promenade.
8:40	Opening ceremony and lookout.
10:00	Travel to Dung Gate.
10:15	Western Wall excavations (professional guide, emphasis on Jewish life during the Second Temple period).
11:30	Visit to Western Wall.
12 noon	Lunch in Culinarium restaurant, the Cardo.
12:45	Tour of Herodian quarter excavations.
13:45	Visit to David's Tomb.
14:15	Travel to Jerusalem Forest youth hostel for siesta.
17:30	Travel to town centre.
18:00	Free evening in pedestrian mall.
21:00	Return to hostel.

Counsellors: Israelis – group leader and counsellor; Americans – male and female counsellor and tour guide from Archaeological Seminars guiding the group at the sites.

Programme 2

7:45am	Breakfast at Kiryat Moriah.
8:45	Travel to Ammunition Hill.
9:20	Visit to Ammunition Hill and film (emphasis on the divided city, Six Day War).
11:00	Travel to Mt Herzl.
11:30	Visit to grave of Yitzhak Rabin, with explanations.
12:15pm	Visit to Herzl's grave.
12:20	Ceremony at Jabotinsky's grave (Beitar youth group).
1:00	Travel to Rose Garden for lunch (box lunch).
2:00	Explanation of the Menorah opposite the Knesset.
2:15	Travel to Gush Etzion.
3:00	Visit to Kfar Etzion museum (documenting the rise, fall and revival of Gush Etzion).
4:15	Return to Jerusalem.
5:00	Free time in Jerusalem Mall.
6:00	Return to Kiryat Moriah.
6:30	Dinner at Kiryat Moriah.

Counsellors: Israeli counsellor and tour guide, two foreign counsellors and a teacher, and an Israeli medic.

Programme 3

7:15am	Breakfast at Kiryat Moriah.
8:30	Travel to downtown.
8:45	Enter Nachlaot, briefing for neighborhoods game.
9:30	Neighbourhoods game in Nachlaot, including Mahane Yehuda market (highlight on independent activities relating to Jewish history and Jewish life in Jerusalem).
11:30	Conclusion of game.
12 noon	Walk to town centre, lunch in 'Subway' restaurant.
1:15 pm	Travel to Israel Museum.
1:45	Tour of the Shrine of the Book and Sculpture Garden (highlighting the Dead Sea Scrolls and Essene life).
4:00	Free time in the museum.
4:45	End of visit, return to Kiryat Moriah (cancellation of visit to Knesset Menorah because of campers' tiredness).
6:00	Dinner at Kiryat Moriah.
7:30	Evening out: See a play at the Khan Theatre.
9:30	Return to Kiryat Moriah.

Notes

1. Retrieved June 24, 2007 from: http://www.israelexperience.org.il/NewSite/index1.asp?PageID=56&DepIDMain=3&Language=english. This particular web page is no longer active, as the website is updated regularly to show the current programmes. A choice of 'Sample Programmes' can be found on the general website (www.israelexperience.org.il; accessed 11.1.07).
2. 'Special' programmes are those carried out at the responsibility of the movement bringing the youngsters or at the responsibility of a sub-contractor (module).

References

Abrams, S., Klein-Katz, S. and Schachter, L. (1996) Standing within the gates: A study of the impact of the Cleveland Israel Educators' Seminar on the personal and professional lives of its participants. *Journal of Jewish Communal Service* 73 (1), 83–88.

Ackerman, W. (1986) New models of Jewish education: Formal and informal, what is most worth? *Jewish Education* 51 (1), 3–7.

Adams, W. (1988) Still shooting after all these years. *Mother Jones* 13, 47–49.

AJC (American Jewish Committee) (1996) *Rebuilding Jewish Peoplehood: Where Do We Go From Here? A Symposium in the Wake of the Rabin Assassination*. New York, Jerusalem: American Jewish Committee

AJC (American Jewish Committee) (1997) *The Condition of Jewish Peoplehood: A Symposium One Year After the Rabin Assassination*. New York, Jerusalem: American Jewish Committee.

Amar, R. and Toledano, S. (2002) *HUDAP: Hebrew University Data Analysis Package*. Jerusalem: Computation Center of the Hebrew University, Louis Guttman Israel Institute of Applied Social Research.

Anti-Defamation League (2001) *The Debate Over US-Jewish Tourism to Israel*. Jerusalem: ADL Israel Office.

Appadurai, A. (1996) *Modernity at Large: Cultural Dimensions of Globalization*. Minneapolis, MN: University of Minnesota Press.

Askénazi, L. (1984/2005) L'identité d'un peuple. In *La parole et l'écrit* (Vol. 2): *Penser la vie juive aujourd'hui*. Paris: Albin Michel, 141–149.

Avivi, O. (2000) *Birthright Israel Mifgashim: A Summary of the Planning, Implementation and Evaluation of Mifgashim During Birthright Israel Programs. Executive Report: Winter Launch 1999–2000*. Jerusalem: Bronfman Mifgashim Center.

Barkat, A. (2007) More than half of Israelis support Diaspora Jews' right to criticize Israel. *Haaretz*, 20 March.

Bar-Shalom, Y. (1998) *Encounters with the Other: An Ethnographic Study of Mifgashim Programs for Jewish Youth: Summer 1997*. Jerusalem: The Charles R. Bronfman Centre for the Israel Experience.

Bar-Shalom, Y. (2002) From a negative point of view: Reactive Jewish identity amongst Jewish youngsters in south-western USA. *Ba Michlala* 13, 97–108.

Barth, F. (1969) *Ethnic Groups and Boundaries*. London: Allen and Unwin.

Beilin, Y. (1999) *Death of the American Uncle*. Jerusalem: Miskal-Yedioth Ahronoth Books/Chemed Books.

Beilin, Y. (2000) *His Brother's Keeper: Israel and Diaspora Jewry in the Twenty-First Century*. New York: Schocken Books.

Bekerman, Z. (1997) *Constructivist Perspectives on Language, Identity and Culture: Implications for Jewish Identity and the Education of Jews*. Jerusalem: Hebrew University.

Bekker, V. (2006) Wave of bias attacks sweeps Diaspora. *Jewish Daily Forward*, 1 September.
Ben Rafael, E. (1997) *Crisis and Transformation: The Kibbutz at Century's End*. Albany, NY: State University of New York Press.
Ben-Shalom, U. and Horenczyk, G. (2003) Acculturation orientations: A facet theory perspective on the bi-dimensional model. *Journal of Cross-Cultural Psychology* 34 (2), 176–188.
Bensimon, D. and Della Pergola, S. (1986) *La Population Juive de France: Socio-démographie et Identité* (Jewish Population Studies, No. 17). Jerusalem: The Institute of Contemporary Jewry, Hebrew University of Jerusalem.
Berger, P. (1979) *The Heretical Imperative*. Garden City, NY: Anchor Books.
Berkman, J. (2006) *The Jewish Standard*, 3 August.
Berry, J. (1976) *Human Ecology and Cognitive Style*. New York: John Wiley.
Berry, J. (1984) Cultural relations in plural societies: Alternatives to segregation and their socio-psychological implications. In N. Miller and M. Brewer (eds) *Groups in Contact* (pp. 11–27). New York: Academic Press.
Berry, J. (1990) Psychology of acculturation: Understanding individuals moving between cultures. In R.W. Brislin (ed.) *Applied Cross-Cultural Psychology* (pp. 232–253). Thousand Oaks, CA: Sage.
Berry, J. (1997) Immigration, acculturation and adaptation. *Applied Psychology* 46 (1), 5–34.
Berry, J., Poortinga, Y., Segall, M. and Dasen, P. (2002) *Cross-Cultural Psychology: Research and Applications* (2nd edn). Cambridge: University Press.
Blumberg, A. (1998) *The History of Israel*. Westport, CT: Praeger.
Bochner, S. (ed.) (1982) *Cultures in Contact: Studies in Cross-Cultural Interaction*. Sydney: Pergamon Press.
Boorstin, D. (1964) *The Image: A Guide to Pseudo-Events in America*. New York: Harper & Row.
Borg, I. (ed.) (1981) *Multidimensional Data Representations: When and Why*. Ann Arbor, MI: Mathesis Press.
Bourdieu, P. (1979) *La Distinction: Critique Sociale du Jugement*. Paris: Éditions de Minuit. English translation: (1984) *Distinction: A Social Critique of the Judgment of Taste* (R. Nice, trans.). London: Routledge.
Bramwell, B. and Lane, B. (2000) *Tourism Collaboration and Partnerships: Politics, Practice and Sustainability*. Clevedon: Channel View Publications.
Brettschneider, M. (1996) *The Narrow Bridge: Jewish Views on Multiculturalism*. New Brunswick, NJ: Rutgers University Press.
Brodsky-Porges, E. (1981) The grand tour: Travel as an educational device, 600–1800. *Annals of Tourism Research* 8 (2), 171–186.
Bruner, E. (1996) Tourism in Ghana: The representation of slavery and the return of the black Diaspora. *American Anthropologist* 98 (2), 290–304.
Bubis, G. and Marks, L. (1975) *Changes in Jewish Identification: A Comparative Study of a Teen Age Israel Camping Trip, a Counsellor-in-Training Program, and a Teen Age Service Camp*. Los Angeles, CA: Florence G. Heller/JWB Research Center.
Burns, P. (2005) Social identities, globalization and the cultural politics of tourism. In W. Theobald (ed.) *Global Tourism* (3rd edn) (pp. 390–406). Amsterdam: Elsevier, Butterworth-Heinemann.
Canter D. (ed.) (1985) *Facet Theory: Approaches to Social Research*. New York: Springer Verlag.

Carlson, J. and Widaman, K. (1988) The effects of study abroad during college on attitudes toward other cultures. *International Journal of Intercultural Relations* 12 (1), 1–18.

Chazan, B. (1991) What is informal Jewish education? *Journal of Jewish Communal Service* 67 (4), 300–308.

Chazan, B. (1992) The Israel trip as Jewish education. *Agenda-Jewish Education* 1 (1), 30–33.

Chazan, B. (1993) The metamorphosis of Jewish education. In B. Reisman (ed.) *Adult Education Trips to Israel: A Transforming Experience.* Jerusalem: JCC, Melitz, Melton Center for Jewish-Zionist Education in the Diaspora

Chazan, B. (1994) The Israel trip: A new form of American Jewish education. In B. Chazan (ed.) *Youth Trips to Israel: Rationale and Realization* (pp. 1–26). New York: CRB Foundation and the Mandell L. Berman Jewish Heritage Center at JESNA.

Chazan, B. (2000) Through a glass darkly: Israel in the mirror of American Jewish education. In A. Gal and A. Gottschalk (eds) *Beyond Survival and Philanthropy: American Jewry and Israel* (pp. 123–130). Cincinnati, OH: Hebrew Union College Press.

Chazan, B. (ed.) (2002) *Studies in Jewish Identity and Youth Culture.* Jerusalem: Keren Karev.

Cohen, B. and Schmida, M. (1997) Informal education in Israel and North America. *Journal of Jewish Education* 63, 122.

Cohen, E. (1979) A phenomenology of tourist experiences. *Sociology* 13 (2), 179–201.

Cohen, E. (1984) The sociology of tourism. *Annual Reviews in Anthropology* 10, 373–392. (Reprinted in Aostolopoulos, Y., Leivadi, S. and Yiannakis, A. (eds) (1996) *The Sociology of Tourism.* London: Routledge.)

Cohen, E. (1985) The tourist guide: The origins, structure and dynamics of a role. *Annals of Tourism Research* 12 (1), 5–29.

Cohen, E. (2007) Authenticity in tourism studies: Aprés la lutte. *Tourism Recreation Research* 32 (2), 75–82.

Cohen, E. and Avieli, N. (2004) Food in tourism, attraction and impediment. *Annals of Tourism Research* 31 (4), 755–778.

Cohen, E.H. (1974) *The Youth & Hechalutz French-Speaking 1974 Summer Programs: An Analytical Data Report.* Jerusalem: Youth and Hachalutz Department.

Cohen, E.H. (1986) Les volontaires Juifs de France vers Israel durant la Guerre de Kippour, contribution à l'étude des relations Israel–Diaspora. PhD dissertation, Université de Nanterre.

Cohen, E.H. (1991) *L'Etude et l'Education Juive en France.* Paris: Editions du Cerf.

Cohen, E.H. (1992a) Jewish education in France and the State of Israel as perceived by leaders and professionals. In B. Pinkus and D. Bensimon (eds) *French Jewry, Zionism and the State of Israel* (pp. 271–298). Paris, Be'er Sheva: Ben Gurion Research Center, INALCO.

Cohen, E.H. (1992b) *The World of Informal Jewish Education: Staff and Settings.* Jerusalem: Joint Authority for Jewish Zionist Education.

Cohen, E.H. (1994a) *A Compilation of Direct Quotes of Participants' Personal Comments and Evaluations.* Jerusalem: Israel Experience Ongoing Survey & Evaluation.

Cohen, E.H. (1994b) *Towards a Strategy of Excellence.* Jerusalem: Israel Experience Ongoing Survey & Evaluation.

Cohen, E.H. (1995a) *The 1987–1992 Sherut La'am Program Alumni: A Follow-Up Survey.* Jerusalem: Israel Experience Ongoing Survey & Evaluation.

Cohen, E.H. (1995b) *Existing Marketing Network: A First Review: The Participants of the Israel Experience Short-Term Programs*. Jerusalem: Israel Experience Ongoing Survey & Evaluation.
Cohen, E.H. (1995c) Toward a strategy of excellence: A systemic analysis and policy research based on external variables in SSA. In J.J. Hox, G.J. Mellenbergh and P.G. Swanborn (eds) *Facet Theory Analysis and Design* (pp. 55–62). Amsterdam: University of Amsterdam.
Cohen, E.H. (1995d) *The Summer 1993 Israel Experience American Alumni: A Follow-up Survey*. Jerusalem: Israel Experience Ongoing Survey & Evaluation.
Cohen, E.H. (1995e) *Kibbutz: Special Data Report, Summer 1995*. Jerusalem: Research and Evaluation.
Cohen, E.H. (1996a) *Formative Evaluation of the 'Miracle Mission for Teens'*. Detroit, MI: Jewish Federation of Metropolitan Detroit.
Cohen, E.H. (1996b) *The UJA Federation of Bergen County & North Hudson: The 1995 Israel Experience Alumni, a Follow-Up Evaluation*. Jerusalem: Research and Evaluation.
Cohen, E.H. (1996c) *The 1994–1995 Mifgashim Programs, Questionnaires & Observation Survey*. Jerusalem: Israel Experience Ongoing Survey & Evaluation.
Cohen, E.H. (1997a) *Educational Shlihut: An International Systemic and Policy Analysis*. Jerusalem: Research and Evaluation.
Cohen, E.H. (1997b) *World Jewish Student Organization Activists: A Cross-Cultural Survey*. Jerusalem: Student Department of the WZO, World Union of Jewish Students.
Cohen, E.H. (1997c) *A Visit to Prague*. Jerusalem: Israel Experience Ongoing Survey & Evaluation.
Cohen, E.H. (1997d) Formal and informal Jewish education: A structural comparison. In M. Ito (ed.) *Sixth International Facet Theory Conference: Contributing to Cumulative Science* (pp. 58–72). Liverpool: University of Liverpool.
Cohen, E.H. (1997e) *The Israel Experience Logistics Aspects: A Pilot Study*. Jerusalem: Israel Experience Ongoing Survey & Evaluation (Hebrew).
Cohen, E.H. (1997f) *1996 CIS Summer Camps for Adolescents and Students*. Jerusalem: Research and Evaluation.
Cohen, E.H. (1998) *The Israel University Experience: A Comprehensive Survey of Visiting Students in Israel (1994–1997)*. Jerusalem: Council for Higher Education in Israel, Youth and Hechalutz Department.
Cohen, E.H. (1999a) Prior community involvement and 'Israel Experience' educational tours. *Evaluation and Research in Education* 13 (2), 76–91.
Cohen, E.H. (1999b) What is an excellent *Madrich*? The Israel Experience participants' view of their counsellors. In R.M. Schweizer (ed.) *Seventh International Facet Theory Conference, Design and Analysis* (pp. 367–383). Berne: Facet Theory Association..
Cohen, E.H. (1999c) Informal marketing of Israel Experience educational tours. *Journal of Travel Research* 37 (3), 238–243.
Cohen, E.H. (2000) Mifgashim: A meeting of minds and hearts. *Journal of Jewish Education* 66 (1–2), 23–37.
Cohen, E.H. (2001) A structural analysis of the R. Kahane code of informality: Elements toward a theory of informal education. *Sociological Inquiry* 71 (3), 357–380.
Cohen, E.H. (2002a) *The Jews of France: Values and Identity, Highlights*. Jerusalem: United Jewish Social Fund.

Cohen, E.H. (2002b) *Market Penetration of the Israel Experience Programs: A Worldwide Data Analysis. A Preliminary Report.* Jerusalem: Research and Evaluation Group.
Cohen, E.H. (2003a) A questionable connection: Community involvement and attitudes to intermarriage of young American Jews. *Jewish Journal of Sociology* 45 (1), 5–19.
Cohen, E.H. (2003b) Images of Israel: A structural comparison along gender, ethnic, denominational and national lines. *Tourist Studies* 3 (3), 253–280.
Cohen, E.H. (2003c) Tourism and religion: A case study: Visiting students in Israeli universities. *Journal of Travel Research* 42 (1), 36–47.
Cohen, E.H. (2004a) *From Four Corners of the World: Executive Summary of the Survey of Birthright Israel Participants from Argentina, Australia/New Zealand, Brazil and France 2002–2003* (study commissioned by Birthright Israel Foundation). Jerusalem: Research & Evaluation
Cohen, E.H. (2004b) Components and symbols of ethnic identity: A case study in informal education and identity formation in Diaspora. *Applied Psychology* 53 (1), 87–112.
Cohen, E.H. (2004c) Preparation, simulation and the creation of community: Exodus and the case of Diaspora education tourism. In T.E. Coles and D.J. Timothy (eds) *Tourism, Diasporas and Space* (pp. 124–138). London: Routledge.
Cohen, E.H. (2005a) *Facet Theory Bibliography.* Jerusalem/Rome. Online http://micro5.mscc.huji.ac.il/~kerenguttman/Facet_Theory_Bibliography.pdf. Accessed 12.11.07.
Cohen, E.H. (2005b) *Touristes Juifs de France en 2004.* Paris/Jerusalem: AMI.
Cohen, E.H. (2006a) Research in religious education: Contents and methods for the postmodern and global era. *Religious Education* 101 (2), 147–152.
Cohen, E.H. (2006b) Excellence in educational youth tourism: The case of the Israel Experience Program. Paper presented at the 24th EuroCHRIE Congress. Makedonia Palace Hotel, Thessaloniki. October 25–28.
Cohen, E.H. (in press-a) Comparison of attitudes, behaviours and values of French Jewish families with children enrolled in Jewish Day Schools and other school systems. In A. Pompson and H. Deitcher (eds) *Jewish Day Schools, Jewish Community: A Reconsideration.* Oxford: Littman Library of Jewish Civilization.
Cohen, E.H. (in press-b) French Jewish students in Israel: A structural study of values. In E. Yaniv and D. Elizur, *Facet Theory: Theory and Research in Social Sciences.* Jerusalem: Akademon.
Cohen, E.H. and Amar, R. (1993) *External Variables in WSSA1 (Including External Profiles and POSAC Regions): A Contribution.* Prague: Fourth International Facet Theory Conference.
Cohen, E.H. and Amar, R. (1999) External variables as points in SSA: Comparison with unfolding techniques. Paper presented at the 7th International Facet Theory Conference. Berne. July 26–28.
Cohen, E.H. and Amar, R. (2002) External variables as points in Smallest Space Analysis: A theoretical, mathematical and computer-based contribution. *Bulletin de Méthodologie Sociologique* 75, 40–56.
Cohen, E.H. and Bar-Shalom, Y. (2006) Jewish youth in Texas: Towards a multi-methodological approach to minority identity. *Religious Education* 101 (1), 40–59.
Cohen, E.H. and Cohen, E. (2000) *Ha-Chavayah Ha-Yisraelit (The Israel Experience: An Educational and Policy Analysis).* Jerusalem: The Jerusalem Institute for Israel Studies.

Cohen, E.H. and Horenczyk, G. (2003) The structure of attitudes towards Israel–Diaspora relations among Diaspora youth leaders: An empirical analysis. *Journal of Jewish Education* 69 (2), 78–88.

Cohen, E.H., Ifergan, M. and Cohen, E. (2002) The madrich: A new paradigm in tour guiding: Youth, identity and informal education. *Annals of Tourism Research* 29 (4), 919–932.

Cohen, E.H. and Keisar, A. (1993) *The 1992 Summer Israel Experience Educational Programs*. Jerusalem, Israel: CRB Foundation and Mandel Associated Foundations.

Cohen, S. (1986a) *Jewish Travel to Israel: Incentives and Inhibitions among US and Canadian Teenagers and Young Adults*. Jerusalem: Jewish Education Committee, Jewish Agency for Israel.

Cohen, S. (1986b) *Participants in Educational Programs in Israel: Their Decision to Join the Programs & Short-Term Impact of Their Trips*. Jerusalem: Nativ Policy & Planning Consultants.

Cohen, S. (1991) *Committed Zionists and Curious Tourists: Travel among Canadian Jewish Youth*. Montreal: CRB Foundation.

Cohen, S. (1992) *Youth Travel to Israel: The Good Trip to Israel*. Montreal: CRB Foundation.

Cohen, S. (1995) The impact of varieties of Jewish education upon Jewish identity: An inter-generational perspective. *Contemporary Jewry* 16, 68–96.

Cohen, S. (1996a) *UJA Missions to Israel: A Qualified Success Story. An Evaluation Study for the Missions Department of the UJA*. Jerusalem: Hebrew University of Jerusalem.

Cohen, S. (1996b) *Deconstructing the Outreach–Inreach Debate*. Jerusalem: Melton Center for Jewish Education in the Diaspora.

Cohen, S. and Horenczyk, G. (eds) (1999) *National Variations in Jewish Identity: Implications for Jewish Education*. New York: State University of New York Press.

Cohen, S. and Wall, S. (1994) Excellence in youth trips to Israel. In B. Chazan (ed.) *Youth Trips to Israel: Rationale & Realization* (pp. 45–67). New York: CRB Foundation, JESNA.

Cohen, S. and Wertheimer, J. (2006) Whatever happened to the Jewish people? *Commentary*, 33–37.

Coles, T., Duval, D. and Hall, C. (2005) Tourism, mobility and global communities: New approaches to theorizing tourism and tourist spaces. In W. Theobald (ed.) *Global Tourism* (3rd edn; pp. 463–481). Amsterdam: Elsevier, Butterworth Heinemann.

Coles, T.E. and Timothy, D.J. (eds) (2004) *Tourism, Diasporas and Space*. London: Routledge.

Comet, T. (1965) *Research Findings on the Effect of a Summer Experience in Israel on American Jewish Youth*. Philadelphia: AZYF.

Conger, J. and Petersen, A. (1984) *Adolescence and Youth*. New York: Harper Row.

Coombs, P. and Ahmed, M. (1974) *Attacking Rural Poverty: How Non-formal Education Can Help*. Baltimore, MD: Johns Hopkins University Press.

Coombs, P.H. with Prosser, C. and Ahmed, M. (1973) *New Paths to Learning for Rural Children and Youth*. New York: International Council for Educational Development.

CRB Foundation (1993) *The Israel Experience: Planning for 1994: Over 200 Selected Educational Modules*. Jerusalem: The Joint Authority for Jewish Zionist Education, the CRB Foundation.

CRIF (2003) *Déclaration du Grand Rabbin de France, Joseph Sitruk*. Paris: Conseil Représentatif des Institutions Juives de France.

Dann, G. and Seaton, A.V. (2001) *Slavery, Contested Heritage, and Thanatourism*. Binghamton, NY: Hawthorn Press.
Dashefsky, A. (ed.) (1976) *Ethnic Identity in Society*. Chicago, IL: Rand McNally.
Davis, T. (1996) *Open Doors 1995–1996: Report on International Educational Exchange*. New York: Institute of International Education.
Della Pergola, S., Dror, Y. and Wald, S. (2005) *Jewish People Policy Planning Institute Annual Assessment 2005 Executive Report: Facing a Rapidly Changing World*. Jerusalem: Jewish People Policy Planning Institute.
Elazar, D. (1999) Jewish religious, ethnic, and national identities: Convergences and conflicts. In S. Cohen and G. Horenczyk (eds) *National Variations in Jewish Identity: Implications for Jewish Education* (pp. 35–52). New York: State University of New York Press.
Elazar, D. and Trigano, S. (1995) *How European Jewish Communities Can Choose and Plan Their Own Futures*. Jerusalem: Jerusalem Center for Public Affairs. Online at http://www.jcpa.org/dje/articles2/eurjewcomm.htm. Accessed 11.11.07.
Erikson, E. (1963) *Childhood and Society*. New York: W.W. Norton.
Erikson, E. (1968) *Identity: Youth and Crisis*. New York: W.W. Norton.
Erikson, E. (1974) *Dimensions of a New Identity: The 1973 Jefferson Lectures in the Humanities*. New York: W.W. Norton and Co.
Ezrachi, E. and Sutnick, B. (1997) *Israel Education Through Encounters with Israelis: Israel in Our Lives*. Jerusalem: CRB Foundation.
Featherstone, M. (ed.) (1990) *Global Culture: Nationalism, Globalization and Modernity*. London: Sage Publications.
Finestein, I. (1986) *Post-Emancipation Jewry: The Anglo-Jewish Experience*. Oxford: Oxford Centre for Postgraduate Hebrew & Jewish Studies.
Forman, D. (1989) Youth tours to Israel, message and mission. *Journal of Reform Judaism* 36 (4), 49–53.
Freidenreich, H. (2002) *Female, Jewish, and Educated: The Lives of Central European University Women*. Bloomington, IN: Indiana University Press.
Friedlander, D., Morag-Talmon, P. and Moshayov, D.R. (1991) *The One Year Program in Israel: An Evaluation, North America Jewish Students in the Rothberg School for Overseas Students at the Hebrew University*. Jerusalem: American Jewish Committee, Institute on American Jewish–Israeli Relations.
Furnham, A. and Bochner, S (1986) *Culture Shock: Psychological Reactions to Unfamiliar Environments*. London: Routledge.
Gale, N. (1999) Residence, social mobility and practice theory: The case of Sephardic Jews of Sydney. *Journal of Sociology* 35 (2), 149.
Gale, N. (1997) Religious involution: Sacred and secular conflict among Sephardic Jews in Australia. *Ethnology* 36 (4), 321–334.
Gans, H. (1979) Symbolic ethnicity: The future of ethnic groups and cultures in America. *Ethnic and Racial Studies* 2, 1–20.
Gans, H. (1994) Symbolic ethnicity and symbolic religiosity: Towards a comparison of ethnic and religious acculturation. *Ethnic and Racial Studies* 17, 577–592.
Geertz, C. (1973) *The Interpretation of Cultures: Selected Essays*. New York: Basic Books.
Gibson, H. and Yiannakis, A. (2002) Tourist roles: Needs and the lifecourse. *Annals of Tourism Research*, 29 (2), 358–383.
Gitelman, Z., Kosmin, B. and Kovács, A. (2003) *New Jewish Identities: Contemporary Europe and Beyond*. New York: Central European University Press.
Goffman, E. (1959) *The Presentation of Self in Everyday Life*. New York: Anchor Books.

Goffman, E. (1961) *Encounters: The Studies in the Sociology of Interactions*. New York: Bobbs-Merrill.
Gold, P. (2003) *Making the Bible Modern: Children's Bibles and Jewish Education in Twentieth Century America*. Cornell, NY: Cornell University Press.
Goldberg, H. (2002) A summer on a NFTY safari 1994: An ethnographic perspective. In B. Chazan (ed.) *Studies in Jewish Identity and Youth Culture* (pp. 23–142). Jerusalem: Keren Karev.
Goldberg, H. (2003) *Jewish Passages: Cycles of Jewish Life*. Berkeley, CA: University of California Press.
Goldfarb Consultants (1992) Attitudes toward travel to Israel among Jewish adults and Jewish youth. In *The Israel Experience*. Jerusalem: CRB Foundation.
Goldman, E. (1911) Francisco Ferrer and the modern school. In E. Goldman (ed.) *Anarchism and Other Essays* (2nd edn; pp. 151–172). New York: Mother Earth Publishing Association.
Goodman, H. (1994) Jewish in the new South Africa: Not all black or white. *The Jerusalem Report*, 28.
Gordin, J. (1995) *Ecrits: Le Renouveau de la Pensée Juive en France*. Paris: Collection Présences du Judaïsme, Editions Albin Michel.
Gordon, M. (1964) *Assimilation in American Life: The Role of Race, Religion and National Origins*. Oxford: Oxford University Press.
Grant, L. (2006) What British Jews think of Israel. *The Independent*, 18 July. Online at http://news.independent.co.uk/uk/this_britain/article1183428.ece. Accessed 11.11.07.
Grant, L. and Pomson, A. (2003) *From In-Service Training to Professional Development: Alternative Paradigms in Israel for Diaspora Educators*. Jerusalem: JAFI.
Grauer, T. (2001) A drastically bifurcated legacy: Homeland and Jewish identity in contemporary Jewish American literature. In D. Dash-Moore and S.I. Troen (eds) *Divergent Jewish Cultures, Israel and America* (pp. 37–64). New Haven, CT: Yale University Press.
Guibernau, M. and Rex, J. (eds) (1997) *The Ethnicity Reader: Nationalism, Multiculturalism and Migration*. New York: Polity Press.
Guttman, L. (1968) A general nonmetric technique for finding the smallest coordinate space for a configuration of points. *Psychometrika* 33, 469–506.
Guttman, L. (1982) Facet Theory, Smallest Space Analysis, and Factor Analysis. *Perceptual and Motor Skills* 54, 491–493.
Guttman, L. (1986) Coefficients of polytonicity and monotonicity. In S. Kotz, N. Johnson and C. Read (eds) *Encyclopedia of Statistical Sciences* (Vol. 7; pp. 80–87). New York: John Wiley and Sons.
Habib, J. (2004) *Israel, Diaspora, and the Routes of National Belonging*. Toronto, University of Toronto Press.
Hall, C. and Lew, A. (1998) *Sustainable Tourism: A Geographical Perspective*. Boston, MA: Addison Wesley Longman
Halpern, B. and Reinharz, J. (1998) *Zionism and the Creation of a New Society*. London: Oxford University Press.
Head, J. (1997) *Working with Adolescents: Constructing Identity*. London: Falmer Press.
Heilman, S. (2002) A Young Judea Israel discovery tour: The view from inside. In B. Chazan (ed.) *Studies in Jewish Identity and Youth Culture* (pp. 143–268). Jerusalem: Keren Karev.

Henze, R. (1992) *Informal Teaching and Learning: A Study of Everyday Cognition in a Greek Community*. Hillsdale, NJ: Lawrence Erlbaum Associates Publishers.
Herman, S. (1962) American Jewish students in Israel: A social psychological study in cross-cultural education. *Jewish Social Studies* 34, 3–29.
Herman, S. (1970) *American Students in Israel*. Ithaca, NY: Cornell University Press.
Herman, S. (1977a) *Jewish Identity: A Social Psychological Perspective*. Beverly Hills, CA: Sage Publishers.
Herman, S. (1977b) Criteria for Jewish identity. In M. Davis (ed.) *World Jewry and the State of Israel* (pp. 163–181). New York: Arno Press
Hertzberg, A. (1968) *The French Enlightenment and the Jews: The Origins of Modern Anti-Semitism*. New York: Columbia University Press (chapter originally published in *Historia Judaica* volume XVIII, 1956).
Hochstein, A. (1986) *The Israel Experience: Educational Programs in Israel*. Jerusalem: Jewish Education Committee, Jewish Agency for Israel.
Hollinshead, K. (1998) Tourism, hybridity and ambiguity: The relevance of Bhabha's 'third space' cultures. *Journal of Leisure Research* 30 (1), 121–157.
Hollinshead, K. and de Burlo, C. (eds) (in press) *Journeys into Otherness: The Representation of Difference and Identity in Tourism*. Amsterdam: Pergamon Press.
Homer, S. (2005) *Jacques Lacan*. London: Taylor & Francis.
Horowitz, T. *et al.* (1971) Volunteers for Israel during the Six Day War: Their motives and careers. *Dispersion and Unity* 13–14, 68–115.
Jack, G. and Phipps, A. (2005) *Tourism and Intercultural Exchange: Why Tourism Matters*. Clevedon: Multilingual Matters.
Jeffs, T. and Smith, M. (1990) *Using Informal Education*. Philadelphia, PA: Open University Press.
Jeffs, T. and Smith, M. (1996) *Informal Education: Conversation, Democracy and Learning*. Ticknall: Education Now.
Jensen, L. (2003) Coming of age in a multicultural world: Globalization and adolescent cultural identity formation. *Applied Developmental Science* 7 (3), 189–196.
Jewish Information and Referral Service. (2006) *JAFI-support for Jewish Schools in Latin America*. Online at http://www.jirs.org/jirs/jirs0063bi.html. Accessed 11.11.07.
Jiobu, R (1988) *Ethnicity and Assimilation*. Albany: State University of New York Press.
Kafka, R., London, P., Bandler, S. and Frank, N. (1992) The impact of 'summer in Israel' experiences on North American Jewish teenagers: Executive summary. In Goldfarb Consultants, *The Israel Experience*. Jerusalem: CRB Foundation.
Kahane, R. (1974) *Structures and Uses of Informal Youth Educational Organization: An Analytical Framework*. Jerusalem: Hebrew University.
Kahane, R. (1975) Informal youth organizations: A general model. *Sociological Inquiry* 45 (4), 17–28.
Kahane, R. (1988) Multicode organizations: A conceptual framework for the analysis of boarding schools. *Sociology of Education* 61 (4), 211–226.
Kahane, R. (1997) *The Origins of Postmodern Youth: Informal Youth Movements in a Comparative Perspective*. New York: Walter de Gruyter.
Kahane, R. and Rapoport, T. (1988) Informal socialization and role development. *Sociological Inquiry* 58, 49–74.
Kallen, H. (1954) *'Of Them Which Say They are Jews' and Other Essays on the Jewish Struggle for Survival*. New York: Bloch Publishing Company.
Kauffmann, N.L., Martin, J.N., Weaver, H.D. and Weaver, J. (1992) *Students Abroad, Strangers at Home: Education for a Global Society*. Yarmouth, ME: Intercultural Press.

Kelner, S. (2002) Almost pilgrims: Authenticity, identity and the extra-ordinary on a Jewish tour of Israel. PhD dissertation, University of New York.
Kelner, S. and Phil, M. (2001) Authentic sights and narratives on Taglit. Paper presented at the 33rd Annual Meeting of the Association for Jewish Studies. Washington, DC, December 16.
Kelner, S., Saxe, L., Kadushin, C., Canar, R., Lindholm, M., Ossman, H., Perloff, J., Phillips, B., Teres, R., Wolf, M. and Woocher, M. (2000) *Making Meaning: Participants' Experience of Birthright Israel*. Waltham, MA: Cohen Center for Modern Jewish Studies, Brandeis University.
Kerem, M. (1988) Project Oren, background information. Presented at the Israel Experience Committee, Board of Governors of the Jewish Agency for Israel, Haifa.
Kerem, M., Shkedi, A. Mittleberg, D., Bialy, A. and Maizel, I. (1989) *Can the Israel Experience for Jewish Youth From the Diaspora be Developed as an Educational Enterprise for the Kibbutz Movement?* Jerusalem: Jewish Agency.
Klein-Katz, S. (1991) *The Planning of an Israel Experience as a Jewish Educational Resource: The Cleveland Teachers' Seminar in Israel: A Case Study*. Jerusalem: Jerusalem Fellows.
Klein-Katz, S.G. (1990) Encountering Israel as an adult learning experience. Jerusalem: Jerusalem Fellows. Unpublished report, May.
Kohn, D. (1999) *Practical Pedagogy for the Jewish Classroom: Classroom Management, Instruction and Curriculum Development*. Westport, CT: Greenwood Press.
Kornberg, J. (1983) *At the Crossroads: Essays on Ahad Ha-am*. Albany, NY: Albany State University of New York Press.
Kosmin, B., Lerman, A. and Goldberg, J. (1998) The attachment of European Jews to Israel: The British experience. *Journal of Jewish Communal Service*, 108–111.
Kronish, R. (1983) Israel as a resource. In H.F. Marcus and R.R. Zwerin (eds) *Jewish Principal's Handbook* (pp. 293–300). Denver, CO: Alternatives in Religious Education.
Kronish, R. (1984) Strengthening the bonds between Israel and the Diaspora in Israeli Jewish education. *Jewish Education* 52 (1), 29–34.
Laborde, C. (2001) The culture(s) of the republic: Nationalism and multiculturalism in French republican thought. *Political Theory* 29, 716–735.
Lacan, J. (1977 [1949]) *Écrits: A Selection* (A. Sheridan, trans.). London: Routledge.
Laubscher, M. (1994) *Encounters With Difference: Student Perceptions of the Role of Out-of-Class Experiences in Education Abroad*. Westport, CT: Greenwood Press.
Lederhendler, E. (ed.) (2000) *The Six Day War and World Jewry* Bethesda, MD: University Press of Maryland.
Levenberg, J. and Isaacs, L. (1991) *Israel Experience Marketing Project Highlights of Findings and Recommendations*. Jerusalem: CRB Foundation, Jewish Agency.
Levinson, T.A. and Zoline, S. (1997) Impact of summer trip to Israel on the self-esteem of Jewish adolescents. *Journal of Psychology and Judaism* 21, 87–119.
Levran, Z. (2004) *Israel Experience Youth Program Statistics Spring/Summer 2004*. Jersualem: The Jewish Agency for Israel.
Levy, S. (1985) Lawful roles of facets in social theories. In D. Canter (ed.) *Facet Theory: Approaches to Social Research* (pp. 59–96). New York: Springer-Verlag.
Levy, S. (ed.) (1994) *Louis Guttman on Theory and Methodology: Selected Writings*. Dartmouth: Aldershot.

Liebman, C. (2003) Jewish identity in transition: Transformation or attenuation? In Z.Y. Gitelman, B.A. Kosmin and A. Kovács (eds) *New Jewish Identities: Contemporary Europe and Beyond* (pp. 341–350). New York: Central European University Press.

Lorge, M. and Zola, G. (eds) (2006) *A Place of Our Own: The Rise of Reform Jewish Camping*. Tuscaloosa, AL: University of Alabama Press.

MacCannell, D. (1973) Staged authenticity: Arrangements of social space in tourist settings. *American Journal of Sociology* 79 (3), 589–603.

MacCannell, D. (1976) *The Tourist: A New Theory of the Leisure Class*. New York: Schoken Books.

MacCannell, D. (1992) *Empty Meeting Grounds: The Tourist Papers*. London: Routledge.

Macdonald, S. (2006) Mediating heritage: Tour guides at the former Nazi party rally grounds, Nuremberg. *Tourist Studies* 6 (2), 119–138.

Magonet, J. (1995) How do Jews interpret the Bible today? *Journal for the Study of the Old Testament*, 20 (66), 3–27.

Mandel, M. (1991) *A Time to Act. Report of the Commission on Jewish Education in North America*. Lanham, MD: University Press of America.

McClintock, M. and Sutherland, J. (2004) *Anti-Semitism in Europe: Challenging Official Indifference*. New York: Human Rights First, Lawyers Committee for Human Rights.

McKee, M. (1999) Alcohol in Russia. *Alcohol and Alcoholism* 34, 824–829.

McLoyd, V. and Steinberg, L. (eds) (1998) *Studying Minority Adolescents: Conceptual, Methodological and Theoretical Issues*. London: Lawrence Erlbaum Associates Publishers.

Mead, G. (1934) *Mind, Self, and Society*. Chicago, IL: University of Chicago Press.

Miller, H. (2001) Meeting the challenge: The Jewish schooling phenomenon in the UK. *Oxford Review of Education* 27 (4), 501–513.

Mittelberg, D. (1988) *Strangers in Paradise: The Israeli Kibbutz Experience*. New Jersey: Transaction Books.

Mittleberg, D. (1994) *The Israel Visit and Jewish Identification*. New York: Institute on American Jewish–Israeli Relations, American Jewish Committee.

Mittelberg D. (1997) *Summary Interim Report on the Evaluation of the Kibbutz*. Jerusalem: Institute for Jewish Experience, Institute for Research of the Kibbutz and the Cooperative Idea.

Mittelberg, D. and Lev-Ari, L. (1991) *The Kibbutz as an Educational Environment for Jewish Youth From Abroad*. Haifa: The Kibbutz Center of the Institute for the Study of the Kibbutz and the Communal Concept, Haifa University.

Mittelberg, D. and Lev-Ari, L. (1994) From kibbutz experience to Jewish identity: Project Oren evaluation. In A. Shkedi (ed.) *An Encounter Between Cultures*. Tel Aviv: Ach Publishers.

Moss, A.R. (1988) *Theories of Adolescence*. Tel Aviv: Sifriyat Hapoalim.

Müller, J. (2002) *Memory and Power in Post-War Europe: Studies in the Presence of the Past*. Cambridge: Cambridge University Press.

Munar, A. (2007) Rethinking globalization theory in tourism. *Tourism, Culture & Communication* 7, 99–115.

Noy, C. (2002a) You must go trek there: The persuasive genre of narration among Israeli *tarmila'im*. *Narrative Inquiry* 12, 261–290.

Noy, C. (2002b) The great journey: Narrative analysis of Israeli trekking stories. PhD dissertation, Hebrew University of Jerusalem.

Noy, C. (2003a) Narratives of hegemonic masculinity: Representations of body and space in Israeli backpackers' trekking narratives. *Israeli Sociology* 5, 111–142.
Noy, C. (2003b) The write of passage: Reflections on writing a dissertation in narrative methodology. *Forum: Qualitative Social Research* 4 (2).
Noy, C. (2004a) This trip really changed me: Israeli backpackers' narratives of self-change. *Annals of Tourism Research* 31(1), 78–102.
Noy, C. (2004b) Performing identity: Touristic narratives of self-change. *Text and Performance Quarterly* 24 (2), 115–138.
Noy, C. and Cohen, E. (2006) *Israeli Backpackers: A View From Afar*. New York: State University of New York Press.
Ohayon, S. (2004) *Students from North America in Israel: The Machon Gold One-Year Program Compared to University Program*. Philadelphia, PA: Schechter Institute.
ORT (2006) *Latin American Review: 2006*. Online at http://www.ort.org/asp/article.asp?id=335. Accessed 11.11.07.
Poria, Y., Butler, R. and Airey, D. (2003) The core of heritage tourism. *Annals of Tourism Research* 30 (1), 238–254.
Pratt, M. (1992) *Imperial Eyes: Travel Writing and Transculturation*. London: Routledge.
Rein, R. (2004) Together yet apart: Israel and Argentine Jews. 12th International Latin American Jewish Studies Assocation (LAJSA) Research Conference. Dartmouth College, Hanover, NH. June 26–29.
Reisinger, Y. and Steiner, C. (2006) Reconceptualising interpretation: The role of tour guides in authentic tourism. *Current Issues in Tourism* 9 (6), 481–498.
Reisinger, Y. and Turner, L. (2003) *Cross-Cultural Behaviour in Tourism: Concepts and Analysis*. Oxford: Butterworth-Heinemann.
Reisman, B. (1990) *Informal Jewish Education in North America*. Jerusalem: Mandel Commission on Jewish Education in North America.
Reisman, B. (1993) *Adult Education Trips to Israel, A Transforming Experience*. Jerusalem: JCC, Melitz, Melton Center for Jewish-Zionist Education in the Diaspora.
Reisman, B. and Chazan, B. (1978) Israel as Jewish education: An analysis of the short-term study program in Israel. *Forum* 30–31, 54–73.
Richards, S. (2005) What is to be remembered? Tourism to Ghana's Slave Castle-Dungeons. *Theatre Journal* 57 (4), 617–638.
Ritchie, B., Carr, N. and Cooper, C. (2003) *Managing Educational Tourism*. Clevedon: Multilingual Matters.
Robertson, R. (1997) *Theodor Herzl and the Origins of Zionism*. Edinburgh: Edinburgh University Press.
Rosenak, M. (1987) *Commandments and Concerns: Jewish Religious Education in Secular Society*. Philadelphia, PA: Jewish Publication Society.
Rovner, R. (1976) Preparing a group for a short-term experience in Israel: Some conceptual guidelines. *Journal of Jewish Communal Service* 54 (2), 138–146.
Sales, A. and Saxe, L. (2004) *How Goodly are Thy Tents: Summer Camps as Jewish Socializing Experiences*. Hanover, CT: Brandeis University Press.
Sarup, M. (1996) *Identity, Culture and the Postmodern World*. Athens, GA: University of Georgia Press.
Saxe, L., Kadushin, C., Pakes, J., Kelner, S., Horowitz, B., Sales, A.L. and Brodsky, A. (2000) *Birthright Israel Launch Evaluation: Preliminary Findings*. Waltham, MA: Cohen Center for Modern Jewish Studies, Brandeis University.

Saxe, L., Kadushin, C., Hecht, S., Rosen, M., Phillips, B. and Kelner, S. (2004) *Evaluating Birthright Israel: Long-Term Impact and Recent Findings*. Cohen Center for Modern Jewish Studies, Brandeis University.

Saxe, L., Kadushin, C., Kelner, S., Rosen, M.I. and Yereslove, M. (2001) *A Mega-Experiment in Jewish Education: The Impact of Birthright Israel*. Waltham, MA: Cohen Center for Modern Jewish Studies, Brandeis University.

Saxe, L., Kadushin, C., Kelner, S., Rosen, M.I. and Yereslove, M. (2002) *A Mega-Experiment in Jewish Education: The Impact of Birthright Israel*. Waltham, MA: Cohen Center for Modern Jewish Studies, Brandeis University.

Saxe, L., Sasson, T. and Hecht, S. (2006) *Taglit-Birthright Israel: Impact on Jewish Identity, Peoplehood and Connection to Israel*. Boston, MA: Cohen Center for Modern Jewish Studies, Brandeis University.

Schick, M. (2004) *A Census of US Day Schools, 2003–2004: Executive Summary*. New York: Avi Chai Foundation. Online at http://www.avi-chai.org/Static/Binaries/Publications/execsumm_0.pdf. Accessed 11.11.07.

Schmidt, H. (1962) Chief Rabbi Nathan Marcus Adler (1803–1890): Jewish educator from Germany. *Leo Baeck Year Book* 18, 289–311.

Schoem, D. (1982) Explaining Jewish student failure. *Anthropology & Education Quarterly* 13 (4), 308–322.

Schwartz B. (1997) Collective memory and history, how Abraham Lincoln became a symbol of racial equality. *The Sociological Quarterly* 38 (3), 469–496.

Shackel, P. (2001) *Myth, Memory and the Making of the American Landscape*. Gainesville, FL: University of Florida Press.

Shapiro, F. (2006) *Building Jewish Roots: The Israel Experience*. Montreal: McGill-Queens University.

Shurkin, M. (2000) Decolonization and the renewal of French Judaism: Reflections on the contemporary French Jewish scene. *Jewish Social Studies* 6, 156–171.

Shye, S. (1978) *Theory Construction and Data Analysis in the Behavioral Sciences*. San Francisco, CA: Jossey-Bass.

Shye, S. (1986) *Educational Programs in Israel: A Field Study of Programs, Designed for Visitors From the Diaspora*. Jerusalem: Nativ Policy and Planning Consultants.

Shyovitz, D. (2007) The virtual Jewish history tour: Australia. Online at http://www.jewishvirtuallibrary.org/jsource/vjw/australia.html. Accessed 11.11.07.

Simon, L. (ed.) (1922) *Ten Essays on Zionism and Judaism by Achad Ha-Am*. London: Routledge.

Skelton, T. and Valentine, G. (eds) (1988) *Cool Places: Geographies of Youth Cultures*. London: Routledge.

Skirball, H. (1988) The Israel imperative. *Jewish Education News* 9 (1), 18–19.

Smith, V. (ed.) (1977) *Hosts and Guests: The Anthropology of Tourism*. Philadelphia, PA: University of Pennsylvania Press.

Spicer, E.H. (1980) *The Yaquis: A Cultural History*. Tucson, AZ: University of Arizona Press.

Steinberg, B. (1979) Jewish education in the United States: A study in religio-ethnic response. *The Jewish Journal of Sociology* 21 (10), 5–35.

Steinberg, B. (1984) The present era in Jewish education: A global comparative perspective. *The Jewish Journal of Sociology* 26 (2), 93–109.

Steinhart Foundation (2005) *Transforming Jewish Life in America: Ten Year Inaugural Report 1994–2004*. New York: Jewish Life Network, Steinhart Foundation.

Strenger, M. and Lichtenberg, A. (1996) *Does the Israel Experience End? Keeping the Spirit Alive*. New York: Y&H Department.

Strenski, I. (1997) *Durkheim and the Jews of France*. Chicago, IL: University of Chicago Press.

Sturken, M. (1997) *Tangled Memories: The Vietnam War, the AIDS Epidemic, and the Politics of Remembering*. Berkeley, CA: University of California Press.

Szajkowski, Z. (1970) *Jews and the French Revolutions of 1789, 1830 and 1848*. New York: Ktav.

Trier, T. (1996) Reversed Diaspora: Russian Jewry, the transition in Russia and the migration to Israel. *Anthropology of Eastern Europe Review* 14. Online at http://www.anthrobase.com/txt/T/Trier_T_01.htm. Accessed 11.11.07.

United States Holocaust Memorial Museum (2007) Jewish population of Europe 1933. Online at http://www.ushmm.org/wlc/article.php?lang=en&ModuleId=10005161. Accessed 11.11.07.

Valins, O., Kosmin, B. and Goldberg, J. (2001) *The Future of Jewish Schooling in the UK: A Strategic Assessment of a Faith-Based Provision of Primary and Secondary School Education*. London: Institute for Jewish Policy Research.

Wall, S. and Klein-Katz, S. (2007) Jewish educational Israel experiences. In P. Flexner and R. Goodman (eds) *What We Now Know About Jewish Education: Perspectives on Research for Practice*. Los Angeles, CA: Torah Aura Productions.

Wearing, S. (2001) *Volunteer Tourism: Experiences That Make a Difference*. Oxford: CABI Publishing.

Weber, M. (1922/1991) *The Sociology of Religion*. Boston, MA: Beacon Press.

Weiner, R. (2005) The virtual Jewish history tour: South Africa. Online at http://www.jewishvirtuallibrary.org/jsource/vjw/South_Africa.html. Accessed 11.11.07.

Weisberger, A.M. (1997) *The Jewish Ethic and the Spirit of Socialism*. NY: Peter Lang.

Wieviorka, M. (1999) *Violence en France*. Paris: Editions du Seuil.

World Association of the Scout Movement (1998) Scouting: An educational system. Online at http://www.scout.org/en/content/pdf/3759/Scouting%20an%20Educational%20System.pdf. Accessed 11.11.07.

World Jewish Congress (2001) *Jewish Education in the Diaspora: 2001 Update*. Online at http://www.worldjewishcongress.org/instwjc_dispatch.html#. Accessed 11.1.07.

Zeldin, M. (2006) Making the magic in reform Jewish summer camps. In M. Lorge and G. Zola (eds) *A Place of Our Own: The Rise of Reform Jewish Camping* (pp. 85–116). Tuscaloosa, AL: University of Alabama Press.

Index

Subjects

Adolescence, adolescents (also 'teenage') xii, 1, 2, (3), 3, 8, 23, 24, 25, 31, 34, 45, 60, (73, 74, 77) 73-79, 82, 86-91, 98, 101, 107, 111, 121, 122, 124, 147, 156, 171, 177, 178, 187, (188) 188, 190, 193, (194) 194, 199

Age 8, 10, 17, 26, 29, 30-31, 37, 45, 46, 71, 73, 86, 95, 101, 109, 146, 149, 150, 151, 163, 189, 194, 198, 199

Aliyah (immigration to Israel) 14, 19, 22-25, 38, 54, 59, 90-94, 120-124, 134, 174, 190, 200

Anti-Semitism 36-42, 49, 56, 59, 61-62, 65-68, 78, 117, 133, 137, 158, 196

Argentina, Jews of (*see also* Latin America, Jews of and South America, Jews of) 27, 30, 46, 54-55, 84, 104, 119, 193

Army, Israeli Defense Forces 64, 74, 90, 93, 95, 96, 109, 127, 130, 142, 148-150, 167-168, 196, 204

Ashkenazi Jews 79, 200

Assimilation 7, 8, 16, 20, 37, 39, 40, 42, 45, 48, 49, 50, 51, 56, 61-63, 189, 190, 194

Australia and New Zealand, Jews of 27, 29, 30, 33, 37, 44, 54, 56, 71, 72, 79, 84, 100, 107, 114, 118, 120, 177

Bar/Bat Mitzvah 31, 50, 73, 102, 150-151, 194-195 Belgium, Jews of (*see also* Western Europe, Jews of) 27, 30

Brazil, Jews of (*see also* Latin America, Jews of and South America, Jews of) 30, 46, 84, 104

Canada, Jews of (*see also* North America, Jews of) 29, 30, 34, 37, 41, 44, 46, 76, 82, 83, 84, 90, 91, 93, 94, 104, 180

Commonwealth of Independent States (CIS), Jews of (*see also* Soviet Union and Soviet States, former, Jews of) 29, 30

Community (in general) 12, 16, 17, 18, 20, 24, 26, 29, 39, 41, 43, 45, 46, 48, 49, 50, 51, 52, 55, 56, 60, 61, 62, 63, 64, 71, 73, 75, 80, 83, 87, 98, 102, 110, 118, 119, 123, 124, 133, 139, 154, 157, 158, 161, 168, 169, 171, 174, 181, 188, 190, 193

Community
- Institutions, organizations, centres 7, 14, 34, 47, 48, 51, 53, 54, 59, 85, 87, 96, 105, 122, 176, 179, 181, 182, 192, 195, 196, 198
- Leaders 1, 7, 8, 40, 41, 50, 51, 77, 87, 97, 119, 121, 122, 123, 179, 185, 198
- Nature or character of local 29, 50, 51, 78, 91, 97, 148, 169, 174, 188, 199
- Participation, involvement in 7, 9, 19, 31, 32, 34, 46, 77, 84, 97, 106, 107, 109, 113, 117, 118, 122, 124, 153, 155, 160, 170, 176, 181, 182, 183, 184, 185, 190. 191
- Temporary 75, 94

Conservative Jews, Judaism 20, 49, 50, 77, 79, 93, 95, 151, 153,

Counsellor(s) (madrich(im)) ix, x, 3, 10, 74, 86, 87, 97, 100-103, 105, 109, 111, 113, 114, 129, 134, 135, 137, 139, 142, 143, 144, 148, 149, 156, 157-164, 165-175, 179, 188, 192, 197, 198, 200, 204, 207, 208

Cross-cultural 1, 2, 26, 94, 121, 144, 159

Culture 1, 3, 7, 11, 16, 17, 18, 19, 20, 25, 38, 39, 43, 44, 47, 49, 52, 53, 54, 58, 59, 62, 65, 66, 68, 69, 70, 73, 74, 75, 81, 91, 94, 96, 105, 112, 141, 142, 143, 145, 155, 160, 162, 168, 169, 171, 188, 189, 194, 196, 199

Eastern Europe, Jews of 27, 29, 32, 33, 49, 51, 53-55, 56, 67, 68, 71, 72, 79, 100, 107, 114, 117, 118, 119, 120, 121, 132, 136, 173, 174, 175, 178, 198

Ethnicity, ethnic identity xii, 1, 2, 12, 38, 44, 45, 46, 49, 52, 54, 60, 61, 62, 63, 66, 68, 73, 75, 80, 94, 189, 196, 198, 199

Exodus boat tour 109, 136-139

Exogamy (intermarriage) 17, 31, 55, 59, 76-78, 81, 102, 170-173

Expectations for the tour (*see also* goals and objectives) 3, 14, 15, 21, 23-25, 31, 37, 43, 48, 58, 59, 60, 82, 83, 84, 87, 89, 98, 99, 106, 108, 111, 112, 113, 116, 119, 141, 145, 152, 153, 155, 168, 175, 188, 193

224

Index

Facet Theory 4-6
France, Jews of; French Jews (see also Western Europe, Jews of) 9, 22, 23, 25, 27, 29, 30, 32, 42, 44, 46, 51, 52, 62, 67, 71, 73, 75, 76, 78, 84, 85, 90-94, 104, 113, 114, 136, 152, 153, 167, 172, 173, 174, 183, 184, 188, 193, 196, 198

Gender (male/female) 4, 31, 58, 65, 86, , 93-96, 121-122, 151, 175
Germany, Jews of (see also Western Europe, Jews of) 29, 30, 79, 156
Goals and objectives of the tour 2, 8, 11, 14-19, 21, 23-25, 43, 55, 60, 65, 67, 75, 78, 80, 82, 89, 98, 112, 115, 117, 121, 128, 138, 141, 148, 151, 152, 153, 162, 173, 179, 185-188, 190-193, 199

Hebrew language 13, 16-17, 25, 30, 38, 47, 53, 55, 64, 67, 70, 90, 93, 137, 142, 145, 153-155, 158, 168, 171, 196, 200-201
Heritage tourism xii, 1-3, 14, 58, 59, 61, 80, 91, 139, 141, 155, 187, 198-199
Holocaust (Shoah) 12, 16, 36-37, 41, 44-45, 51, 53-54, 56, 61, 65, 67, 69, 102, 131-138, 156, 158, 193, 198, 201
– Holocaust Memorial Museum in Jerusalem (Yad Vashem) 12-13, 44, 69, 90-93, 127, 130-136, 159, 193, 198, 204-207
Home hospitality 109, 127, 144, 148, 159, 204, 206-207
Hungary, Jews of (see also Eastern Europe, Jews of) 30, 79, 85

Identity development xii-xiii, 1-3, 17, 22, 24, 31, 35, 38, 57, 60-63, 67, 69, 73-74, 76, 80, 90, 93-94, 121-122, 138, 145, 161-162, 167, 186, 187-188, 193, 197, 199
– Jewish identity 1-3, 7-8, 11-12, 15-16, 18, 20-24, 35, 38-39, 43-45, 49-57, 60-72, 78, 80-85, 87, 91, 94-95, 102, 110, 113, 115-119, 122-125, 129, 131, 137, 141-142, 151-153, 155, 162, 170-171, 175, 177, 179, 181, 184, 187-190, 192-193, 197, 199
Immigration 14, 15, 19, 24, 26, 36, 39, 53, 90, 92-94, 121, 136, 137, 190, 200
Informal education 3, 10, 16, 32, 34, 44-46, 57, 61, 78, 121-122, 126, 138, 157-164, 166, 186, 187-188, 193
Israel–Diaspora relations 35-43, 61, 78, 102, 148, 175, 177, 187, 192

Jewish Day Schools 32, 46-56, 94, 133, 151, 155, 176, 178, 199

Jewish religious ritual 16, 45, 54, 56, 70-71, 78
Jewish religious sites 12-13, 25, 71, 89
– Western Wall (Kotel) 129-130, 151, 158, 161, 191, 205-207

Kibbutz 11-13 38, 74, 86, 90-93, 102, 111-112, 127, 129, 130, 134, 139-141, 149, 159, 161, 200, 203-207
– Oren kibbutz Hebrew programme 83, 153, 154-155

Latin America, Jews of 29, 30, 46, 54, 55,
Leisure 1, 3, 46, 47, 57, 100, 101, 102, 147, 148, 188
Logistics xii, 89, 108, 110, 111, 127, 139, 163, 166-169, 180, 183, 191, 202
Longer study programmes 10, 23, 30, 86, 119, 149, 155
– MASA 7-8, 26, 107, 131, 188, 190, 200
– Visiting students 31, 151-155

Marketing 10, 29, 86, 176-185
Mexico, Jews of (see also Latin America, Jews of and South America, Jews of) 27, 29, 30, 46, 112
Module (educational) 11, 98, 126-130, 146, 157, 161, 165, 193, 209
Memorial sites 11, 132, 141-144, 198

North America, Jews of 29, 32, 33, 67, 68, 71, 76, 95, 100, 107, 114, 118, 119, 120, 132, 173, 175

Orthodox Jews, Judaism 16, 34, 49, 50, 53, 54, 55, 56, 62, 64, 77, 78, 93, 95, 151, 155, 178, 179, 188, 189, 193, 196, 199

Palestinian conflict, intifada xii, 26, 27, 35, 39-40, 85, 128, 135, 143, 158, 195, 200
Parents 14, 15, 16, 17, 20-25, 31-34, 43, 45, 57, 64, 70, 71, 73, 75-77, 87, 97, 107, 116, 142, 160, 173, 177, 178, 181, 182, 186, 188, 192, 194, 199
Pilgrimage 2, 38, 43, 57-59, 89, 90, 92-95, 142, 187
Post-modernity 60, 157, 199

Recreation 9, 11, 14, 16, 23, 24, 25, 58, 59, 73, 89, 126, 127, 129, 131, 144, 148, 157, 161, 184, 185, 188, 193
Reform Jews, Judaism 49, 50, 64, 77, 79, 92, 93, 95, 128, 134, 145, 155, 193, 199
Religion 12, 14, 16, 18, 38, 49, 52, 54, 62, 63,

65, 66, 68, 70, 71, 72, 89, 90, 93, 94, 102, 115, 119, 126, 153, 154, 170, 171, 172, 196

Satisfaction 30, 50, 83, 97-114, 129, 130, 138, 154, 159, 160, 175, 183, 190, 193, 194
Secular 2, 44, 47, 48, 49, 51, 52, 53, 59, 62, 69, 83, 93, 95, 145, 153, 171, 172
Sephardi Jews 52, 62, 79, 201
Shelter 91-95
Six Day War (1967) 13, 27, 38, 49, 71, 203, 205, 208
Smallest Space Analysis, data analysis 4, 42, 65, 92, 101, 129, 130
South Africa, Jews of 30, 32, 46, 55-56, 71, 72, 104, 105, 136, 151, 173, 174, 177, 178,
South America, Jews of (*see also* Latin America) 32, 33, 54, 67, 68, 72, 100, 107, 114, 118, 119, 120, 130, 132, 151, 173, 199
Soviet Union, Jews of (*see also* Commonwealth of Independent States, Jews of) 39, 49, 64, 69, 70, 79, 196
Soviet States, former, Jews of (*see also* Commonwealth of Independent States, Jews of) 27, 29, 30, 53-55, 59, 86, 117
Spirituality 11, 38, 90-96, 150, 193
Summer camps 10, 47, 57, 75, 78, 81, 86, 116-117, 122, 138, 162-163, 166, 175, 179, 192,
Symbols
– of Jewish identity 12, 68-71, 91, 196
– in informal education 25, 129, 138, 141-143, 160, 162, 192

Taglit-birthright israel xii, 7-8, 10, 27-29, 31, 34, 41, 75, 83-84, 95-96, 101, 105, 107, 112-113, 116, 121, 124, 133, 149, 151,
176-177, 180, 188, 190, 194-195, 201
Tourism, sociological theory of 57-60, 78, 144, 187-189

United States of America, Jews of (*see also* North American Jews) 9, 13, 17, 20-25, 27, 29, 30, 32-34, 36, 37, 38, 40, 41, 45, 46, 48-50, 54, 62, 63, 64, 72, 76, 80, 81, 83, 84, 85, 87, 90-95, 104, 106, 108, 109, 110, 113, 114, 116, 122, 124, 132, 138, 145-148, 151, 152, 159, 166, 167, 169, 171, 172, 173, 181, 185, 188, 191, 194, 199
United Kingdom, Jews of; British Jews (*see also* Western European Jews) 22, 23, 27, 29, 30, 41, 53, 67, 76, 90, 91, 93, 94, 104, 105, 113, 143, 167, 183

Values 3, 7, 13, 19, 39, 45, 52, 60, 62-64, 73-78, 109, 115, 126, 138, 141, 153, 157, 159, 162, 164, 169, 184, 186, 193
Volunteering, volunteers 12, 30, 64, 69, 71-72, 85-87, 102, 127, 131, 149-150, 159, 193

Western Europe, Jews of 51, 53, 54, 67, 68, 72, 106

Youth movements 7, 10, 32, 34, 36-37, 47, 49, 56, 77, 87, 96, 105, 113, 134, 157, 160-163, 165-166, 168, 182-184, 193

Zionism
– Zionist movement 36-39, 49, 132, 139, 141, 201
– tour to Israel and Zionism 9, 12, 19, 42-43, 55, 82, 92-94, 115, 119-120, 127, 137, 161, 170, 174, 185, 190, 192

Names

Abrams, S. 82
Ackerman, W. 158, 164
Adams, W. 198, 199
Ahad Ha-am 37, 78
Ahmed, M. 164
Alkalai, Y. 78
Allen, Woody 64, 70
Amar, R. 4, 5
Amir, Y. 140
Appadurai, A. 61
Askénazi, L. 61
Avieli, N. 111
Avivi, O. 144

Barkat, A 41

Barnett, R. 151
Bar-On, M. 19, 20, 45, 171
Bar-On Cohen, E. xv
Bar Shalom, Y. 2, 63, 75, 116, 144, 145, 149
Barth, F. 60
Beilin, Y. 8, 40, 78
Bekerman, Z. 20, 65
Bekker, V. 41
Ben Rafael, E. 139
Ben-Shalom, U. 61
Bensimon, D. 51
Ben-Yehuda. E. 78
Berger, P. 60
Berkman, J. 41
Berry, J. 61

Index

Blumberg, A. 37
Bochner, S. 61
Boorstin, D. 57, 58
Borg, I. 4
Bourdieu, P. 60
Bramwell, B. 58
Brettschneider, M. 78
Brodsky-Porges, E. 2
Bronfman, C. 8
Bruner, E. 134
Bubis, G. 81, 107, 115, 116, 122
Burns, P. 59

Canter, D. 4
Carlson, J. 2
Chagall, Marc 70
Chazan, B. 35, 94, 97, 157, 164
Cohen, B. 164
Cohen, E. 58, 59, 111, 189, 197
Cohen, E.H. 2, 4, 5, 19, 24, 25, 29, 30, 31, 41, 42, 43, 46, 52, 56, 60, 63, 65, 71, 73, 75, 77, 84, 85, 86, 91, 93, 94, 96, 98, 101, 102, 105, 116, 119, 121, 124, 126, 129, 134, 137, 140, 146, 152, 153, 156, 157, 161, 162, 166, 167, 172, 180, 186
Cohen, J. 150
Cohen, S. 82, 94, 97, 107, 145, 164, 171, 185
Coles, T. xv, 59
Comet, T. 13, 15, 31, 80
Conger, J. 75
Coombs, P. 164

Dahan, D. 167
Dann, G. 139, 199
Dashefsky, A. 60
Davis, T. 2
de Burlo, C. 59
de Rothschild, E. 78
Della Pergola, S. 51, 53, 55, 172
Durkheim, É. 78

Einstein, Albert 70
Elazar, D. 51, 55
Erikson, E. 60, 73
Ezrachi, E. 144

Featherstone, M. 61
Finestein, I. 53
Forman, D. 64, 65, 128
Frank, Anne 70
Freidenreich, H. 78
Friedman, P. 20
Friedlander, D. 82, 152, 153
Furnham, A. 61

Gale, N. 79
Gans, H. 46, 61, 63, 69
Geertz, C. 60, 68
Gibson, H. 95
Gitelman, Z. 54, 61
Goffman, E. 60, 75
Gold, P. 61
Goldberg, H. 77, 83, 145, 199
Goldman, E. 78
Goodman, H. 55
Gordin, J. 61
Gordon, M. 61
Grant, L. 53, 186
Grauer, T. 94
Gravetz, S. 8, 9, 105
Guibernau, M. 61
Guttman, L. 4

Habib, J. 197
Halberthal, M 74
Hall, C. 58
Halpern, B. 37
Harman, D. 79
Head, J. 73
Heilman, S. 77, 83, 145
Henze, R. 164
Herman, S. 80, 81, 116, 152
Hertzberg, A. 94
Herzl, T. 78, 127
Hildesheimer, A. 78
Hochstein, A. 26, 82, 176
Hollinshead, K. 59
Homer, S. 189
Horenczyk, G. 41, 42, 61, 94, 171
Horowitz, T. 71, 72

Infeld, A. 12, 20, 145
Isaacs, L. 24, 32, 181

Jack, G. 144, 197
Jeffs, T. 164
Jensen, L. 60
Jiobu, R. 61

Kafka, R. 122
Kahane, R. 3, 126, 157, 159-163
Kalischer, Z. 78
Kallen, H. 48
Kauffmann, N. 2
Keisar, A. 156
Kelner, S. 83, 105, 197
Kerem, M. 140, 152
Klein-Katz, S. 82, 105, 163
Kohn, D. 56

Kornberg, J. 37
Kosmin, B. 53
Kronish, R. 21

Laborde, C. 94
Lacan, J. 189
Landsmann, C. 133
Lane, B. 58
Laubscher, M. 2
Lederhendler, E. 27, 38
Lev-Ari, L. 83, 152, 154, 155,
Levenberg, J. 24, 32, 181
Levian, G. 151
Levinson, T. 122
Levran, Z. 27, 92
Levy, S. 4
Lew, A. 58
Lichtenberg, A. 112
Liebman, C. 64
Lorge, M. 57
Lubavitcher rebbe 70

MacCannell, D. 57, 58, 144, 189
Macdonald, S. 199
Magid, J. 140
Magonet, J. 61
Mandel, M. 50
Marks, L. 81, 107, 115, 116, 122
McClintock, M. 52
McKee, M. 64
McLoyd, V. 60
Miriam the prophetess 70
Mittelberg, D. 28, 83, 139, 140, 152, 154, 155
Montefiore, M. 78
More, D. 20, 32, 112
Moss, A. 74
Müller, J. 198
Munar, A. 196

Natonek, J. 78
Noy, C. 197

Ohayon, S. 18, 60, 83

Petersen, A. 75
Phil, M. 105, 197
Phipps, A. 144, 197
Pinsker, L. 78
Pomson, A. 186
Poria, Y. 58
Pratt, M. 134

Queen Esther 70

Rabin, Y. 14, 78, 90, 93, 130, 142-144, 167, 205, 208
Rapoport, T. 160
Rein, R. 55
Reinharz, J. 37
Reisinger, Y. 57, 147, 192
Reisman, B. 21,46, 63, 97, 106, 163, 164
Rex, J. 61
Richards, S. 134, 156
Ritchie, B. 155, 184
Robertson, R. 37
Rosenak, M. 2, 43, 56, 64
Rovner, R. 112
Rozner, I. 32, 52

Sales, A. 116, 162
Sarup, M. 61
Saxe, L. 31, 34, 75, 83, 84, 116, 121, 124, 162, 177, 180
Schick, M. 49, 50
Schmida, M. 164
Schmidt, H. 53
Schoem, D. 56, 63
Schwartz, B. 141
Seaton, A. 139, 199
Seinfeld, J 64
Shackel, P. 198
Shapiro, F. 108
Sharon, A. 78
Shurkin, M. 94
Shye, S. 4, 19, 82, 108, 115
Shyovitz, D. 56
Simon, L. 43
Sitruk, J. 52
Skelton, T. 17
Skirball, H. 74
Smith, M. 164
Smith, V. 58
Spicer, E. 63, 69
Spielberg, S. 133
Steinberg, B. 44
Steinberg, L. 60
Steinhart, M. 8, 41
Steiner, C. 192
Streisand, Barbra 70
Strenger, M. 112
Strenski, I. 78
Sturken, M. 198, 199
Sutherland, J. 52
Sutnick, B. 144
Szajkowski, Z. 94

Timothy, D. xv
Toledano, S. 4

Trier, T. 29
Trigano, S. 51
Turner, L. 57, 147

Valentine, G. 17
Valins, O. 53

Wall, S. 97, 105
Wearing, S. 149
Weber, M. 60
Weiner, R. 55

Weisberger, A. 69
Wertheimer, J. 164
Widaman, K. 2
Wieviorka, M. 94

Yiannakis, A. 96
Zeldin, M. 75, 116, 166

Zola 57
Zoline 122

For Product Safety Concerns and Information please contact our EU Authorised Representative:

Easy Access System Europe

Mustamäe tee 50

10621 Tallinn

Estonia

gpsr.requests@easproject.com

www.ingramcontent.com/pod-product-compliance
Lightning Source LLC
Chambersburg PA
CBHW070601300426
44113CB00010B/1356